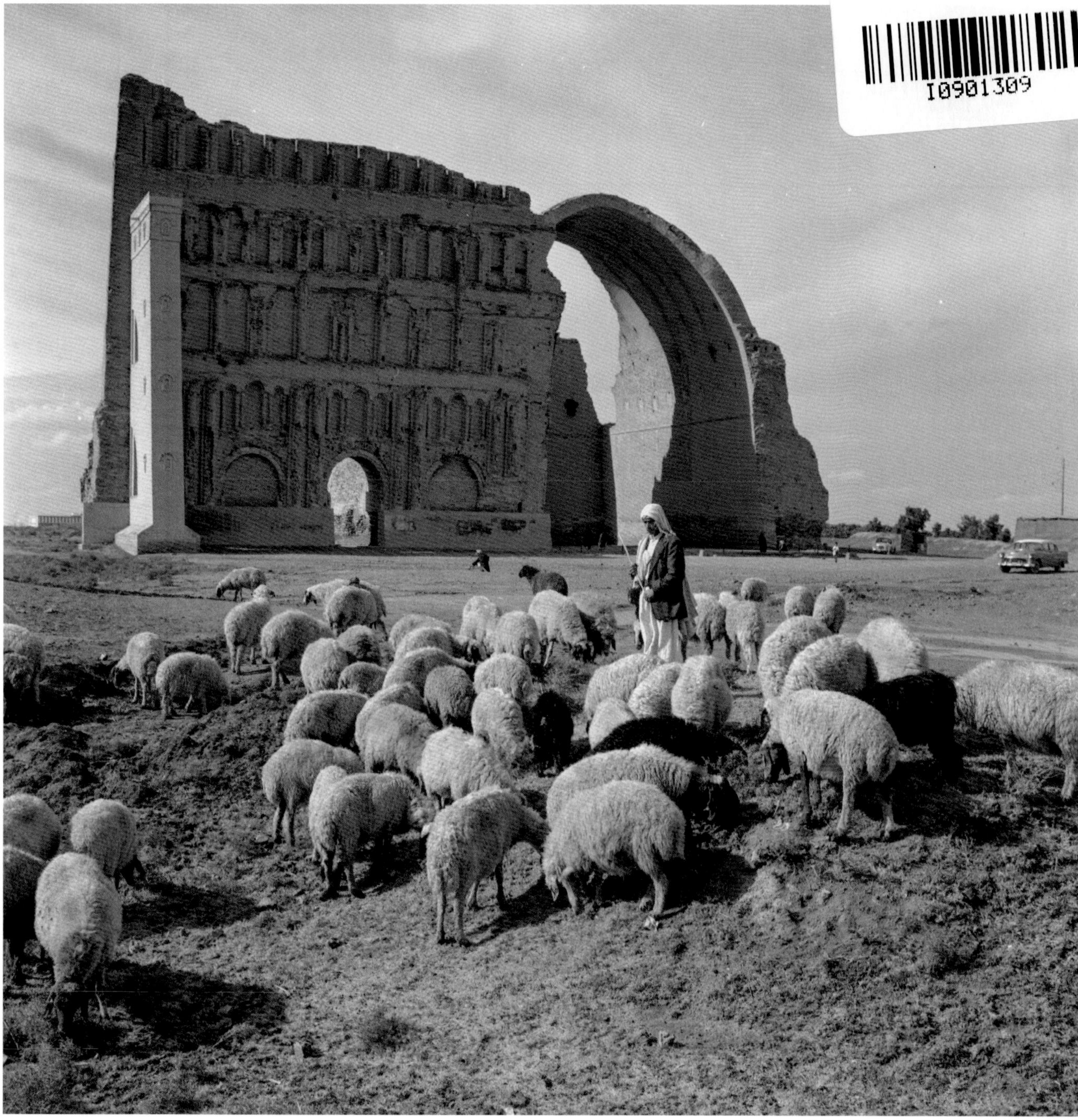

Edited by Pedro Azara

Including contributions by
Adel Abidin
Narmin Amin
Pedro Azara
Roberta Casagrande-Kim
Abdulrahman K. Darwesh
Nelida Fuccaro
Nadine Hattom
Hanaa Malallah
Nat Muller
Mahmoud Obaidi
and Ala Younis

Institute for the Study of the Ancient World
at New York University

Princeton University Press, Princeton and Oxford

THROUGH THE LENS

Latif Al Ani's Visions of Ancient Iraq

This catalogue is published by the Institute for the Study of the Ancient World at New York University and distributed by Princeton University Press on the occasion of the *Through the Lens: Latif Al Ani's Visions of Ancient Iraq* at the Institute for the Study of the Ancient World, November 8, 2023 – February 25, 2024.

CONCEPT AND DIRECTION
Roberta Casagrande-Kim

EXHIBITION

Curatorial Team
Pedro Azara
Roberta Casagrande-Kim

Exhibitions Registrar and Installations Manager
Joanna Salicki

Publications and Interpretive Manager
Taylor McBride

Financial Analyst
Sophy Chu

Exhibition Designer
Ian Sullivan

Graphic Designer
Laura Grey

Lighting Designer
Mary Ann Hoag

CATALOGUE

Editor
Pedro Azara

Managing Editor
Taylor McBride

Designer
Laura Grey

Copy Editor
Mary Cason

Proofreader
Mary Gladue

Color Separations and Printing
Graphius NV

LENDERS

Arab Image Foundation
Jurgen Buedts
Galerie Tanit
Library of the Institute for the Study of the Ancient World
Nadine Hattom
Sahim Omar Kalifa
Hanaa Malallah
The Metropolitan Museum of Art
Mahmoud Obaidi
Walid Siti
Swansea Museum

This exhibition and its accompanying catalogue were made possible by generous support from the Violet Jabara Charitable Trust and the Leon Levy Foundation. Additional funding provided by Joyce F. Menschel and Mr. and Mrs. Lawrence Tucker.

CONTENTS

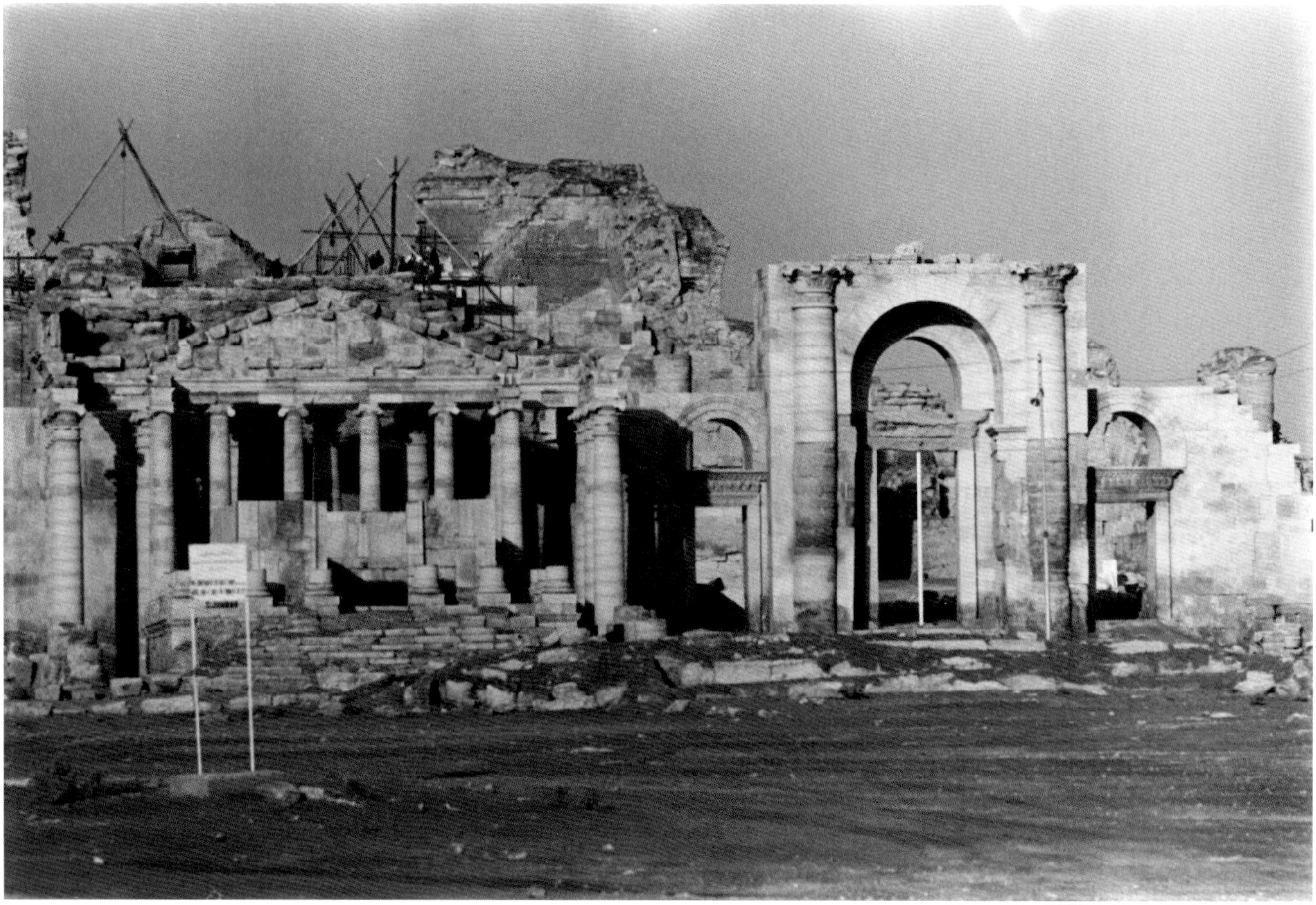

Latif Al Ani. Hatra, Temple (Iwan) of the sun god Shamash. Gelatin silver negative on cellulose acetate film.
Ca. 1960. AIF: 0190an01781. Checklist no. 67.

LETTER FROM ISAW

Alexander R. Jones,
Leon Levy Director, ISAW

When the Iraq Pavilion opened at the 2015 Venice Biennale, many were introduced to the vision of the pioneering Iraqi photographer Latif Al Ani (1932–2021) for the first time. When a young man, Al Ani traveled across the country as a photographer for the Iraqi Petroleum Company's magazine *Ahl al-Naft*. In subsequent decades, however, Al Ani's artistic voice was silenced by the Saddam Hussein regime until recent scholarship brought Al Ani's influence back to life.

Latif Al Ani's story serves as the focal point for *Through the Lens: Latif Al Ani's Visions of Ancient Iraq*, where his photographs of ancient monuments offer a lens to conceptualize and understand how archaeologists and artists have reckoned with Iraq's past. Images of early 1850s excavations, which had been mired by Western colonial practices, and the works of contemporary Iraqi artists accompany Al Ani's photographs. This unique combination of early archival documents, 1960s photography, and contemporary art brings to the forefront complex issues of Iraqi cultural identity and heritage by reclaiming the stories of those who recorded, codified, and currently grapple with the ramifications of such a past.

Shortly before the fallout of the COVID-19 pandemic in 2020, ISAW's exhibition *A Wonder to Behold* also looked to the ancient Near East—particularly the Ishtar Gate, the jewel of Babylon. Then as now, we remain focused on connecting Mesopotamian civilizations to our present day. With *Through the Lens*, we highlight the voices of those who explored the past and the deeply personal stories of living artists who confront its legacy.

As with all our exhibitions, ISAW relies on lenders far and wide. Special thanks go to the Arab Image Foundation and the Al Ani family and estate for lending over fifty images that constitute the core of *Through the Lens*. Our gratitude also goes to the five contemporary Iraqi artists who generously contributed their works or created new commissions specifically for this project: Adel Abidin and Galerie Tanit, Nadine Hattom, Hanaa Malallah, Mahmoud Obaidi, and Walid Siti. We are also grateful to Sahim Omar Kalifa, director, and Jurgen Buedts, producer, for the group of still images from their documentary *Iraq's Invisible Beauty*. We are fortunate to have sourced works from ISAW's own library for this exhibition. David Ratzan, Head of ISAW's library, along with Librarian for Collections and Services, Gabriel McKee, were instrumental to this loan. Finally, I would also like to acknowledge the private collector who generously contributed three maps from the James Felix Jones memoirs to our exhibition.

My gratitude also goes to the curator of the exhibition, Pedro Azara, with whom we are glad to collaborate again after the groundbreaking show *From Ancient to Modern: Archaeology and Aesthetics*. A warm thank-you to the authors of this catalogue for their expertise in such a wide field of study, and the Iraqi artists who wrote so eloquently about their art and shared with us their personal journeys and inspirations.

This exhibition would not have been possible without the generosity and support of our donors, who enable us to explore innovative ideas and bring stunning works of art to ISAW's audience. We thank the Violet Jabara Charitable Trust, Joyce F. Menschel, and Mr. and Mrs. Lawrence Tucker. We wish to acknowledge the Leon Levy Foundation, whose ongoing support ensures that our institute continues its established tradition of thought-provoking exhibitions.

Our exhibitions could not exist without the ever-growing list of individuals who offer their invaluable guidance and expertise. We thank longtime collaborator Laura Grey for her impeccable eye, which lends cohesive yet innovate graphic design to ISAW's exhibitions and catalogues; Ian Sullivan, our Exhibition Designer, for his talent in creating new spaces and experiences tailored to each of our shows. Gratitude to Taylor McBride, ISAW Publications and Interpretive Manager, and the team of collaborators who assisted us in the creation of this catalogue and the exhibition didactics: Mary Cason, Mary Gladue, Graphius NV, Full Point Graphics, and Duggal. No exhibition would be possible without the work of Joanna Salicki, our assiduous Registrar and Installations Manager, and her team of consummate professionals: MaryAnn Hoag, lighting designer; Scott Hoefer at Insight Exhibits; Amy Haskins and Beth Brideau at Object Mounts; and Corrado Verini, LD and AV supervisor. At ISAW, I also want to acknowledge Nour Ammari, our graduate Practicum Student, who fielded many Arabic translation requests and very enthusiastically took on myriad curatorial tasks. Last but not least, Sophy Chu, Exhibition Finance Analyst, tirelessly worked at keeping the exhibition team within the budget and oversaw the gallery-attendants program.

This is the first exhibition for which Roberta Casagrande-Kim has led the exhibition team as the interim Bernard and Lisa Selz Director of Exhibitions and Gallery Curator. Roberta has offered exceptional direction, and we thank her for her work during this stage of transition in the department's leadership.

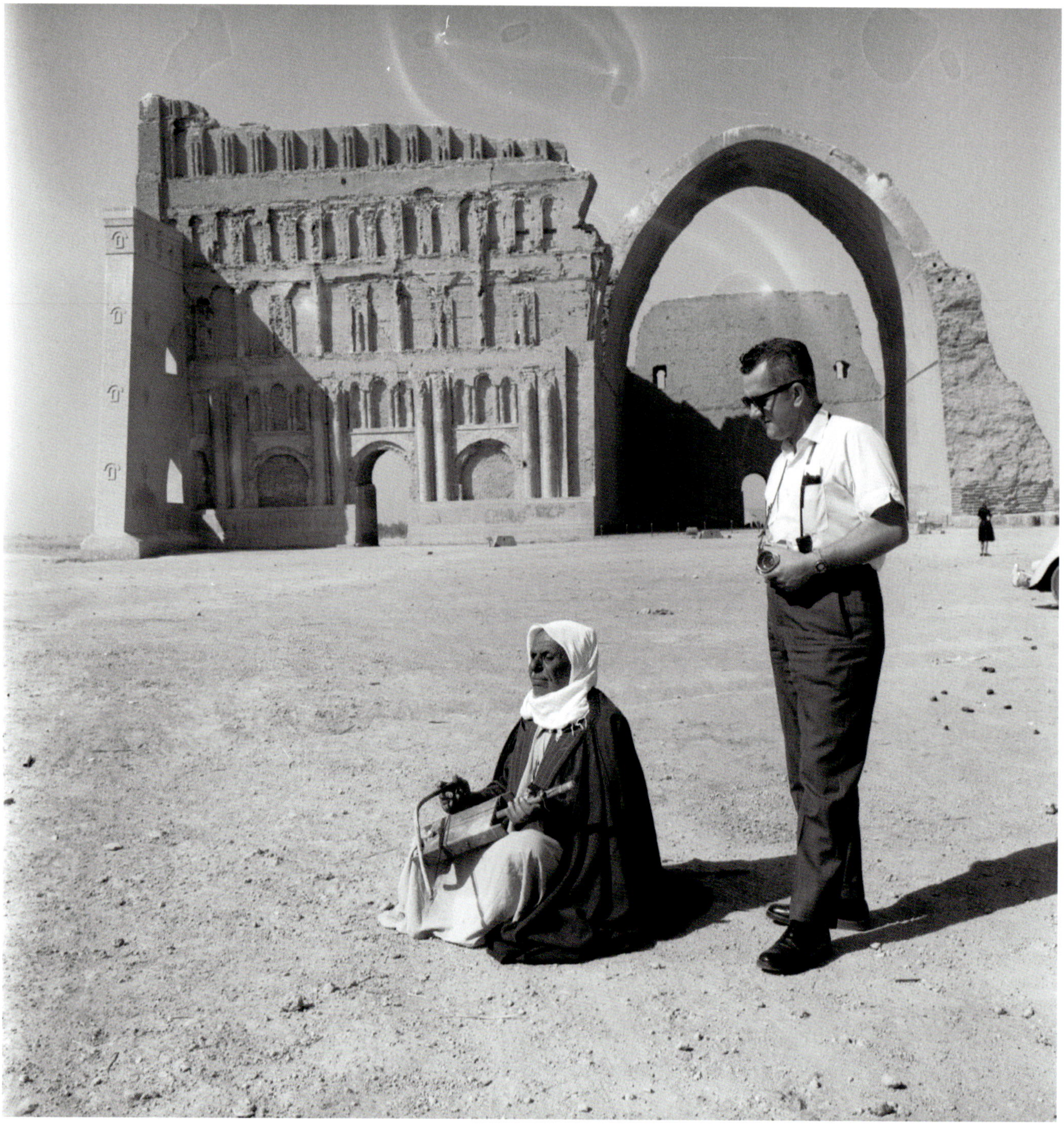

CHAPTER 1

IRAQ'S PAST— FILTERED

Roberta Casagrande-Kim

Latif Al Ani (1932–2021), a pioneering Iraqi photographer active in the 1950s and '60s, paradoxically spent a large part of his life without taking photographs. Silenced by the Saddam Hussein regime (1979–2003), he moved from being a promoter of his art at the highest levels of political and cultural life, including the Iraqi Ministry of Culture and the Iraqi News Agency, to become a bystander to the increasing destruction of his country, observing it all but unable to document it.

As in his life, Al Ani's photographs also present a paradox: mostly in black and white, they are quiet, balanced views of what was in fact a rapid and tumultuous social and economic transformation that took place during the reign of King Faysal II (r. 1939–1958), when Iraq transitioned from a modest, rural society to an educated and urban one (**SEE CHAPTER 4**). Baghdad, a sleepy town under the Ottoman Empire (1453–1922), abandoned its architectural monumentality, reminiscent of early twentieth-century British colonial power, in favor of new forms that better embodied the push for modernity. The transformation that started with Faysal II continued after the 1958 revolution, when newly appointed Iraqi officials promoted the building of large residential neighborhoods with rows of identical houses, and incentivized the urbanization of the city's periphery, now punctuated by grids of roads and avenues with rotundas.

Alongside photographs documenting the urban change, Latif Al Ani took a large number of images of well-known archaeological sites: Babylon, Ctesiphon, Dur-Kurigalzu, Hatra, and Samarra. He is, in fact, the first photographer of Iraqi origins to extensively document the vestiges of his own country. The photographs show the timelessness of the ruins—standing stoically, immune to the changing

FIG. 1-1. Latif Al Ani. Ctesiphon, tourist in front of the ruins of the Tāq Kasrā (Arch of Ctesiphon) with a musician playing the rebab. Gelatin silver negative on cellulose acetate film. 1964. AIF: 0190an01177. Checklist no. 44.

times, quiet witnesses to humanity's transient nature—but also how modernity influences one's perception of the past. At the time when Al Ani visited the main Iraqi archaeological sites, tourists—especially wealthy foreigners—were also flocking there. Often posing in Bedouin garb, they mimicked the customs of a people whose lifestyle was by now on the brink of extinction. In capturing these highly choreographed moments, Al Ani showed the viewer an antiquity filtered through a Western gaze. The archaeological ruins became much more than an idealized background against which elite tourists disguised themselves as "actors" in the middle of the desert: they were transformed into powerful symbols that actively contributed to the formulation of each individual's social persona (**FIGS. 1-1** to **1-6**).

Through the Lens: Latif Al Ani's Visions of Ancient Iraq challenges the narrative of an Iraqi past dominated by Westerners, scholars, and thrill seekers alike. Centered on the images by Al Ani, the exhibition explores the role of recent and distant histories as vehicles in the creation of national identity and heritage, and

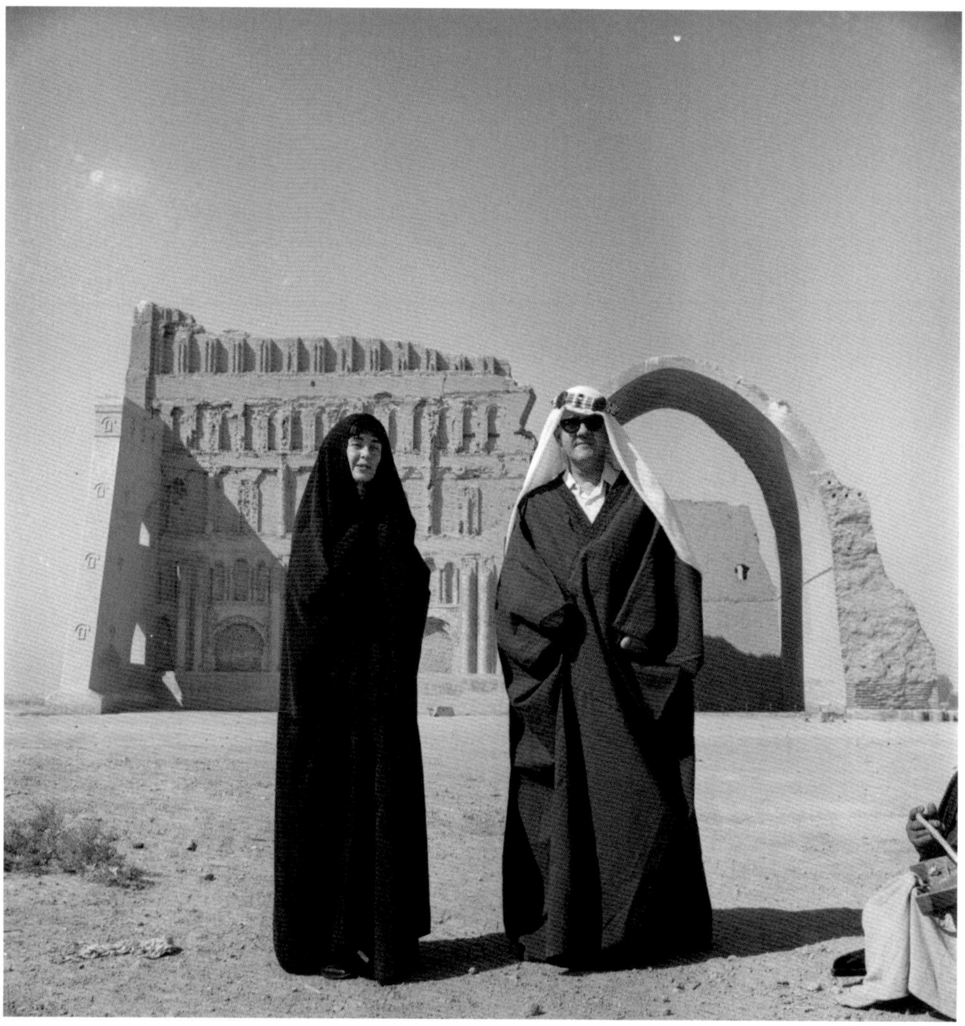

ABOVE: FIG. 1-2. Latif Al Ani. Ctesiphon, tourists in front of the ruins of the Tāq Kasrā (Arch of Ctesiphon). Gelatin silver negative on cellulose acetate film. 1964. AIF: 0190an00919. Checklist no. 37. **OPPOSITE, TOP: FIG. 1-3.** Latif Al Ani. Ctesiphon, tourists in front of the ruins of the Tāq Kasrā (Arch of Ctesiphon) with a musician playing the rebab. Gelatin silver negative on cellulose acetate film. 1964. AIF: 0190an01179. Checklist no. 39. **OPPOSITE, BOTTOM: FIG. 1-4.** Latif Al Ani. Ctesiphon, tourists in front of the ruins of the Tāq Kasrā (Arch of Ctesiphon). Gelatin silver negative on cellulose acetate film. 1964. AIF: 0190an00918. Checklist no. 40.

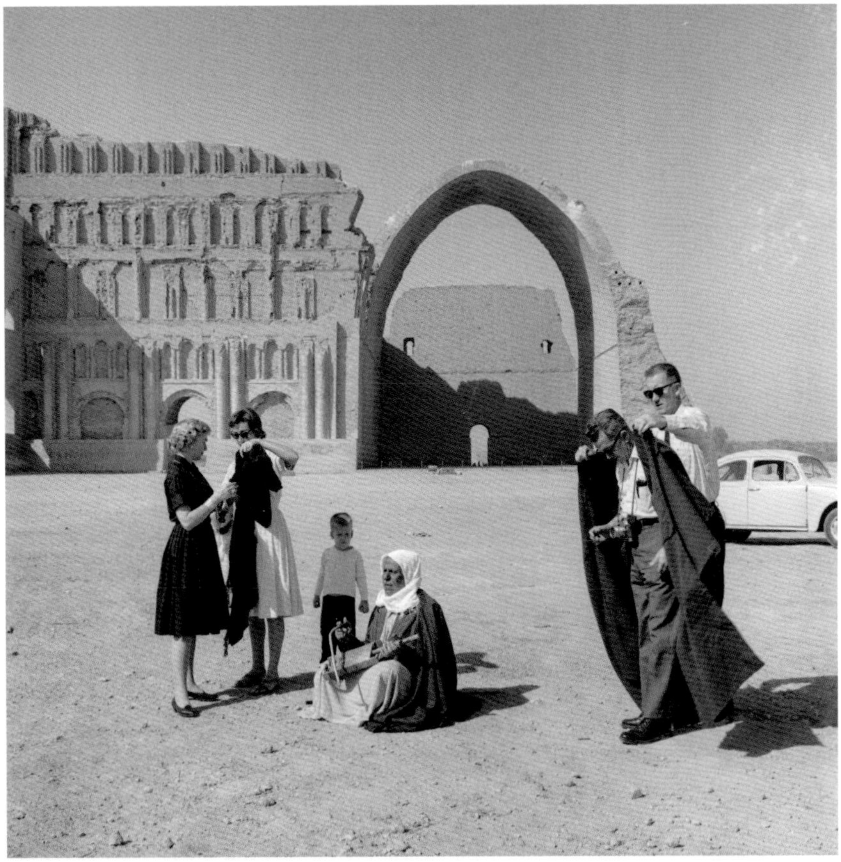

FIG. 1-3

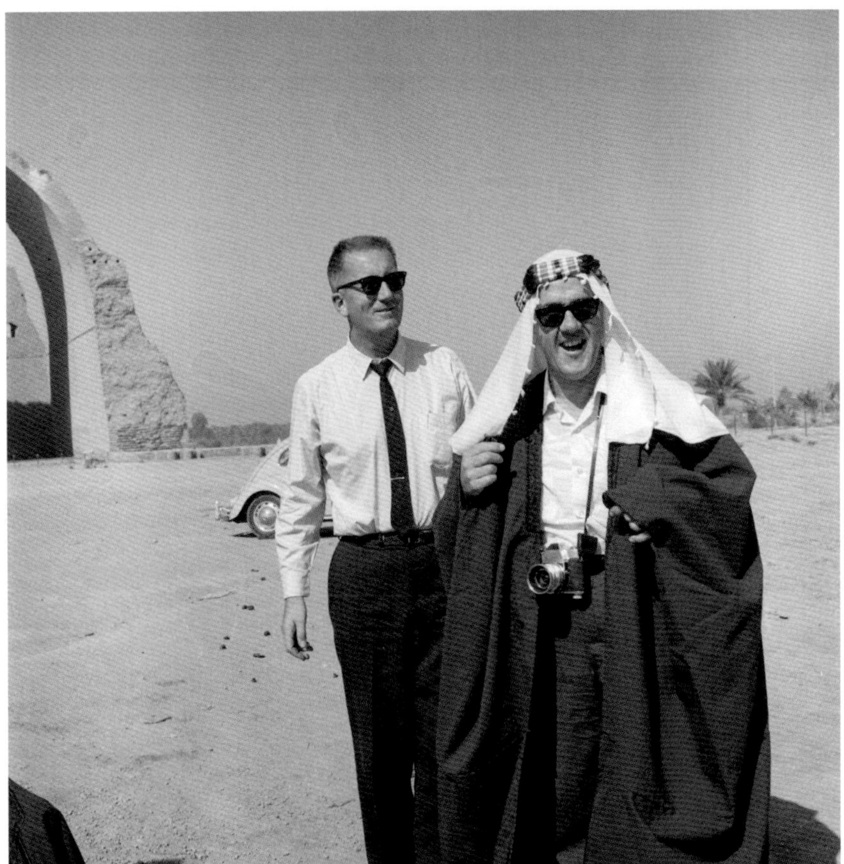

FIG. 1-4

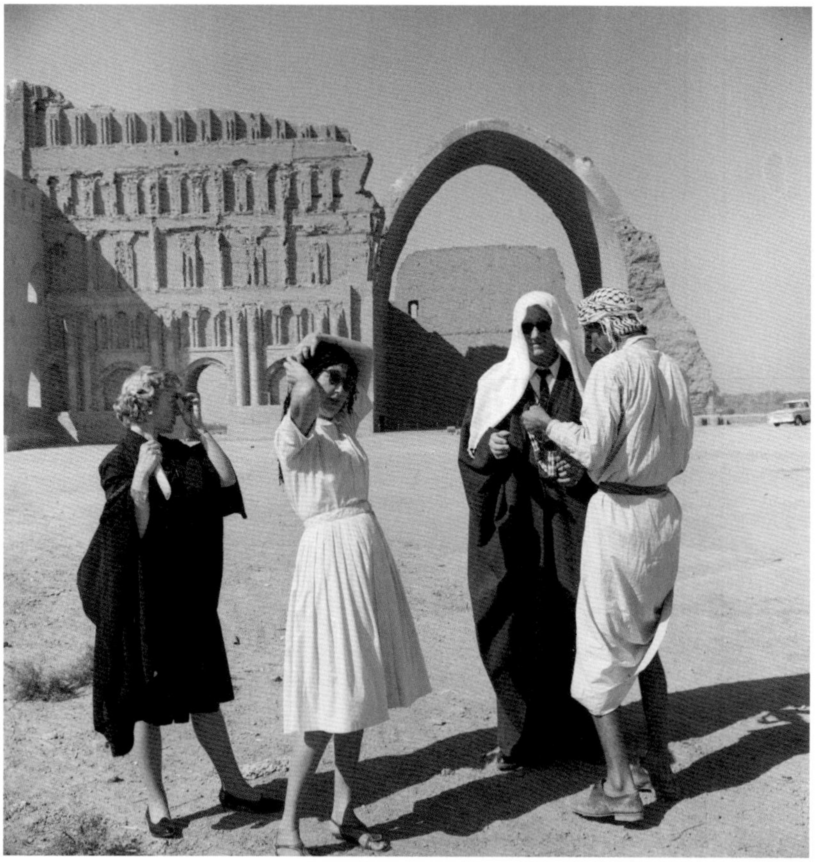

FIG. 1-5

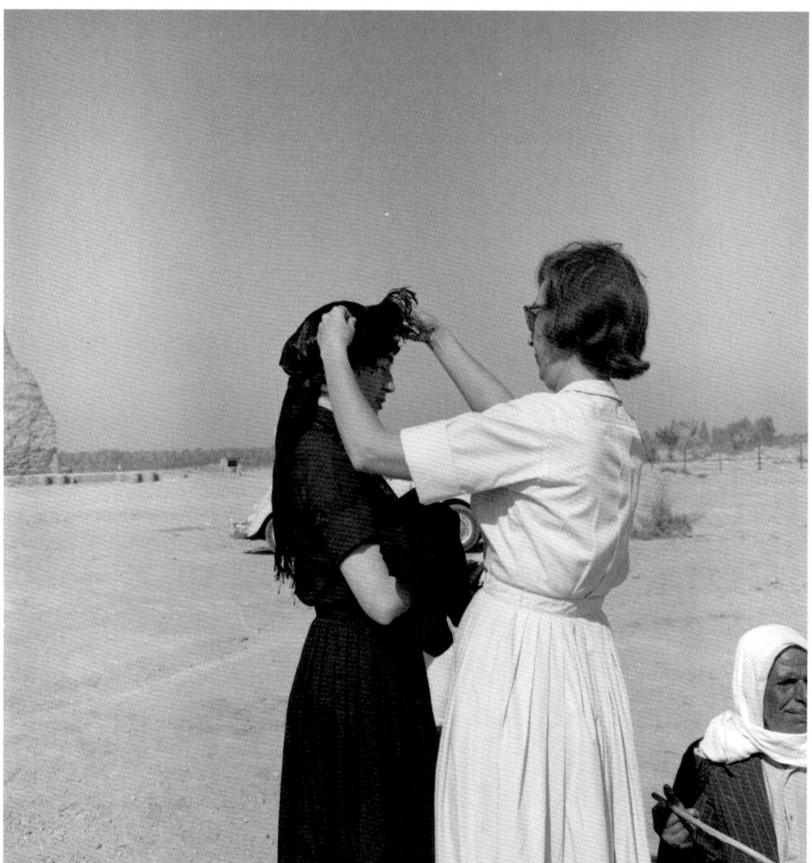

FIG. 1-6

the complex topic of the appropriation of the past via the lenses of Western cultural colonization. By focusing on the figure and role of selected Iraqi individuals, *Through the Lens* presents case studies highlighting how different life experiences translate into varied reverberations of shared, reconstructed pasts.

Mesopotamian and early Islamic ruins entered Western art historical thought through colonial archaeological missions that routinely dismissed the role and knowledge of the communities that had inhabited those lands for hundreds, if not thousands, of years. Hormuzd Rassam (1826–1910), a Christian from Mosul with political connections in both the Ottoman and British Empires, represents the epitome of this fraught relationship. Among the first autochthonous archaeologists, Rassam discovered some of the most important finds of the time by acting as Sir Henry Austen Layard's (1817–1894) right-hand man. In chapter 2, Narmin Amin and Abdulrahman K. Darwesh explore how Rassam was consistently overlooked despite his impressive contributions to the field of ancient Iraqi archaeology, his discoveries routinely attributed to British colleagues. Neither fully accepted by his fellow countrymen because of his Western associations nor fully embraced by British society, Rassam spent most of his career as a de facto outsider. Ultimately, he was forced to resort to the British courts to defend his work and legacy.

In the exhibition, his presence is evoked through absence: a single portrait photograph, taken in England but showing Rassam in Ottoman clothing, strikingly and deliberately contrasts with a large group of plates from Layard's early publications. These drawings and pseudo-scientific reconstructions were assigned to British nationals, most often officers employed by the East Indian Company, who had limited formal training in archaeology or Mesopotamian history. ISAW's galleries are dominated by three large maps from James Felix Jones's (1813–1878) memoirs (**FIGS. 1-7** to **1-9**) that intentionally dwarf Rassam's portrait. A career officer who mapped vast portions of the Middle East, Jones embodied this generation of early British explorers, whose work for the crown encompassed military expeditions, business ventures, and political interventions in the reformulation of states that were rising from the dissolving Ottoman Empire. On this complex political checkboard, the archaeological missions and surveys carried out by the likes of Layard and Jones became one means through which Britain exerted tight control over large swaths of the modern Middle and Near East, a tool that ultimately resulted in the almost exclusive Western monopoly over the formulation of the Iraqi past. When images of local workmen appear on the lithographs illustrating excavation activities, they are either used as a reference scale next to oversize sculptural figures (**FIG. 1-10**) or as anonymous masses whose visual function is to celebrate the grandiosity of the mission. Often shown barefoot with clothing reminiscent of local tribal attire, these figures are associated with manual labor, quite openly implying that the study and interpretation of what was unearthed was beyond their intellectual abilities, and thus in the exclusive purview of the Western project directors.

Rassam is by no means the only Iraqi scholar or artist who reckoned with his history. The essays by both Nelida Fuccaro and Ala Younis (**CHAPTERS 3** and **5**)

OPPOSITE, TOP: FIG. 1-5. Latif Al Ani. Ctesiphon, tourists in front of the ruins of the Tāq Kasrā (Arch of Ctesiphon). Gelatin silver negative on cellulose acetate film. 1964. AIF: 0190an01181. Checklist no. 41. **OPPOSITE, BOTTOM: FIG. 1-6.** Latif Al Ani. Ctesiphon, tourists in front of the ruins of the Tāq Kasrā (Arch of Ctesiphon). Gelatin silver negative on cellulose acetate film. 1964. AIF: 0190an00917. Checklist no. 42.

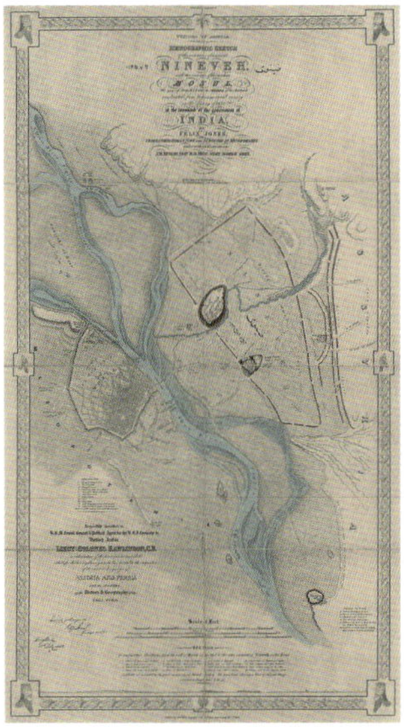

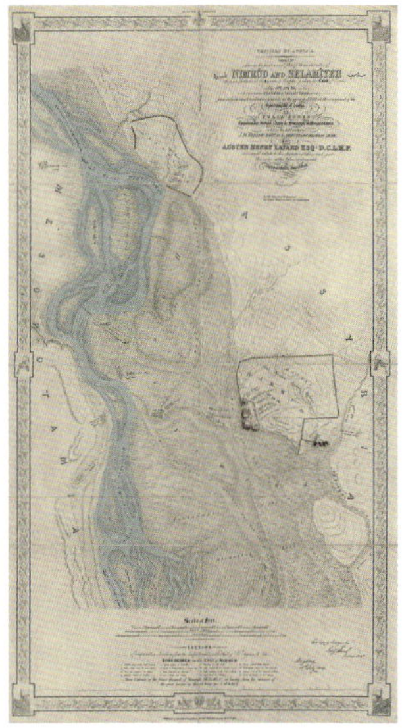

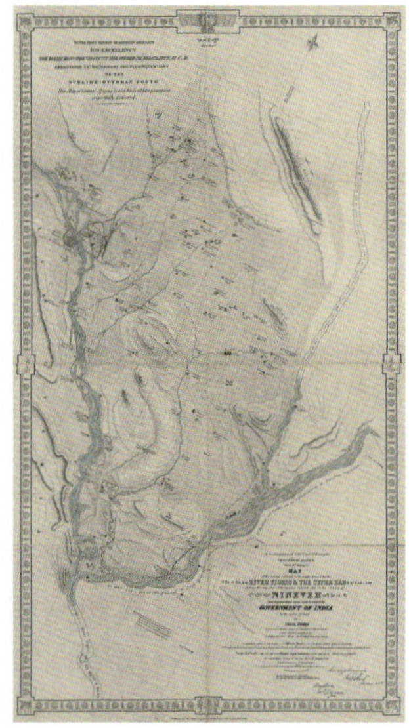

ABOVE, FROM LEFT TO RIGHT: FIG. 1-7. Map of Nineveh. From James Felix Jones, *Memoirs of Baghdad, Kurdistan and Turkish Arabia: Selections from the Records of the Bombay Government*, n.s., no. 63. Hand-colored engraving. 1857. Checklist no. 27. **FIG. 1-8.** Map of Nimrud and Selamiyah. From James Felix Jones, *Memoirs of Baghdad, Kurdistan and Turkish Arabia: Selections from the Records of the Bombay Government*, n.s., no. 63. Hand-colored engraving. 1857. Checklist no. 28. **FIG. 1-9.** Map of Nineveh, the River Tigris, and the Upper Zab. From James Felix Jones, *Memoirs of Baghdad, Kurdistan and Turkish Arabia: Selections from the Records of the Bombay Government*, n.s., no. 63. Hand-colored engraving. 1857. Checklist no. 29.

deal with Latif Al Ani's work for the Iraqi Petroleum Company (IPC), an oil conglomerate founded in 1929 by the largest oil companies from Britain, the Netherlands, and France, together with some of the most prominent investors who survived the demise of the Ottoman Empire. Nationalized in 1962, IPC was at the forefront of Iraq's modernization. In its attempt to normalize oil exploitation, the company employed propaganda tools inspired by Western practices, including the publication of lavishly illustrated magazines meant for a local and international readership. The revisitation of the country's rich ancient history became a favored strategy: long articles about the wonders of ancient Iraq, consistently written by non-Iraqi contributors, promoted the narrative of oil as the primary means to actualize the promise of modern Iraq's return to the prominence it enjoyed during its glorious past.

Through the Lens investigates how the influence of antiquity turned into a leitmotif in Iraq during the 1950s and '60s, one that spread to many aspects of contemporary society. Through Al Ani's images, the exhibition explores Iraqi architectural and artistic trends, as seen in the work of renowned architect Hisham Munir (b. 1930) and in sculptures by Jewad Selim (1919–1961) and Khaled al-Rahal (1926–1987). Educated in the United States, Munir returned to Iraq to become one of the major proponents of architectural modernism. His projects encompassed large public commissions sponsored by the Ministry of Housing and Works, banks, and hotels, but also housing complexes. Munir's buildings changed the urban landscape, especially in Baghdad, to convey a vision that reflected his own interest in contemporary political preoccupations.[1] Though Munir adopted technologies and designs extraneous to the Iraqi past, such as embracing minimalism and widely adopting concrete, his work remained embedded within traditional architecture.

Particularly poignant is the use of brickworks in his Villa (**FIGS. 4-6** to **4-8**). In the gallery space, Latif Al Ani's images of the Villa are juxtaposed with plates

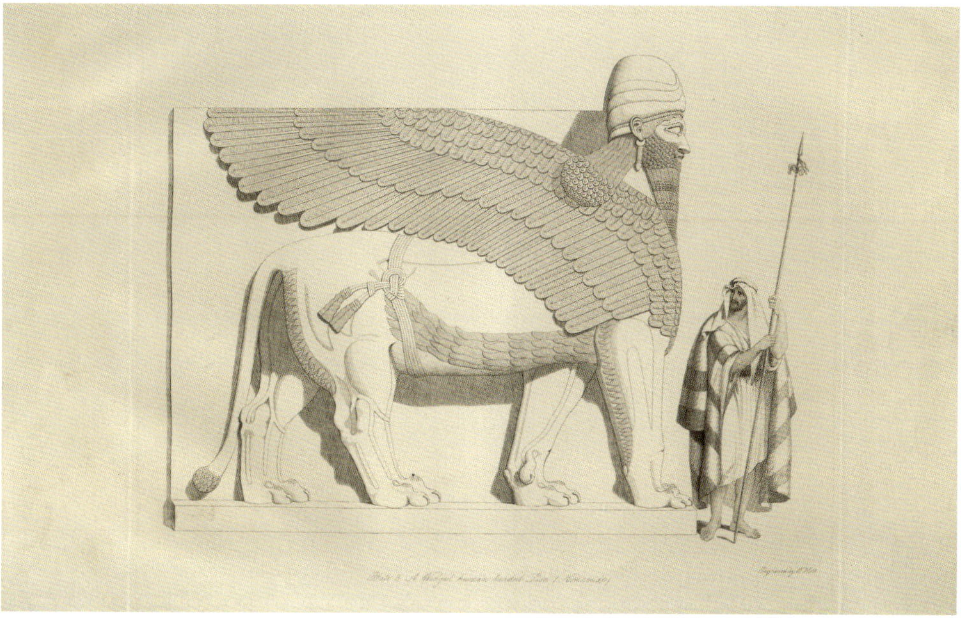

FIG. 1-10. "A Winged Human-headed Lion (Nimroud)." Plate 3 from Austen Henry Layard, *The Monuments of Nineveh: From Drawings Made on the Spot*. Lithograph from an original drawing by Frederick Charles Cooper. 1849. ISAW: N5380 .L3 1849 Folio. Checklist no. 14.

from Layard's publications on Nineveh and Babylon (**FIGS. 1-10** to **1-13**) and with the fragmentary bricks of Adel Abidin's (b. 1973) *Debris* (**FIGS. 6-4** and **6-11**). One cannot overstate the centrality of plain and glazed mud bricks in the construction of Mesopotamian architecture.[2] From the thousands of unadorned bricks comprising monumental ziggurats (**FIG. 4-19**) to individually molded bricks that came together to form highly complex, relief motifs (**FIG. 1-14**), bricks concomitantly constituted a humble, versatile building module and a powerful medium that visually expressed religious, political, and cultural dogmas. The fragmentary glazed bricks in Layard's plates function as a compelling countermelody to the badly damaged concrete blocks that comprise Abidin's installation. Covered in torn images of Islamic imams, *Debris* reaches back to ancient Iraq, where the images prominently on display on building facades were one of the most consequential vehicles in the creation of cultural and religious identity.

Just as Munir incorporated contemporary trends into a millenary building tradition, Jewad Selim and Khaled al-Rahal installed large, commissioned artworks that introduced iconographies strongly tied to ancient Iraq yet reformulated according to new artistic canons. Latif Al Ani captured in his images this interesting commixtion of old and new: fascinated by Selim's *Freedom Monument* and its central location in Baghdad, he produced many images of this sculptural group, both from the ground and in aerial views (**FIGS. 3-7**, **4-9**, and **4-18**).[3] He also documented some of al-Rahal's public works. Interestingly, al-Rahal started his career at the Iraqi Museum, where he was tasked with making replicas of ancient artifacts. Most notably, he was in charge of the copies of the bust of Queen Puabi (2600–2450 BCE) as it was reconstructed by Katharine Woolley immediately after its discovery in 1927. Al-Rahal's exposure to powerful female figures of the past inspired his art throughout most of his career, as attested by the *Motherhood Monument* of 1961, which was prominently displayed in Baghdad's Umma Park (**FIG. 1-15**).

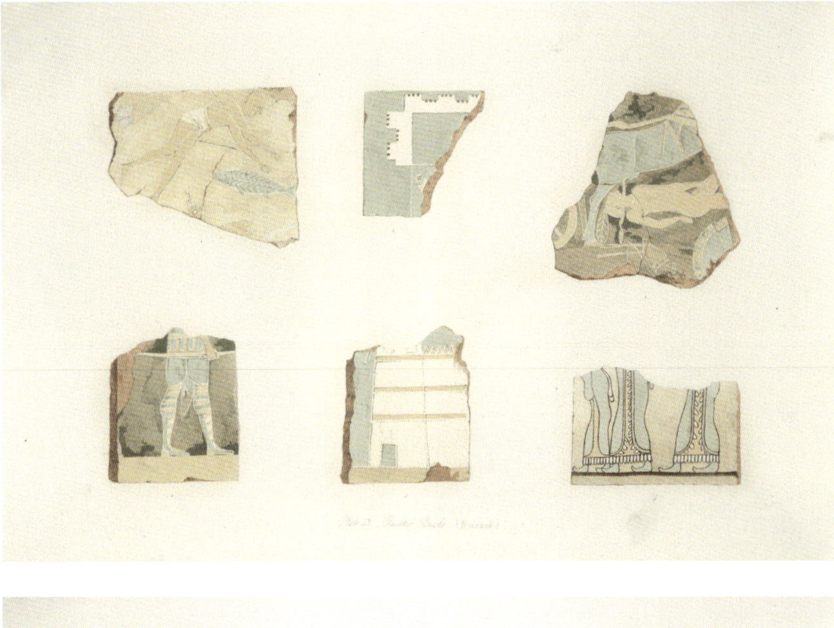

FIG. 1-11

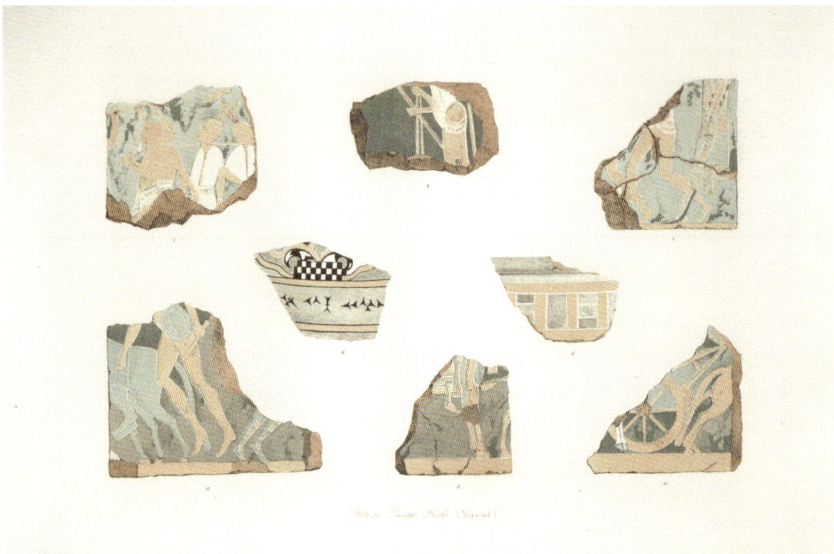

FIG. 1-12

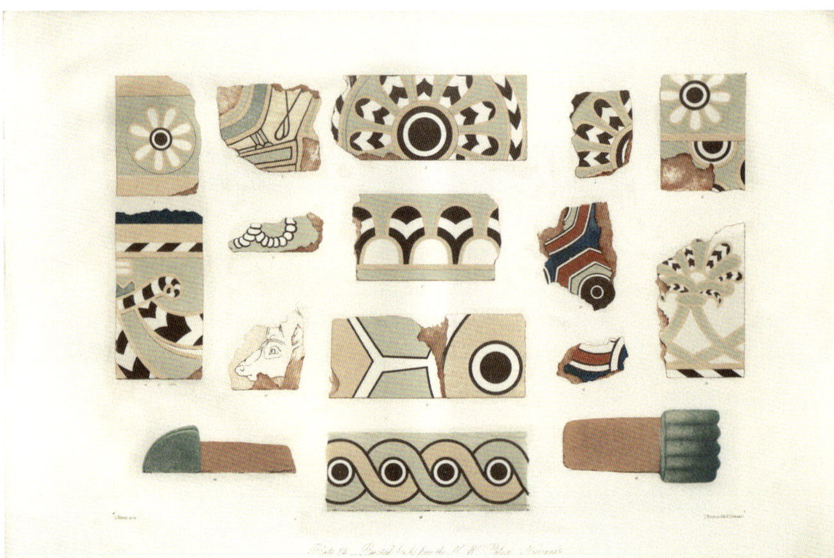

FIG. 1-13

A similarly strong relation with Iraq's ancient history is immediately apparent in the works of the other four contemporary artists on display in *Through the Lens*. However, for each of them this connection takes on very different connotations, filters through which the shared past encounters the personal past. Hanaa Malallah's (b. 1958) approach to antiquity is deeply affected by issues of decolonization (**CHAPTER 8**). Her drawings and videos document the aftermath of Western excavations, addressing how these archaeological missions continue to influence our collective understanding of Mesopotamian civilizations while visually and physically scarring Iraq's land. "Ruination" is for Malallah a process that marks Iraq and, by extension, its very identity. In her *Babylon Curse* drawings, a new commission realized for the ISAW exhibition (**FIGS. 8-6** to **8-9**), the artist makes of ancient Babylon an admonition for humanity's future. The integration of Big Ben, the symbol of London par excellence, transports a long-gone past into the immediacy of the present. Her accompanying videos, made with drones operated by veiled females—hinting at the current debate on the role of women in contemporary Iraqi scholarship and society—are placed within the exhibition space in direct conversation with some of Al Ani's first aerial photographs. This visual dialogue between the two artists emphasizes their very different uses of aerial photography. Whereas Malallah employs it to document the violence of historic Western excavations and of more recent wars, Latif Al Ani's wide-angled views have recorded the monuments as cultural landmarks captured in a serene stillness.

If the work of Malallah comes alive as a protest against the destruction of cultural heritage and modern Iraqi identity, the towers of Walid Siti (b. 1954) embody his nostalgic approach to a past now lost, a past that coincides simultaneously with antiquity and Siti's personal timeline in the years before Saddam Hussein's ascent to power. Siti's spiral minaret of Samarra, revisited both in the video *To the Unknown Architect* (**FIGS. 10-6** and **10-7**) and in his *Seven Towers* drawing (**FIG. 10-8**) strikingly contrast with Al Ani's pictures of the same monument (**FRONT COVER** and **FIG. 10-2**). In the exhibition, Siti's and Al Ani's images of Samarra are placed on the same wall to initiate yet another dialogue between the artists. In her essay on Walid Siti (**CHAPTER 10**), Nat Muller aptly refers to the sense of ephemerality that the artist transmits through his works, a feeling of melancholic fragility that is fully on view in *Arched Tower* (**FIG. 10-10**), a new commission specifically conceived for *Through the Lens*. None of this fragility is implied in Al Ani's views of the Samarra monument. By moving farther away from the minaret, the photographer readdressed the relation between the viewer and the structure: rather than feeling dwarfed by its strong verticality, we are invited to perceive the solidity of the architecture as evidence of its ability to defy time and decay. Siti's world is in flux; Al Ani's is built to persist.

Siti's melancholy for a lost past turns into sorrow in Mahmoud Obaidi's (b. 1966) *Fragments* (**CHAPTER 9**; **FIGS. 9-2** and **9-3**). Hundreds of elements cast in weathering steel, a material that provides a richly toned surface, evoke time

OPPOSITE, FROM TOP TO BOTTOM: FIG. 1-11. "Painted Bricks (Nimroud)." Plate 53 from Austen Henry Layard, *A Second Series of the Monuments of Nineveh*. Lithograph from an original drawing by Frederick Charles Cooper. 1853. ISAW: N5380 .L3 1853 Folio. Checklist no. 5. **FIG. 1-12.** "Painted Bricks (Nimroud)." Plate 54 from Austen Henry Layard, *A Second Series of the Monuments of Nineveh*. Lithograph from an original drawing by Frederick Charles Cooper. 1853. ISAW: N5380 .L3 1853 Folio. Checklist no. 6. **FIG. 1-13.** "Painted Bricks from the N. W. Palace—Nimroud." Plate 84 from Austen Henry Layard, *The Monuments of Nineveh: From Drawings Made on the Spot*. Lithograph from an original drawing by Frederick Charles Cooper. 1849. ISAW: N5380 .L3 1849 Folio. Checklist no. 7.

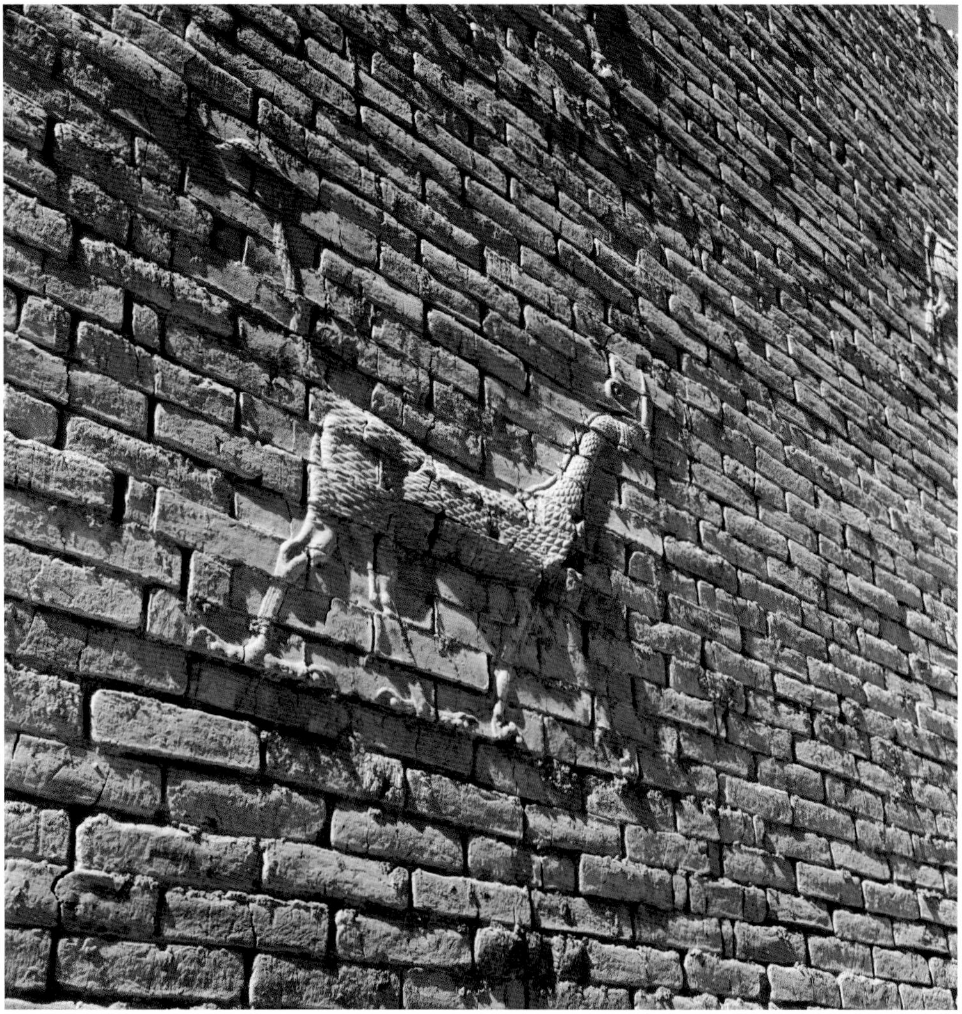

FIG. 1-14. Latif Al Ani. Babylon, detail of a *mušḫuššu* dragon from the Ishtar Gate. Gelatin silver negative on cellulose acetate film. Ca. 1961. AIF: 0190an00630. Checklist no. 12.

passing and trauma. Four modern shoes, meant for a young girl, sit among heaps of flattened votive statues that reproduce Sumerian types excavated at sites such as Khafajah, Tell Asmar, and Diyala. Dust, abrasions, and accretions, all natural results of the weathering process, magnify the feeling of desolation. In the exhibition space, these objects are piled within museum vitrines, as if the viewers were presented with relics of a bygone era reeling from an apocalyptic, all-encompassing event: war.

Conversely, war is digitally erased in Nadine Hattom's (b. 1980) *Shadows* (**CHAPTER 7**; **FIGS. 7-3** to **7-12**). At first glance, Hattom's photographs return the ancient monument to the peaceful, timeless dimension of Al Ani's images. But that peaceful atmosphere is deceptive: not even time can erase the shadows of war. Figments of soldiers past lurk in the space, in the memories of the people who witnessed those events, and in the very identity of generations to come.

Through the Lens: Latif Al Ani's Visions of Ancient Iraq confronts the cultural and political extortion of Iraq's past as seen through the eyes of nineteenth-century archaeologists, twentieth-century photographers, and contemporary artists who experienced it firsthand. In this endeavor, Al Ani's images serve as the primary entry point and connecting thread in our exploration of the filters that have

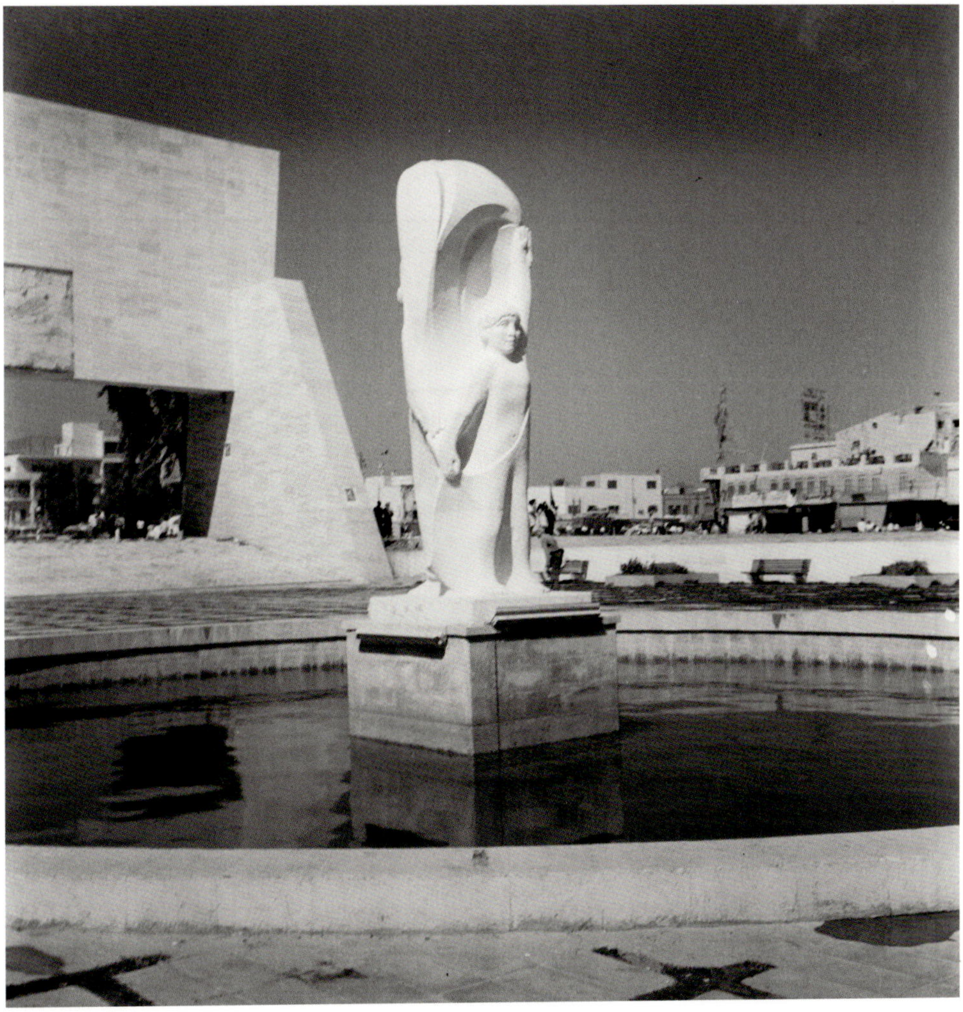

FIG. 1-15. Latif Al Ani. Baghdad, Umma Park: Khaled al-Rahal's Motherhood Monument. Gelatin silver negative on cellulose acetate film. Ca. 1960. AIF: 0190an00612. Checklist no. 80.

affected remote and recent pasts: the nineteenth-century Western appropriation of Iraqi antiquity; the effects of modernization on Iraqi society during the 1960s; and the contemporary response to more recent events that have influenced the relation between visual art, politics, and identity. Ultimately, *Through the Lens* is an exhibition that moves from personal stories and pasts to reveal the complex reality of communal identity, an identity that is the sum of all the filters through which the past is shared.

1 Hisham Munir, "A Perspective into Iraqi Modern Architecture," lecture, Massachusetts Institute of Technology, October 15, 2015, https://www.archnet.org authorities/1286?media_content_id=104347.

2 Fügert and Gries 2019.

3 Al-Tameemi 2020.

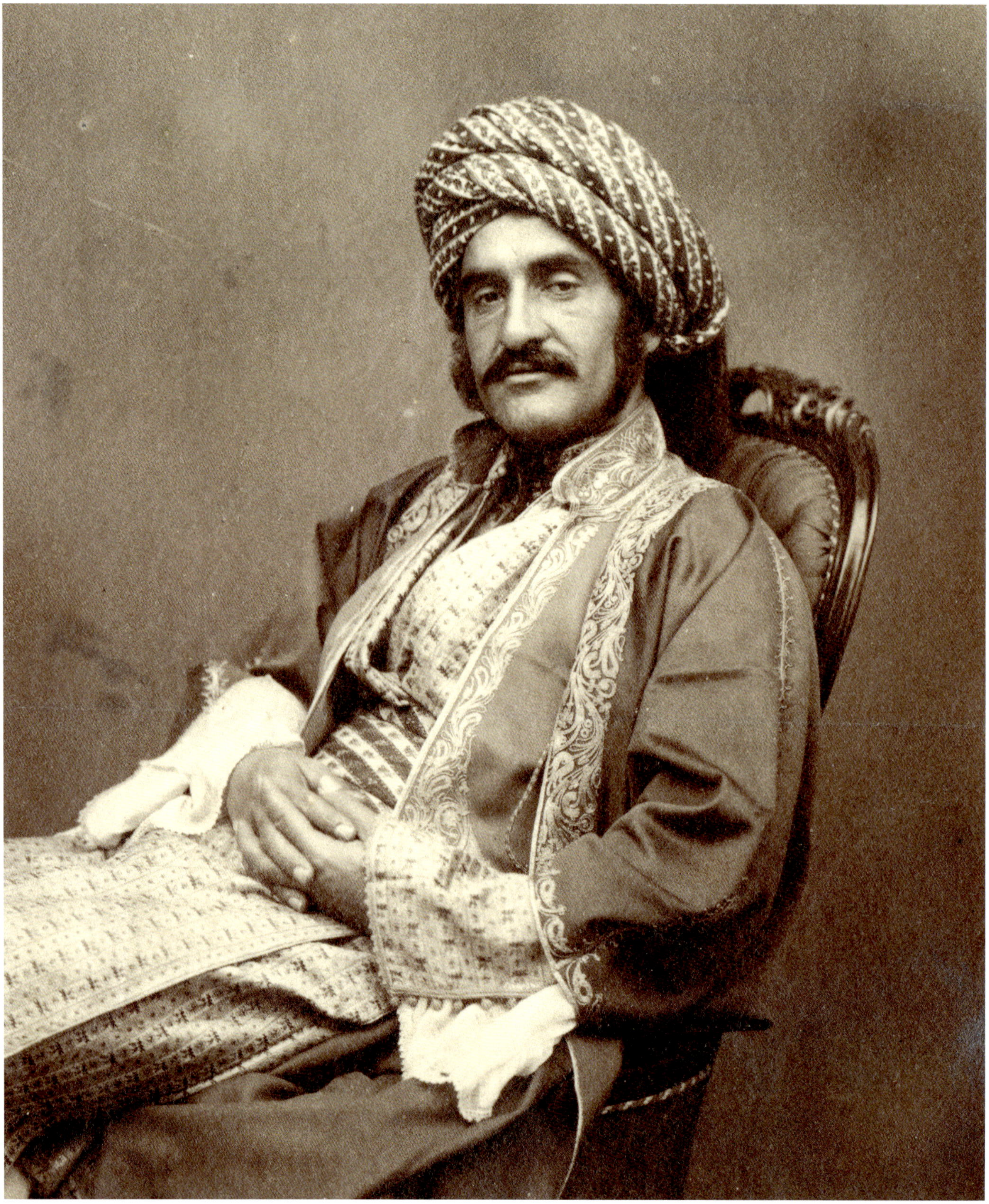

CHAPTER 2

HORMUZD RASSAM: AN IRAQI PERSPECTIVE

Narmin Amin and Abdulrahman K. Darwesh

The character of the archaeologist Hormuzd Anton Rassam (1826–1910; FIG. 2-1) embodies the contradictions of his era. It was a time when states began developing archaeological missions in the Near East, in which the relations between researchers for antiquities were considered more important than reports and archives. Rassam faced the same issues that modern missions face, including a lack of funds. Diving into the past with a new vision, we see that he navigated a difficult and complicated situation created by the diverse political and historical backgrounds of his era.

At the end of the eighteenth century in the Near East, under Ottoman domination, there was little interest in antiquities. Various traditional perspectives constituted a prevailing trend against preserving antiquities. Archaeological discoveries held little importance until the establishment of Western missions at the beginning of archaeological work. The Ottomans shared the discovered objects from the occupied countries. In Mesopotamia, whether through French or British imperialists, the primary focus was on unearthing statues, sculptures, clay cuneiform tablets, and cylinder seals and displaying them in international museums, which led to a competitive atmosphere.

There was initially a legal vacuum for the preservation and excavation of archaeological property. As archaeology was in its early stages within this context, Rassam's personality stands out with all its contradictions in the face of divergent opinions among foreign and Iraqi researchers about the legality of his work. Was Rassam an impulsive figure, enthusiastic about the history and civilization of his country and his understanding of the world? Did he remain in the shadow of other, more prominent characters, such as Assyriologist Sir Austen Henry Layard

FIG. 2-1. Hormuzd Rassam photographed by Philip Henry Delamotte, ca. 1854. SWASM: SM1987.845.79. Checklist no. 31.

(1817–1894)? How can we objectively examine Rassam's personality without fanaticism or discrimination? Yet, how can we discount his contributions, which constitute a significant part of the history of archaeological work in Mesopotamia, including present-day Iraq? We must properly recognize and reintroduce his conceptual perceptions. The continuous criticism that he was and continues to be exposed to from different sides, makes studying Rassam from all aspects an important and essential matter for discovering the many intellectual, political, and social aspects of his time.

—

Hormuzd Anton Rassam was born in 1826 in Mosul, a culturally, religiously, and ethnically diverse environment. He came from a religious Chaldean Catholic family and acquired his knowledge of antiquities from Austen Henry Layard (FIG. 2-2).[1] Rassam studied in Britain at Magdalen College, and in addition to his work in antiquities he was involved in the political and diplomatic fields. Rassam made several significant and independent archaeological discoveries, which sparked intellectual, religious, and political controversies in the nineteenth century. He is regarded as one of the most important pioneers of Assyrian archaeological studies, and was a member of the British Royal Geographical Society. After 1882 he resided primarily in Brighton, England.[2]

Considered one of the greatest archaeologists of his time, Rassam discovered more antiquities than all other British archaeologists combined in the nineteenth century. Over the course of nearly four decades, Rassam made numerous important discoveries, among them the groundbreaking finds in Nineveh (FIG. 2-3) at the end of 1852 and, most notably, the library of King Ashurbanipal.

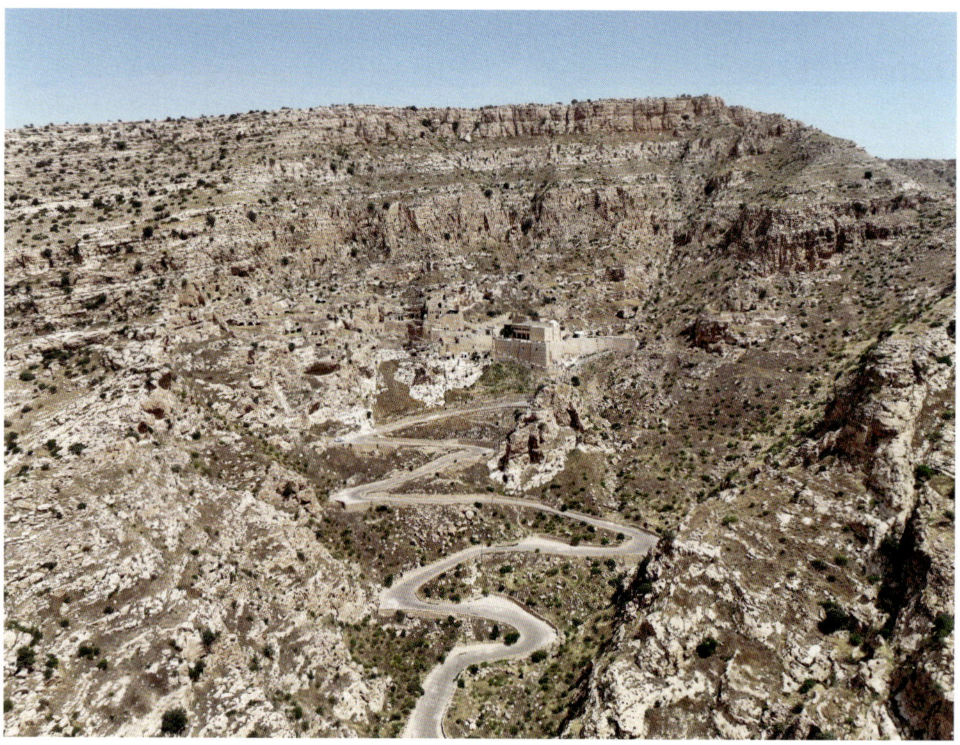

FIG. 2-2. Photo of Rabban Hormizd Monastery of Chaldean Catholic Church. Alqosh, Iraq. Taken by the authors, 2023.

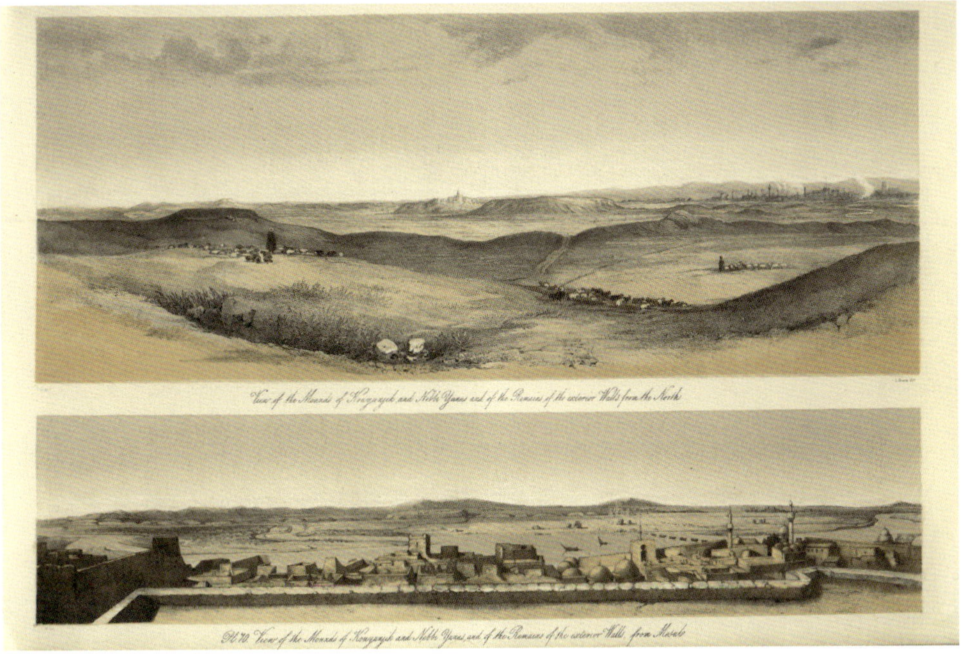

FIG. 2-3. "View of the mounds of Kouyunjik [Quyunjik] and Nebbi Yunus, and of the remains of the exterior walls, from the North." Plate 70 from Austen Henry Layard's *A Second Series of the Monuments of Nineveh*. Lithograph from an original drawing by Frederick Charles Cooper. 1853. ISAW: N5380 .L3 1853 Folio. Checklist no. 35.

This discovery provided invaluable insights into various topics, such as the story of the flood, Noah's ark, Gilgamesh and Ishtar, the tragedy of Tammuz, and Etana. It also contributed to our understanding of cuneiform dictionaries, as well as literature, theology, and economics of that ancient era.[3]

The British missions that followed were able to find approximately twenty-five thousand inscriptions or fragments of inscriptions from the library of Ashurbanipal.[4] Additionally, Rassam supplemented these findings with what Layard discovered in the small temple in front of the palace of the god Nabu (**FIG. 2-4**) and in the palace of Sennacherib (**FIG. 2-5**), as well as with ten thousand inscriptions seized by the Ottomans, most of which are preserved in the Istanbul Archaeology Museums.[5]

Among Rassam's most significant discoveries were the temple built by King Ashurbanipal in Nimrud (**FIG. 2-6**). In 1879 he famously discovered the Cyrus cylinder—a remarkable artifact dating back to 539 BCE, which commemorates the conquest of Babylon by the Achaemenid Empire. Between 1878 and 1882, he uncovered the gates of Balawat, an ancient city near Nineveh. These remarkable achievements solidified Rassam's reputation as a prominent archaeologist in Mesopotamia, leading to his award of a significant financial prize by the Academy of Sciences in Turin in 1882.

In Tell Abu Habba (twenty kilometers south of Baghdad) in 1881, Rassam discovered the Sun Temple in Sippar, where he found the Nabonidus cylinders and the Nebo-Apla-Edina stone tablet from Babylon, featuring relief inscriptions and writing. Additionally, he unearthed around fifty thousand clay tablets containing temple accounts, along with many other discoveries.[6]

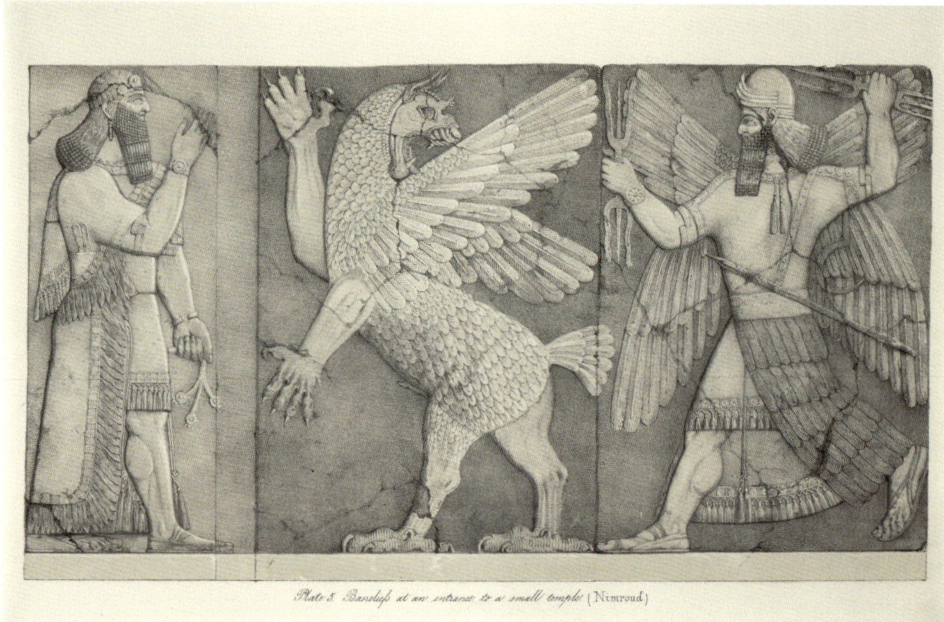

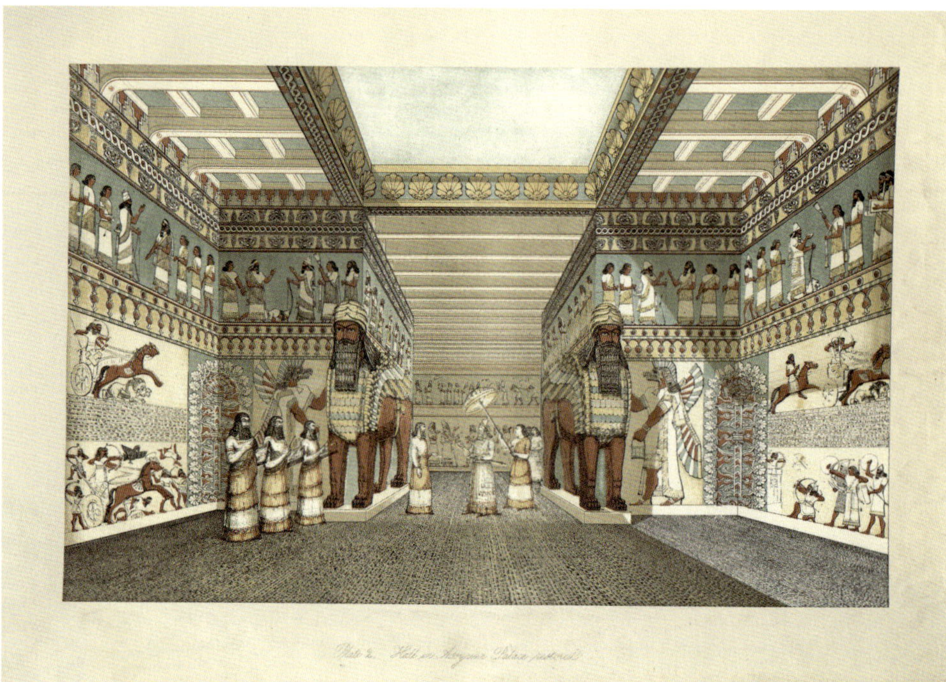

TOP: FIG. 2-4. “Basreliefs at an extrance to a small temple (Nimroud).” Plate 5 from Austen Henry Layard’s *A second Series of the Monuments of Nineveh*. Lithograph from an original drawing by Frederick Charles Cooper. 1853. ISAW: N5380 .L3 1853 Folio. Checklist no. 34. **BOTTOM: FIG. 2-5.** “Hall in Assyrian palace restored.” Plate 2 from Austen Henry Layard’s *The monuments of Nineveh: From Drawings Made on the Spot*. Lithograph from an original drawing by Frederick Charles Cooper. 1849. ISAW: N5380 .L3 1849 Folio. Checklist no. 32.

Many Christian cultural, intellectual, and religious elites in the Nineveh region were influenced by British thought and identity. They abandoned their Catholic doctrine and adopted Protestant beliefs, becoming attached to Britain, defending it, and writing in English. Marie Therese Asmar (1804–1904), known for her book *Memoirs of a Babylonian Princess*, was one of the elites influenced by British

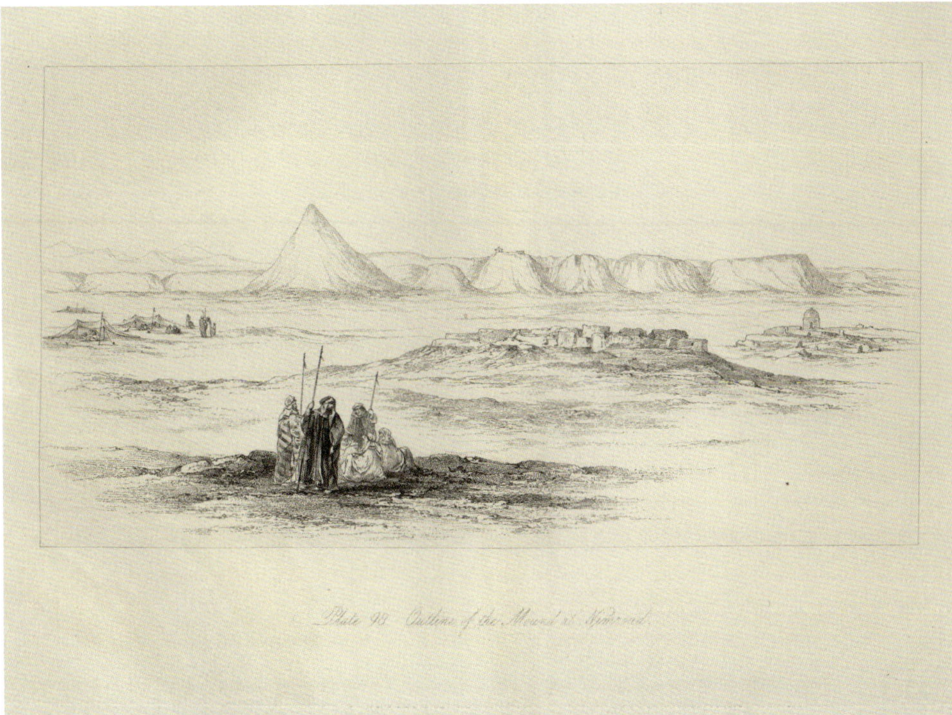

FIG. 2-6. "Outline of the Mound at Nimroud." Plate 98 from *The Monuments of Nineveh: From Drawings Made on the Spot*. Lithograph from an original drawing by Frederick Charles Cooper. 1849. ISAW: N5380 .L3 1849 Folio. Checklist no. 36.

culture, as were many others. Rassam was also among those who embraced British identity, becoming a British citizen and serving Britain exceptionally in various fields.[7]

Rassam's intellectual framework developed in a Catholic religious environment during a time characterized by significant intellectual transformations. He experienced a sense of alienation within the intellectual environment of the Ottoman Empire, which was increasingly leaning toward Islamic religious fundamentalism and Turkish nationalism. Christians in the Near East found European Christian culture to be intellectually and ideologically closer to their own values. Alongside his brother Christian, who became a British citizen and held a consulate position at the British agency in Mosul, Rassam became part of the British circle operating in the region. Both Christian and Rassam were involved in archaeological, political, and diplomatic missions representing the British authority in the area as a family. Rassam exerted his influence in political affairs, in archaeological excavations, and in competition with other archaeological missions.[8]

Rassam was no different from the elites of his time who worked within the archaeological-political framework. He bridged the gap between both realms, as did many before him, his contemporaries, and those who came later. British politicians were involved in antiquities, and archaeologists also dabbled in politics. Rassam, too, engaged in political and diplomatic work in the service of Britain, demonstrating clear political ideas. He worked in various regions, taking on the task of mediation in 1855 between the leader of the Kurdish revolution, Prince YazdanSher, and the Ottoman government, reflecting his extensive connections in the region.[9]

Following the conflict that broke out in Aden in 1861 between the imam of Muscat and his brother, the sultan of Zanzibar, Rassam was assigned to a political mission in Aden. He successfully fulfilled his assignment and received recognition for his efforts in reconciling the two brothers. Subsequently, the British government sent him to Abyssinia in 1864 to rescue an agent of the British government from the captivity of its king. Rassam spent a whole year in Abyssinia, sending letters to the king, requesting his safety. He was welcomed and honored at the royal court, and likely would have succeeded if not for intrigues and conflicting interests. After this Rassam was imprisoned for over two years, but he and the other British agents were eventually released in 1868, as part of one of the most costly and complex conflicts of that era.[10]

—

Archaeological excavations cannot be separated from their religious and political contexts since they support narratives utilized by politicians and clerics in their pursuit of legitimacy as in their countries or in the establishment of sacredness. Archaeologists make the discoveries, and it is possible for them to be influenced by politics or religion, leading to accusations of favoring certain findings over others. They could also encounter numerous complications. In the nineteenth century, the drive for archaeological excavations stemmed from religious perceptions tied to the mentions of various cities in sacred books. The focus was on validating the historical existence of the stories depicted in those sacred texts, but motivations evolved and multiplied as missions diversified and orientations diverged. Additionally, other motives, such as the love of exploration and the desire to acquire ancient artworks for display in numerous museums across Europe—both national and private—should not be overlooked.[11] The prevalence of Eastern romanticism, which captivated Westerners with its alluring mystique, along with explorers' desires and the relatively low cost of comprehensive excavations, were also among the catalysts driving widespread archaeological excavations.[12]

Excavations in the nineteenth century had apparent political consequences, despite the simplicity of the procedures followed, and the extensive history of archaeology reveals its entanglement with political motives. Similar to warfare, excavations became a tool for political maneuvering, albeit through different means. A long history, imbued with political impulses, can be traced in Near Eastern archaeology to the detriment of archaeologists, the material records they unearth, and ethnic minorities in the region.[13] The history of archaeology has demonstrated the potential political misuse of various interpretations stemming from this approach, many of which have been employed to establish political hegemony or to endorse specific political orientations. The fact that many of these travelers participated in diplomatic missions or received early sponsorship from their governments foreshadowed the interdependence of archaeological data and political considerations in the Near East. Consequently, fieldwork became associated with colonial expansion.[14]

This connection between archaeology and political administration persisted into the twentieth century. Gertrude Bell's (1868–1926) activities in Iraq serve as a notable example.[15] It is crucial to acknowledge that archaeologists do not work and excavate solely for themselves; they secure financing for their projects, publish the results, and make decisions regarding the construction of museums to exhibit various aspects of the national past.

The first archaeological excavations in the Nineveh region were carried out by the French archaeologist Paul Emile Botta (1802–1870), who was the French consul in Mosul in 1842, where he began archaeological excavations in the most important cities of Assyria. The British soon emerged as competitors in archeological excavation, taking advantage of their close relationship with the Ottoman sultanate.[16]

The Ottoman Empire did not show much concern for the antiquities within its vast territories, particularly in Mesopotamia and the Greek regions where Classical and other ancient artifacts were found.[17] The empire's policymakers lacked interest in the preservation and protection of antiquities, and their role was not positive. Nevertheless, with the increase in the number of archaeological missions in Mesopotamia and significant Assyrian archaeological discoveries, it can be observed that the Ottomans, influenced by these projects, started paying attention to the results and attempted to claim some of the discoveries for themselves, establishing the Ottoman Imperial Museum in Istanbul to house rare antiquities obtained from European missions operating throughout the empire during that time.

The first Ottoman instructions regarding antiquities and their ownership date back to the nineteenth century.[18] The March Law of 1869 is concise, consisting of only seven items, and its authorship is unknown. The law emphasized that all archaeological work must obtain approval through an Ottoman firman (Decree) and addressed issues of antiquities and their ownership by the state. However, these instructions were not effectively enforced due to amendments made in 1874.[19]

When France initiated its research and archaeological work in the Ottoman Empire, the latter was on the verge of collapse due to the rise of national movements

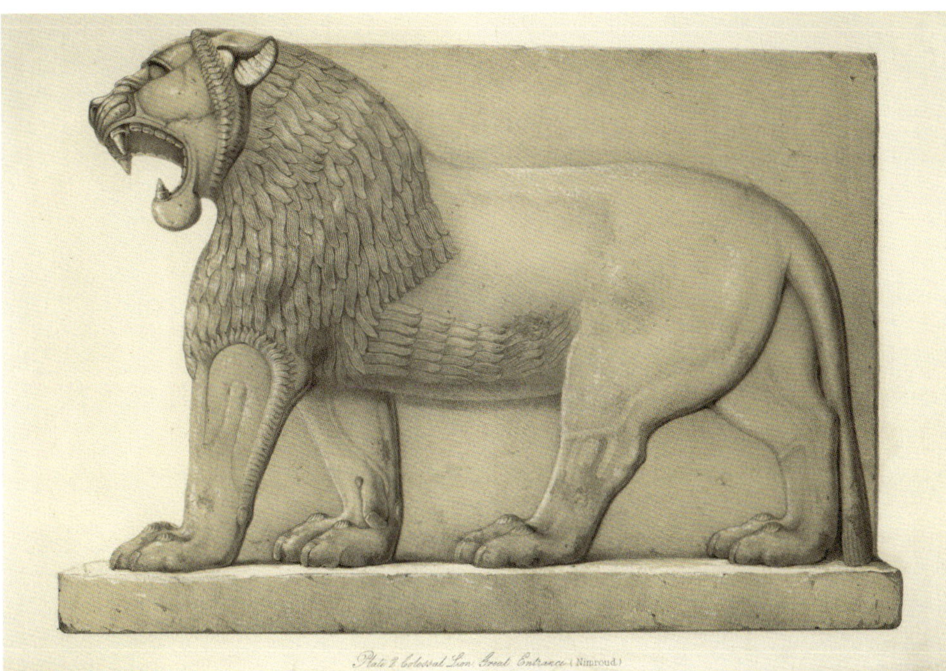

FIG. 2-7. "Colossal Lion, Great Entrance (Nimroud)." Plate 2 from Austen Henry Layard's *A Second Series of the Monuments of Nineveh.* Lithograph from an original drawing by Frederick Charles Cooper. 1853. ISAW: N5380 .L3 1853 Folio. Checklist no. 33.

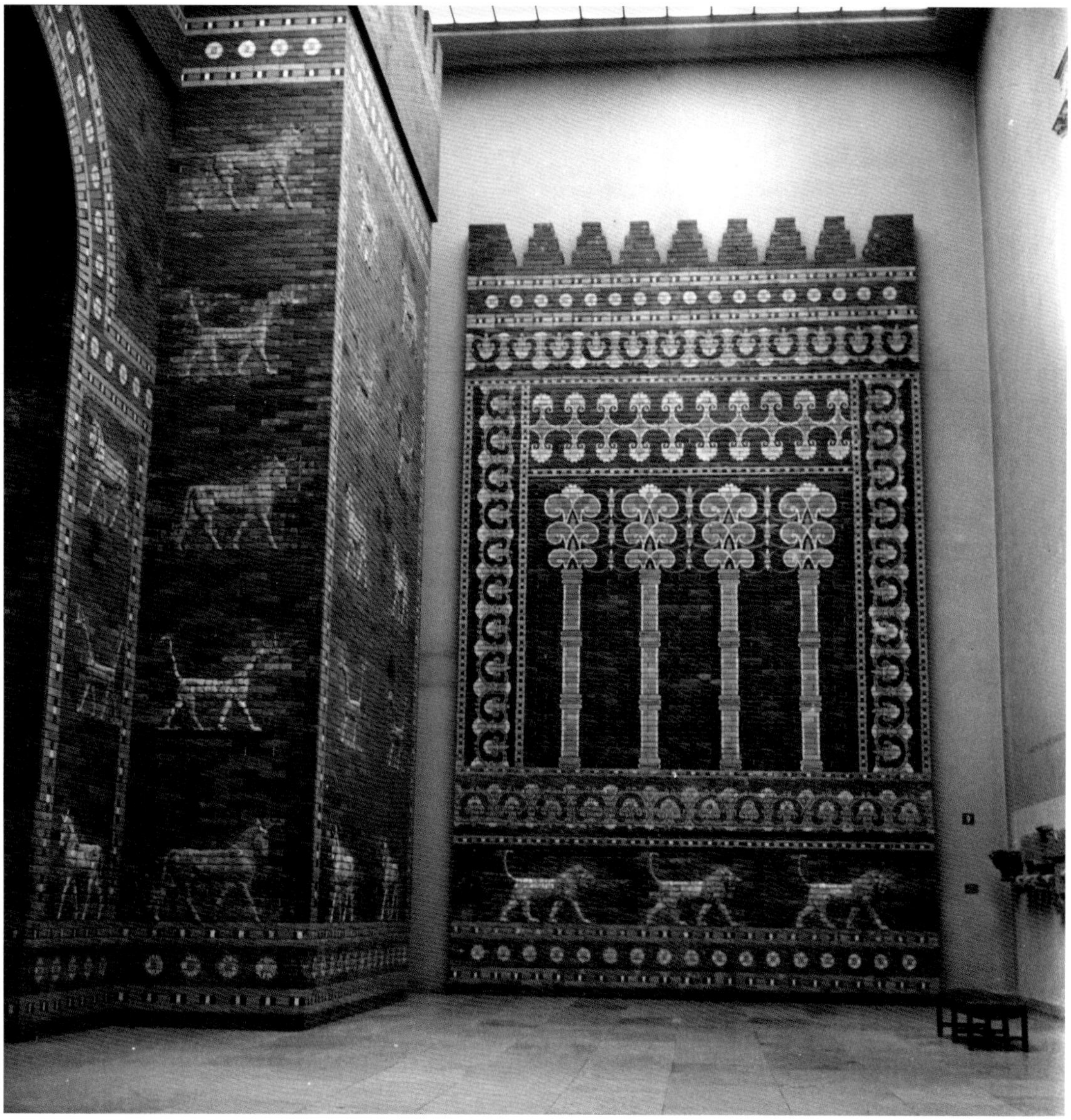

FIG. 2-8. Latif Al Ani. Berlin, Vorderasiatisches Museum: Ishtar Gate. Gelatin silver negative on cellulose acetate film. 1965. AIF: 0190an01345. Checklist no. 17.

and revolutions, and it no longer posed a threat to Europe. During this time, interest in antiquities grew in Mesopotamia, and two important regions, Greece (as per the Treaty of Constantinople in 1832) and Egypt (during the time of Muhammad Pasha in 1840), had separated from Ottoman authority. Additionally, the Russian-Turkish conflict, including the Crimean War between Russia and Turkey in 1854, European interference in Ottoman affairs, and internal tensions further complicated the situation.

Amid this atmosphere, French antiquities policy developed between 1842 and 1855, particularly in the Mosul region of Mesopotamia, influenced by the Ottoman policy of reforms and their organizations (*Tanzimat*). However, discontent began to spread among the local population in Mosul and Baghdad. French and British archaeological missions were initiated to research the lasting influence of Mesopotamia, with the authorization and facilitation of the Ottoman authorities.[20] These missions were led by qualified individuals from European institutions

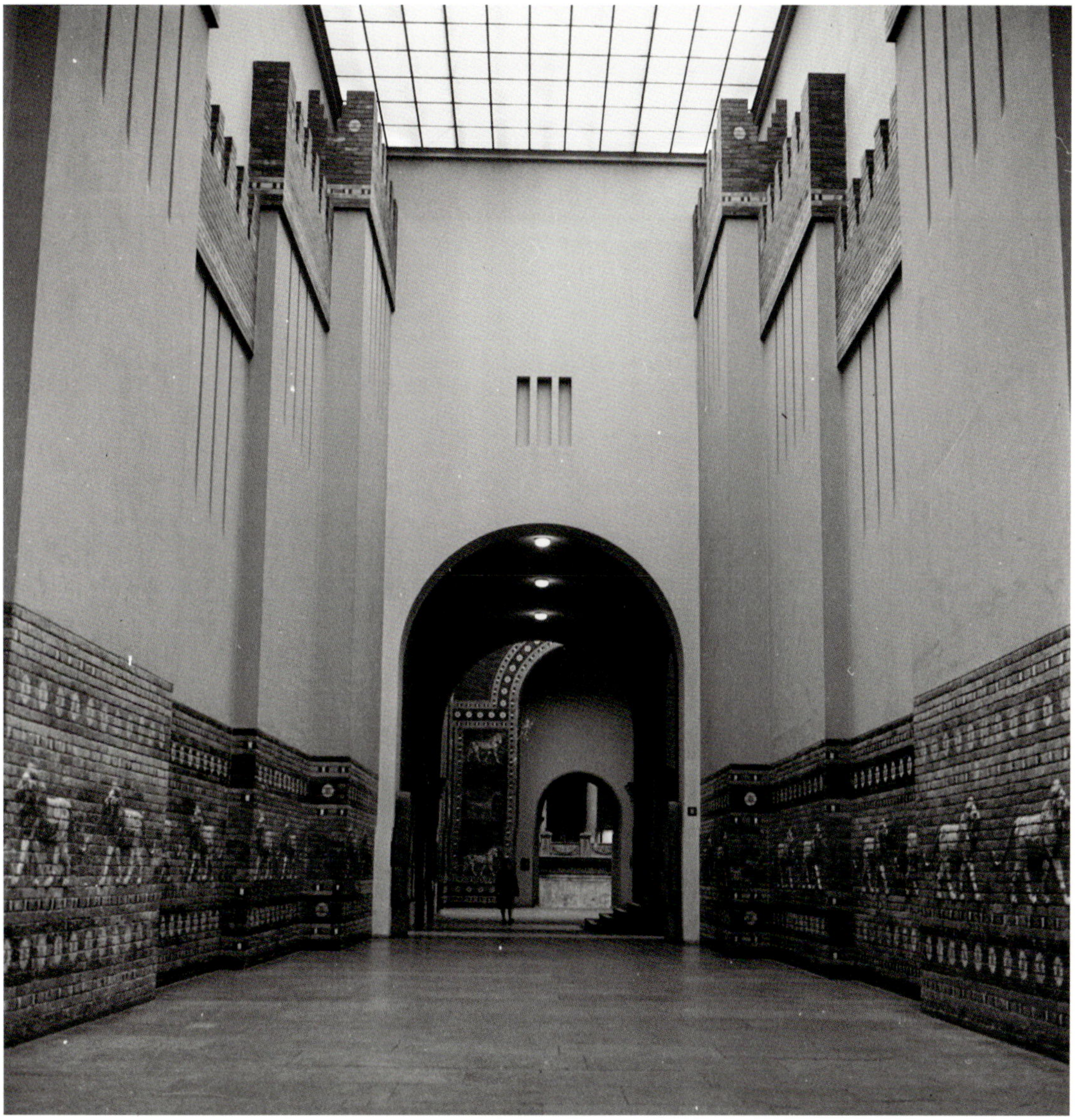

FIG. 2-9. Latif Al Ani. Berlin, Vorderasiatisches Museum: walking lions from the Procession Street of Nebuchadnezzar II. Gelatin silver negative on cellulose acetate film. 1965. AIF: 0190an01348. Checklist no. 18.

and associations, supported by European governments or resident diplomats. The initial motivation behind these expeditions was driven by a spirit of adventure and competition. The primary objective was to collect large quantities of antiquities and trade them to European museums.

In 1851, when the French minister of the interior, Leon Foucher, visited the British Museum and witnessed the collections of Assyrian antiquities amassed by Layard, he was impressed (**FIG. 2-7**). As a result, he requested the continuation of French archaeological work and campaigns in Assyria. A French diplomat and consul in Mosul, Victor Place (1818–1875),[21] took on the responsibility of overseeing the excavations in Khorsabad, followed by Emile Botta.[22]

Beginning in the nineteenth century, British politicians were involved in the collection of ancient antiquities in the region, particularly in Assyria and Babylon, and transported them back to their country (**FIGS. 2-8** and **2-9**). They possessed

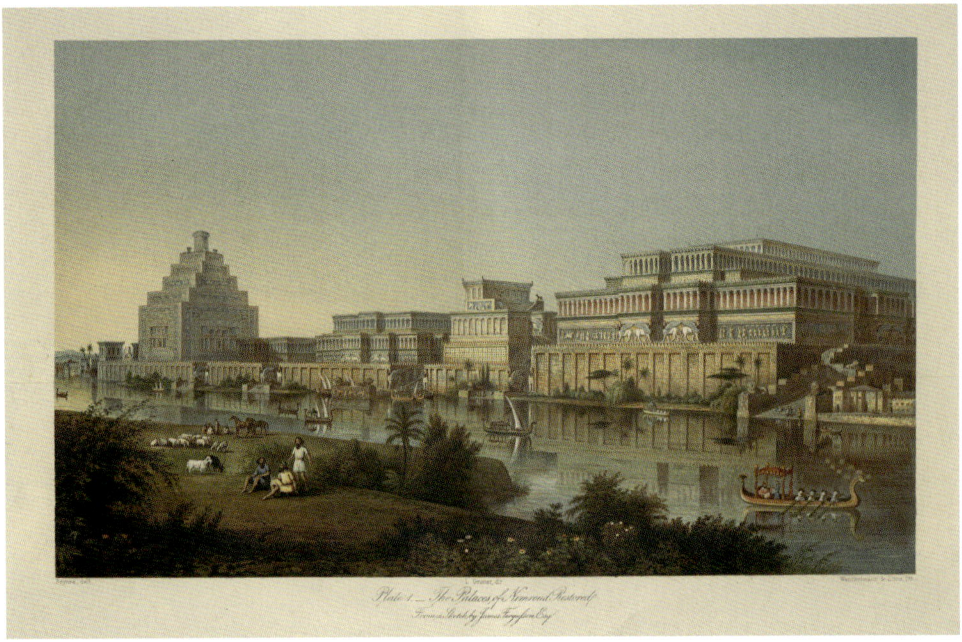

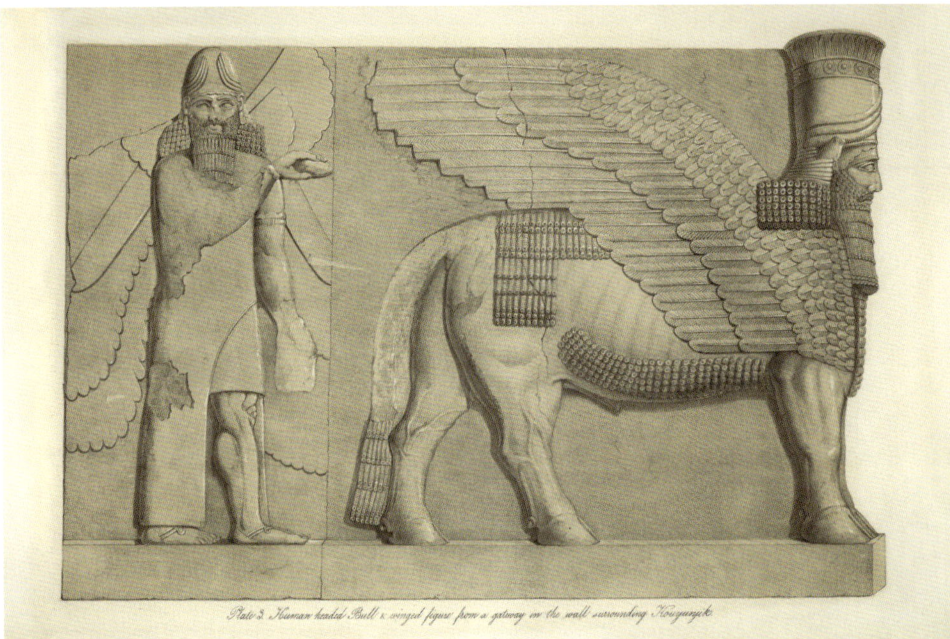

TOP: FIG. 2-10. "The Palace of Nimroud Restored." Plate 1 from Austen Henry Layard's *A Second Series of the Monuments of Nineveh*. Lithograph from an original sketch by James Ferguson, Esq. 1853. ISAW: N5380 .L3 1853 Folio. Checklist no. 30. **BOTTOM: FIG. 2-11.** "Human headed Bull and winged figure from a gateway in the wall surrounding Kouyunjik [Quyunjik]." Plate 3 from Austen Henry Layard's *A second series of the Monuments of Nineveh*. Lithograph from an original drawing by Frederick Charles Cooper. 1853. ISAW: N5380 .L3 1853 Folio. Checklist no. 13.

extensive knowledge of archaeology, as they conducted excavations in Assyria and Babylon, gathering numerous artifacts and transporting them to Britain. One of their notable achievements in Babylon was the creation of a topographical map of the historical city, which became a significant reference for subsequent researchers in identifying the remaining structures in Babylon.

Subsequently, William Heude (1789–1825) embarked on a visit to archaeological sites in 1817. Britain also sent Layard to conduct archaeological excavations in the region. He played a major role in the excavations carried out in Ur and Nineveh, leading several British missions thereafter. In 1829, Colonel Francis Rawdon Chesney (1789–1872),[23] supported by King George IV (r. 1820–1830), was initiated. The British government and the British East India Company jointly funded this campaign. In 1839 the East India Company dispatched Colonel Henry Rawlinson (1810–1895), who had a keen interest in excavation work. Rawlinson made significant progress in Tell Quyunjik, which led to substantial financial support from the British Museum. Known for his meticulousness, enthusiasm, dedication to his work, and expertise in artifact analysis, he excavated numerous cuneiform texts and achieved important results by comparing them.[24]

In the early 1840s, Henry Layard, who was at this point the British ambassador in Istanbul, was tasked with carrying out restoration work in the ruins of Nineveh and Nimrud (**FIG. 2-10**). British excavations took on a broader scope, with missions exploring different regions of Nineveh and Warka (**FIG. 2-11**). The excavations continued until the British military campaign resulted in the British gaining control over the region. In total, there were 108 British archaeological missions between 1811 and 1921.[25]

—

As discussed above, Rassam, along with his family, represented the British presence in the Nineveh region, and was keen on advancing British interests. The Ottomans, with their significant capabilities, were able to marginalize the French role and prevent France from establishing dominance in the field of archaeological excavations in Mosul, Khorsabad, and Tell Quyunjik.[26] In 1852, Rassam clashed with French consul Victor Place and funded a new French campaign in Dur Shurokin, present-day Khorsabad. Simultaneously, British excavations were carried out under the leadership of Rawlinson, who played a major role in deciphering cuneiform script. Rassam conducted archaeological work, collected antiquities, and exerted pressure on the French missions, leveraging his influence and communication with local tribes and powers. He took advantage of logistical problems and complexities that the French faced, and thus he significantly influenced the outcome.[27]

Rassam used his influence and relations in the region to hinder the French in their excavations and gain control over their sites. For instance, he seized the castle of Shirqat, expelling the French from the site. He capitalized on the corruption among the Ottoman authorities to exert pressure on the French mission. This led Place to harbor great bitterness toward Rassam, whom he accused of various offenses, regarding him as merely a greedy collector of sculptures and viewing Rassam's work as "fraud or transgression."[28] However, from Rassam's perspective, the ends justified the means.[29] In his book *Asshur and the Land of Nimrod,* Rassam does not refer to Place's works but rather focuses on the contributions of Layard, Rawlinson, and Loftus. The conflict between the two men had a lasting impact on Place's harsh judgment, and his criticism of Rassam's excavation methods highlighted perceived deficiencies and suggested that he was driven by an obsession to collect sculptures and cuneiform writings, neglecting other important archaeological materials. It is difficult to determine the condition of the excavated and discovered antiquities.

Upon reviewing historical events from the French Archives (*Archives national de France*), it is revealed that Place received telegrams from the Ministry on August 16 and 22, 1853, instructing him to cease work and return to France, resulting in the discontinuation of the nation's antiquities campaign and a focus on the transfer of antiquities and artworks to France.[30]

The controversies described above mark the nineteenth-century beginnings of Assyrian archaeological research and work in Mesopotamia, showcasing the rivalry between the English and the French in the states of Mosul and Assyria, as well as the ambitions of individuals involved in archaeological discoveries.[31] It is clear that Britain greatly benefited from the local influence of Rassam and his family in establishing British dominance over archaeological excavations in the region. Rassam, in turn, played a pivotal role in this conflict, skillfully managing the situation, which resulted in his negative image among the French, who suffered from his policies against them.

—

Archaeological data sometimes allow for multifaceted interpretations, while ideology, politics, and religion contribute to shaping judgments about antiquities and archaeologists, even after significant time has elapsed. Rassam has become a victim of these various aspects, and a century after his death his image continues to suffer in ideological debates.

Despite the great archaeological achievements of Rassam and his significant political and diplomatic activities and contributions, he did not receive the appreciation he deserved. Many believe that he was subjected to persecution, and he firmly believed that he was not accorded appropriate recognition for his services to Britain. As noted above, he discovered a greater number of Assyrian artifacts and clay tablets than all other nineteenth-century British archaeologists combined. Nevertheless, after this remarkable accomplishment, Rassam's name was removed from Assyrian scientific literature and sources. That British society did not accept him as a distinguished archaeological discoverer, just as the administration of the British Museum, discounted his achievements.[32] Others wrongly claimed credit for his discoveries. Wallis Page, the former Keeper of the Ancient Near East Department at the British Museum, accused Rassam and his relatives of stealing artifacts from archaeological sites in Mesopotamia, which led Rassam to take legal action.[33] Following a lengthy trial, Rassam emerged victorious against Wallis, but the court merely fined the curator one English pound, greatly damaging Rassam's reputation. Consequently, he was compelled to withdraw from British society and live the remainder of his life in sadness and seclusion due to the persecution he endured. He was forced to publish *Asshur and the Land of Nimrod*, detailing his activities in excavating ancient Iraqi antiquities and his discoveries, particularly in Ashurbanipal's palace, through a publishing house in the United States.[34]

In *The Buried Book: The Loss and Rediscovery of the Great Epic of Gilgamesh*, David Damrosch details Rassam's suffering and documents the discrimination he was subjected to by the British, who belittled his achievements and regarded him with inferiority.[35] The British removed his name from the books and sources of Assyriology,[36] resulting in his name and work being nearly forgotten. Rassam found himself perplexed when trying to explain the motives behind the lack of recognition despite his numerous accomplishments. Damrosch argues that Rassam was viewed as no more than a Chaldean Christian, considered of insufficient quality to be mentioned with regard to archaeological explorations because of his Near Eastern background, despite being English in his upbringing and serving in the diplomatic corps.[37]

An analysis of the denial and marginalization Rassam faced can have different dimensions. His erasure from history may be related to the nature of British society during that era and the perception of religious, sectarian, and ethnic others, especially those who held influential positions and status among the political, cultural, and scientific elites. It may also be attributed to manifestations of elite conflicts that resulted in the use of discriminatory tactics against him. Additionally, the nature of the conflicts he engaged in at different levels might have played a role. None of these factors justifies the deliberate and irrational rejection of his achievements, and the lack of appreciation for the services he rendered to Britain, which was his homeland and for which he fought. The state of denial and persecution persisted even after Rassam's death. It took several decades for the British Museum to acknowledge his accomplishments, and even then, it was a timid recognition that fell short of what was due.[38]

In addition to the marginalization he experienced in his lifetime, Rassam has been haunted by an unfair curse on the contemporary stage due to various ideological analyses and interpretations. Arab nationalists argue that he personifies someone who served British imperialism and renounced his own identity in favor of aligning with the British crown, only to face humiliation and treatment as an inferior. This discursive interpretation targets the local societies of countries that emerged after World War I, reminding them that those who abandon their identity for the sake of foreign powers will be betrayed and demeaned.[39]

The ideological analysis also accuses Rassam of being a thief of antiquities and civilization for the benefit of imperialism, labeling him as nothing more than a plunderer. His actions and achievements have been demonized, and he has been depicted as a dangerous national traitor.[40] Among the archaeologists affected by the national and religious dimensions in Iraq, some claim that Rassam engaged in looting antiquities for the benefit of European museums and antique collectors. They criticize his work for its haphazard methods of excavation and extraction, particularly in the Tell of the Prophet Yunus.[41]

Rassam belonged to the British sphere of influence at a time when there was no Iraqi national state or even national ideologies among Near Eastern Christians. Rassam's British affiliation provided him and his extensive family with numerous advantages on various levels. The values of Britain were closer to him than those of the Ottoman state, which was leaning toward Islamization and did not treat Christians and other nationalities equitably, often engaging in brutal wars against them. When criticizing his excavation methods and the way he collected and transferred antiquities to museums, it should be noted that such methods were commonly used by archaeological missions (FIGS. 2-12 and 2-13). It is unfair to single out Rassam for those shortcomings. Some argue that he was a victim, manipulated and controlled under the influence of the British, and paid the price for it,[42] but this cannot be considered a valid justification for the ongoing marginalization and distortion of his contributions to significant archaeological discoveries. Regardless of his personal ambition and how he conducted conflicts and interacted with others, Rassam should not have his archaeological achievements denied or be falsely accused of collusion and theft, distorting his image and stealing his accomplishments.

—

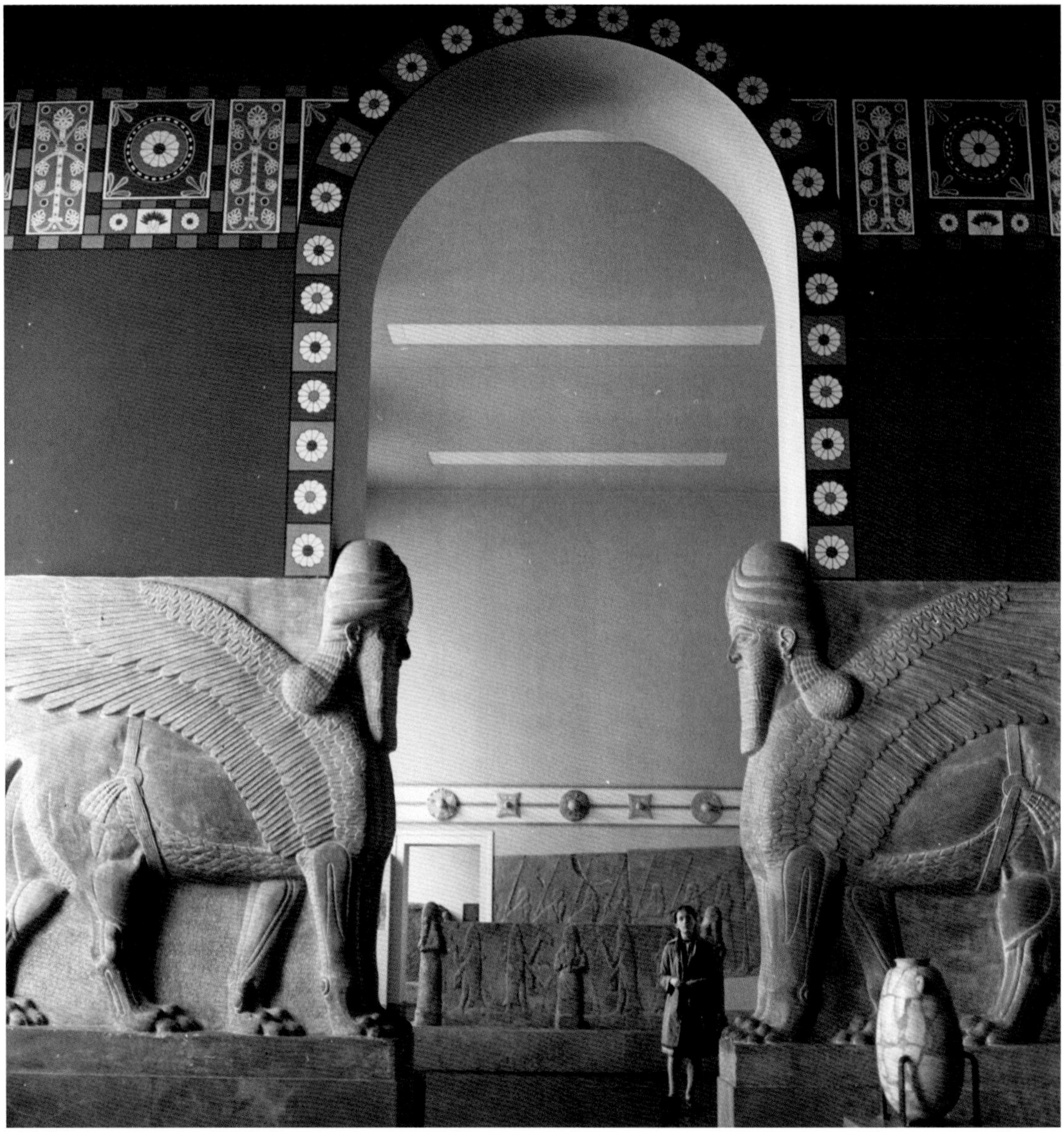

FIG. 2-12. Latif Al Ani. Berlin, Vorderasiatisches Museum: Lamassu reliefs from the palace of Tukulti-Ninurta I. Gelatin silver negative on cellulose acetate film. 1960. AIF: 0190an01133. Checklist no. 15.

The past is not a static, fossilized relic, but rather an inherited product that exerts a significant influence on the present through official and popular texts. It is possible that a conscious, responsible, and globally connected archaeology can serve as a positive force, encouraging, celebrating, and recognizing the true diversity of differences.[43] The challenges faced and the approach taken by Rassam played a crucial role in shaping this formula, which was derived from archaeological excavations and discoveries.

Rassam greatly benefited from his cultural and personal abilities, including his knowledge of the languages spoken in the region and his understanding of the conditions of the inhabitants, as he himself was one of them on his path to archaeological, political, and diplomatic accomplishments. It is not surprising

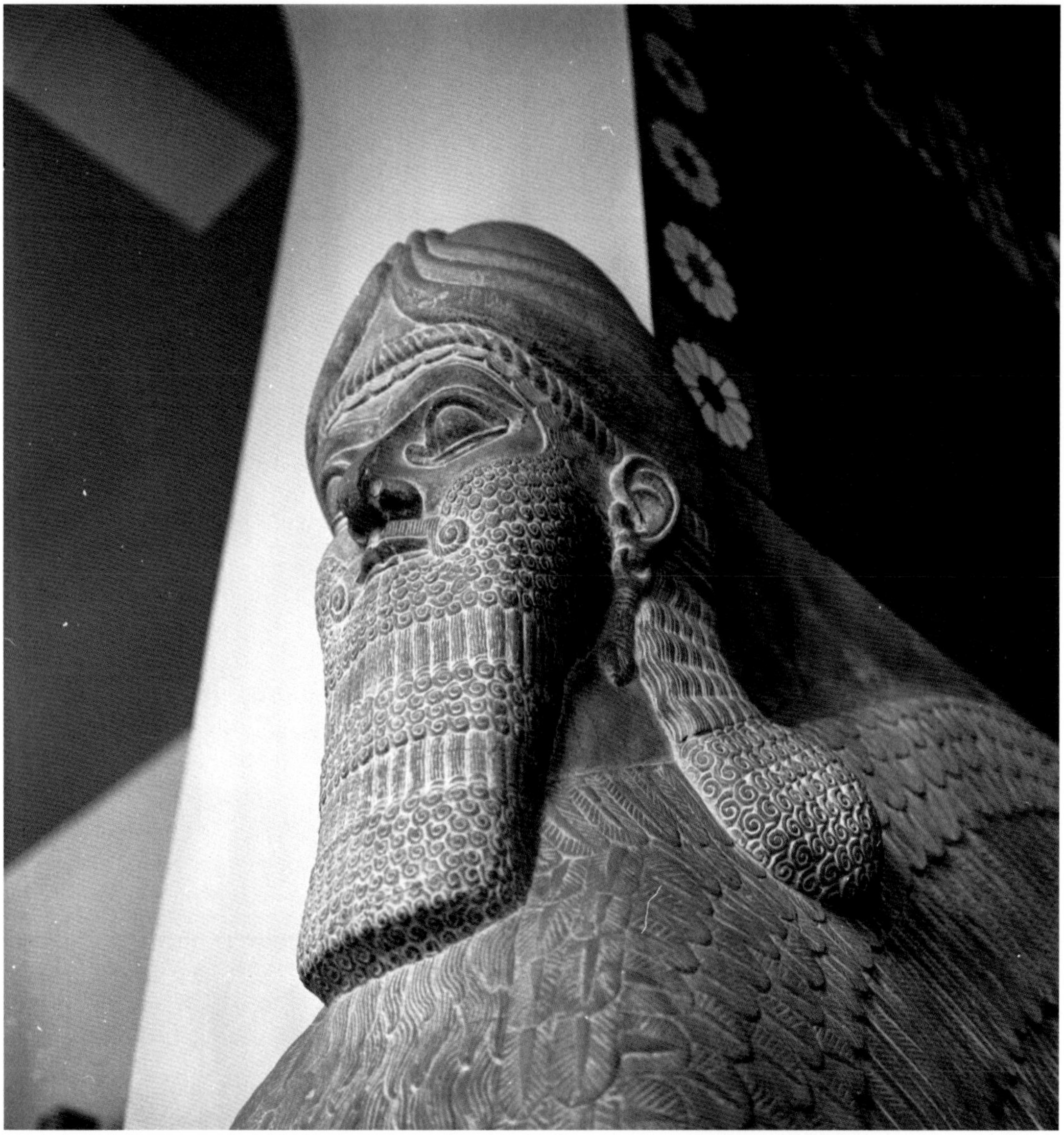

FIG. 2-13. Latif Al Ani. Berlin, Vorderasiatisches Museum: Lamassu reliefs from the palace of Tukulti-Ninurta I. Gelatin silver negative on cellulose acetate film. 1960. AIF: 0190an01132. Checklist no. 16.

that Rassam adopted a British identity, as he felt more closely connected to the British culture than to the Ottoman authority. Embracing a British identity, of course, provided him with numerous privileges in various respects.

The nature of his British political and diplomatic activities aligned with the behavior of British elites during that era, and his method of archaeological excavation was influenced by British archaeologists of the time. Rassam's involvement in the conflict with the French can be understood within the context of the broader British-French rivalry.

While Rassam's marginalization and persecution by the British elites stemmed from various conflicts between archaeologists, of which were primarily based on prevailing beliefs and intellectual ideologies of the time, the negation of his role in archaeological discoveries by the British Museum cannot be justified. It can

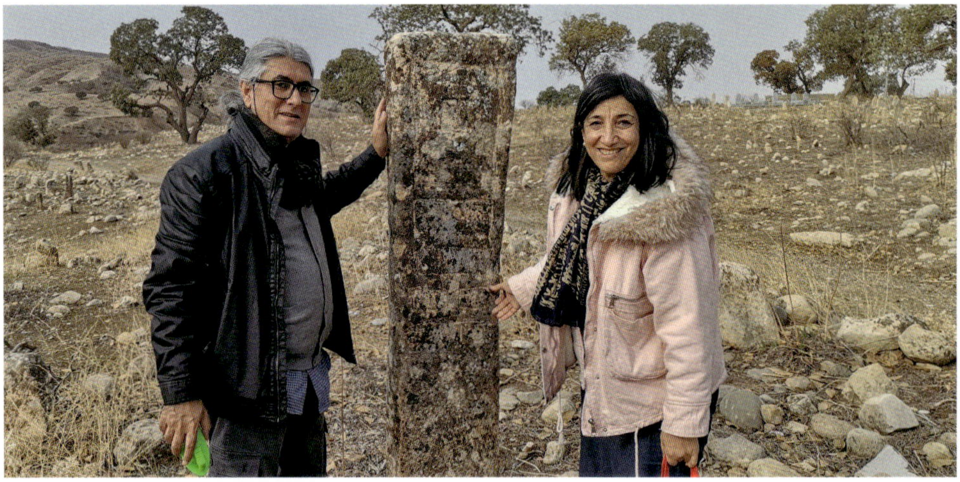

FIG. 2-14: Sanger Hassan. Dr. Narmin Amin (right) and Dr. Abdulrahman K. Darwesh in Hanara (Erbil Governorate) during an aerologist campaign. Digital image. 2022.

be argued that he faced significant historical injustice, and it is more appropriate to separate his personal nature, the complexities of his work and behavior, from acknowledgment of his accomplishments as an archaeologist. Despite the challenges, he was able to uncover many important archaeological facts.

The continued marginalization and criticism of his memory are not devoid of ideological and political dimensions, as contemporary archaeologists and historians from the region have placed him under scrutiny using the logic of their own time, rather than considering the context of his era. Their analyses often serve political purposes, leading them to deviate from a rational assessment of his archaeological achievements.

As researchers (**FIG. 2-14**), we believe it is important at this stage to work toward fairness in acknowledging Rassam as an important archaeological discoverer of his time. More detailed studies should be conducted to uncover the secrets and complexities surrounding his circumstances, to reveal the truth. We believe that studying his case will contribute to a deeper understanding of cultural relations, as well as of the political and intellectual aspects of that period, some of which may have persisted and caused ongoing issues.

1 Layard 1849, 52.

2 Habab 2012, 137–38.

3 Baqer 2012, 136–37.

4 Taha 2016.

5 Margron 1986, 26.

6 Rassam 1897, v–xi. See also Reade 1994, 16–35.

7 Taleb 2015.

8 Rassam 1897, 1–22.

9 Taleb 2015.

10 Marcus 1975, 32.

11 Al-Sabbagh 2022.

12 Wheeler 1964, 35–36.

13 Silberman 1990, 12.

14 Chakravarti 1950, 1–15.

15 For more on her contemporary evolution, see Alajmy and Quraashy 2021, 62–76.

16 Parrot 1953, 39–94, 98, 412.

17 Bahrani, Çelik, and Eldem 2011, 1753–1914.

18 Chevalier 2002, 54–57.

19 Chevalier 2008, 493–507.

20 Chevalier 2008, 513–15.

21 See Place 1867–70, 166.

22 Reade 1994, 116–35. See also Botta 1845, 18.

23 Chesney 2002, 1–20.

24 Kitan 2018.

25 Taylor 2008, 508–12.

26 Kitan 2018.

27 Chevalier 2002, 541. See also Botta 1845, 50–52.

28 Botta 1845, 50–52.

29 Rassam 1897, 24.

30 Chevalier 2002, 57.

31 Baqer 2012 135–40.

32 Qazanjy 2015.

33 Abd al-Latif 2015.

34 Qazanjy 2015.

35 Damrosch 2007, 141–67.

36 Larsen 1996, 45.

37 Damrosch 2007, 182–93.

38 Al-Shammari 2015, 238–39.

39 Al-Humaidhi 2020, 783–819.

40 Al-Shammari 2015, 238–39.

41 Baqer 2012, 136–37. See also Al-Suff 2009, 68; and Khalil 1991, 492–94.

42 Al-Nassery 2019.

43 Meskell 2002, 279–301.

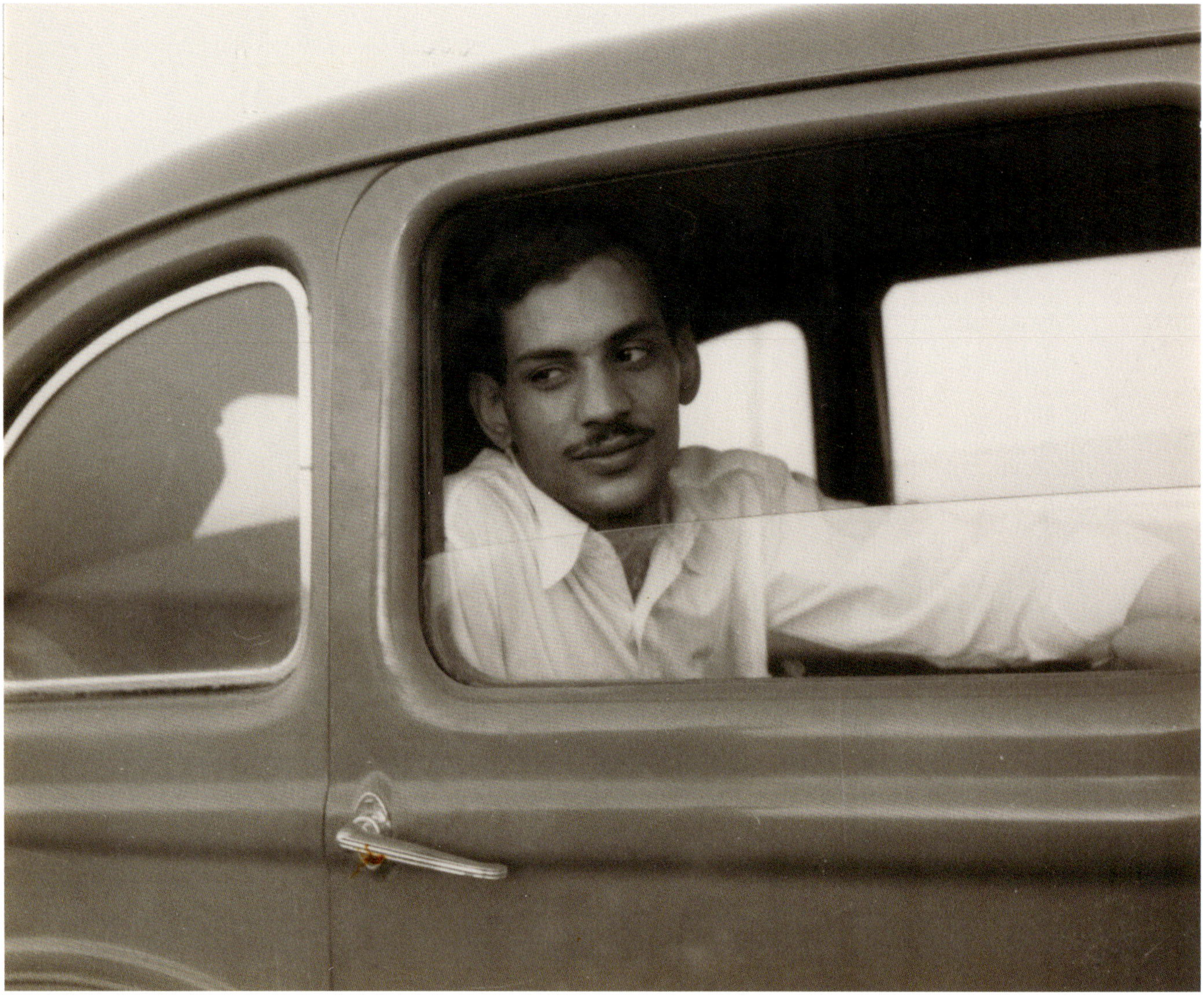

CHAPTER 3

AHL AL-NAFT: OIL'S CORPORATE PHOTOGRAPHY AND THE MODERNIZATION OF IRAQ

Nelida Fuccaro

In August 1951, the monthly illustrated magazine *Ahl al-Naft* (People of Oil), published by the Iraq Petroleum Company (IPC), marked an important moment in the history of the British-controlled firm in the last years of the reign of King Faysal II. With *Ahl al-Naft*, IPC entered a new age of propaganda efforts that targeted its Arabic-speaking workforce. In words and images, the magazine popularized the modernization of the country's infrastructure, the operations of the oil industry, and the close historical connections that bound the Iraqi people to the natural landscape and the rich subsoil of their country. *Ahl al-Naft* also introduced Latif Al Ani (1932–2021, **FIG. 3-1**) to the world of professional photography. Al Ani started an apprenticeship with IPC in the company's newly established Photographic Unit in October 1953 after he had heard of a vacancy from a friend who was a member of the magazine's editorial board. Al Ani remained on the company's payroll until 1960, when he joined the Iraqi Ministry of Information and headed its first photographic department (**FIG. 3-2**). While *Ahl al-Naft* is poignant testimony to a confident, bygone Iraq and to Latif Al Ani's coming of age as a photographer of its people and landscapes, the magazine embodied the tensions of oil modernization and the corporate interests of a company that was deeply intertwined with British colonialism and the Iraqi monarchy, both of which were swept away by the 1958 Revolution.

—

Like *Iraq Petroleum* (IPC's English publication issued in the same year), *Ahl al-Naft* was an exercise in soft power that inaugurated a new era of "prestige publicity"

FIG. 3-1. Photographer unknown. Portrait of Latif Al Ani. Gelatin silver print. 1955. AIF: 0190an01973.

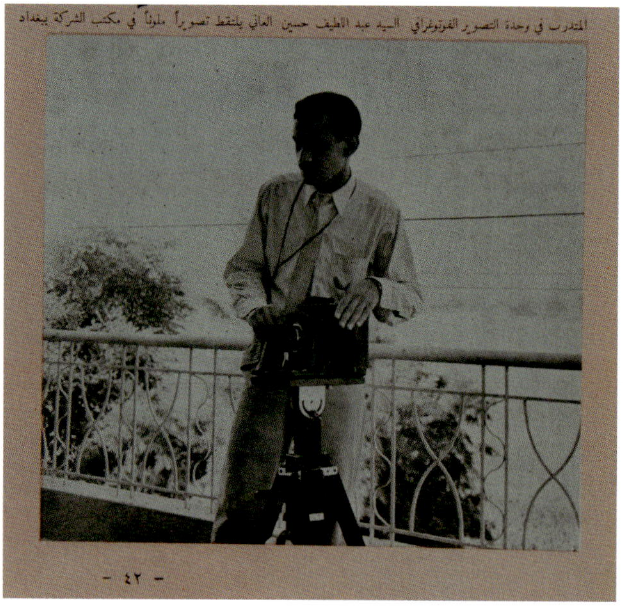

FIG. 3-2. "Abd al-Latif Husayn al-Ani, the trainee in the photographic unit of the company, takes a color photograph in the company's office in Baghdad." From *Ahl al-Naft*, no. 40 (November 1954): 42.

(a term used by IPC executives) for the company's propaganda, which sought to influence Iraqi public opinion while projecting the image of a benevolent modernizer closely connected to the government. Orchestrated as a public relations exercise, the magazine was conceived as IPC's response to a militant era of decolonization, Arabism, and Pan-Arabism that engulfed the Arab world and threatened the privileged position of foreign oil companies, particularly after the nationalization of Iran's oil industry in 1952.[1] Under the tight supervision of the company's public relations office, *Ahl al-Naft* avoided any engagement with the turbulent politics of the day, celebrating and supporting the monarchical regime. Although the last issue hit the newsstands in March 1959, the magazine had stopped regular publication in June 1958, a month before the 1958 Revolution.

Unlike *Iraq Petroleum*, which was aimed at the English-speaking middle and upper classes of Iraq's major urban centers, *Ahl al-Naft* addressed different segments of Iraqi society, showing the benefits of oil development not only to IPC's workforce but also to Iraqis from all walks of life. As suggested by its name—People of Oil—the magazine aimed at crafting a modern petroleum community that bound its employees to the company regardless of their place of residence, or their religious and ethnic affiliations. The editorial board routinely invited employees to share their opinions, as well as personal and family news, which were published in the magazine's news section. IPC's public relations strategy also sought to cement an esprit de corps among the personnel of different centers of oil production, particularly in the secluded oil stations that dotted the pipeline transporting Kirkuk's oil to the Mediterranean Sea through Syria and Lebanon. The magazine had a broad circulation. In the first year alone, IPC printed 96,000 copies, a number that had risen by 1953 to 230,750 with distribution at thirteen oil sites, including Tripoli and Beirut, where the company extended its operations.[2]

As an enterprise in loyalty building, *Ahl al-Naft*'s content mixed indoctrination with leisure and education. On the one hand, the company used the magazine to encourage reading as a new pursuit that defined the IPC model employee: open-minded, cultured, and keen to learn about the oil industry, Iraq, and the world. On the other, the editorial office adopted a focus on content that promoted Iraqi and Arab literature, history, archaeology, and the arts with the publication of articles often lavishly illustrated with photographs, charts, and drawings. In *Ahl al-Naft*'s first issue, the editor invited readers to send poetry, short stories, and photographs for publication, which many of them did during the eight years the magazine was in print.[3] *Ahl al-Naft* also offered a platform for new creative talent, covering art exhibitions and literary events throughout the Arab world. The names of prominent literary figures and artists appeared as guest writers and columnists, or as the subject of features. In 1952 the Iraqi painter and sculptor Jewad Selim (1919–1961) started a column on the emerging art scene in Iraq and the Arab region. His first piece featured an exhibition of modern art held in Baghdad on the celebration of the millennial anniversary of the birth of Ibn Sina, a renowned medieval Muslim scholar and scientist. One of Selim's paintings of his wife, Lorna, framed the opening page of the article (**FIG. 3-3**). Crucially, *Ahl al-Naft* pioneered oil's engagement with the Iraqi art scene, which was extended in *Al Amiloon Fil Naft* (Oil Workers), its post-revolutionary successor, also sponsored by IPC but under the closer scrutiny of Iraq's Ministry of Information.

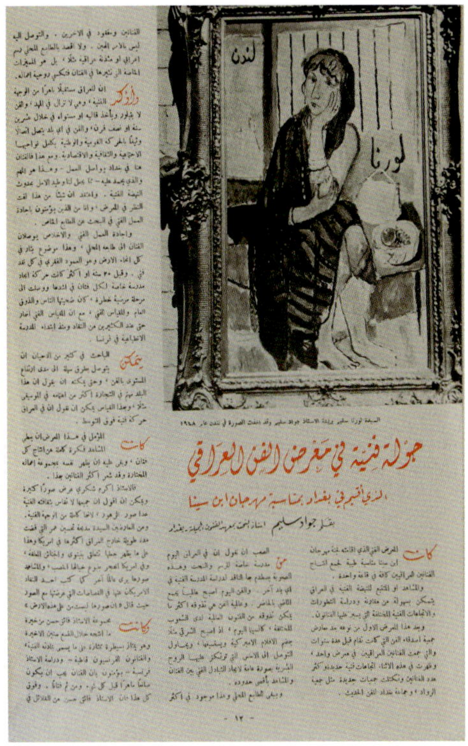

جولة فنية في معرض الفن العراقي

الذي أقيم في بغداد بمناسبة مهرجان ابن سينا

بقلم جواد سليم

FIG. 3-3. "A Tour of Iraqi Art's Exhibition," Jewad Selim, *Ahl al-Naft*, September 1952: 12. The caption of the image on the top of the page reads: "Mrs. Lorna Selim painted by Mr. Jewad Selim. This picture was taken in London in 1947".

—

When Al Ani joined IPC in 1953, photography was becoming increasingly central to the "prestige publicity" of foreign oil companies operating in the Arab world. By the end of the decade, cameras had become popular in Iraq, in part thanks to *Ahl al-Naft*'s photographic competitions, which invited readers to send pictures on subjects ranging from babies and mustaches to landscape. Many years later, Al Ani recalled that working for the company was a comfortable and professionally rewarding experience, in his own words "a school for me in working seriously, having discipline and order." He also remembered the content of *Ahl al-Naft* as more creative than that of *New Iraq,* one of the magazines published by the Ministry of Culture, where Al Ani worked after the revolution. *Ahl al-Naft*'s "more sophisticated editorial line" gave him a sense of freedom before "the element of fear had taken root in me."[4] After he joined Iraq's News Agency in 1970, Al Ani's coexistence with the post-revolutionary regimes became increasingly troubled.

It is difficult to identify Al Ani's IPC portfolio as most of the images published in *Ahl al-Naft* did not include bylines, an indication of the limited professional and artistic visibility of non-Western photographers on the payroll of oil companies.[5] We can surmise, however, that Al Ani's early photographs contributed to shaping the visual language of IPC oil propaganda and that played a role in fulfilling his

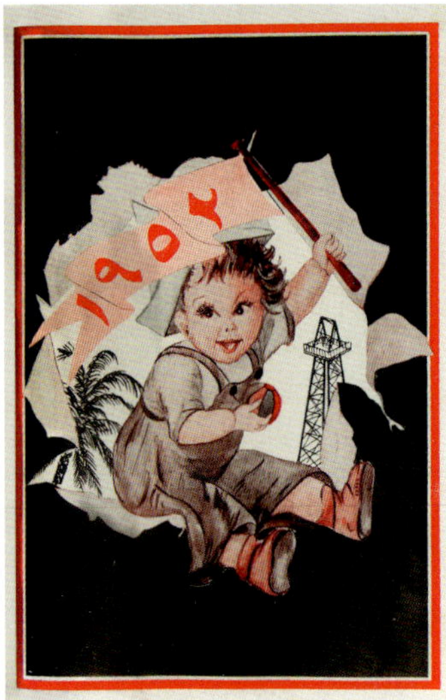

FIG. 3-4. *Ahl al-Naft*, no. 6 (January 1952): back cover.

personal goal that photography become the artistic language *for* and *of* Iraq's future, a language that became established in the 1960s. As an example of the future-oriented editorial line of the magazine, the picture of a smiling baby with oil rigs in the background welcomed readers to *Ahl al-Naft*'s second year of publication, establishing a connection between the industry and Iraq's younger generations (**FIG. 3-4**).

Judging from Al Ani's recollections of his early years of training as a professional photographer, color photography must have shaped much of his work for IPC in the 1950s. Although he has become well-known for his high-contrast black-and-white images of the 1960s (**FIGS. 3-5** and **3-6**), Al Ani was the only Iraqi who knew how to develop color photography when he joined the Ministry of Information in 1960. Oozing company confidence, color images were the pride of the IPC photographic unit, highly prized for attracting the attention of readers and for conveying company messages more effectively than black-and-white photos. *Ahl al-Naft* first included color images after 1953, and by 1957 multi-image color plates with a strikingly bright palette had become a popular feature of the magazine. The 1950s were also Al Ani's training ground in aerial photography (**FIG. 3-7**), which he continued to pursue with great success in the following decades, particularly with images of archaeological sites (**FIG. 3-8**) and urban landscapes. He recalled that taking pictures from planes with the IPC film unit gave him the opportunity to capture a different side of Iraq: "From the air, I saw things in a different way. . . . I saw the contrast more clearly between the ugly and the beautiful. Everything was more exposed. Nothing could be hidden."[6] While a perspective from above revealed to Al Ani aesthetic and social disparities, the company used aerial photography to showcase infrastructure, modern housing projects, and even nature as the uniform and sanitized large-scale spectacle of oil progress. This spectacle was staged to instill awe and wonder in viewers, what David E. Nye called the "technological sublime" with reference to the collective experience of large-scale projects in industrialized societies.[7]

—

In the first year of *Ahl al-Naft*'s publication, oil featured as a mineral substance embedded in the history and archaeology of Iraq's subsoil. An article in the November 1951 issue reported on the Chicago archaeological mission excavating the Neolithic agricultural settlement of Jarmo, one of the oldest in the Middle East. The article's title suggests that the mission was looking for Adam as the archetypal prehistoric man "because he knew of oil," alluding to the archaeologists' claims that Neolithic societies used oil to light their homes.[8] The following month readers were reminded that the fourteenth-century Moroccan traveler Ibn Battuta

OPPOSITE, TOP: FIG 3-5. Latif Al Ani. Babylon, musician playing the rebab in front of the city wall. Gelatin silver negative on cellulose acetate film. Ca. 1961. AIF: 0190an00763. Checklist no. 21.
OPPOSITE, BOTTOM: FIG. 3-6. Latif Al Ani. Hatra, head of a statue. Gelatin silver negative on cellulose acetate film. 1960. AIF: 0190an00707. Checklist no. 71.

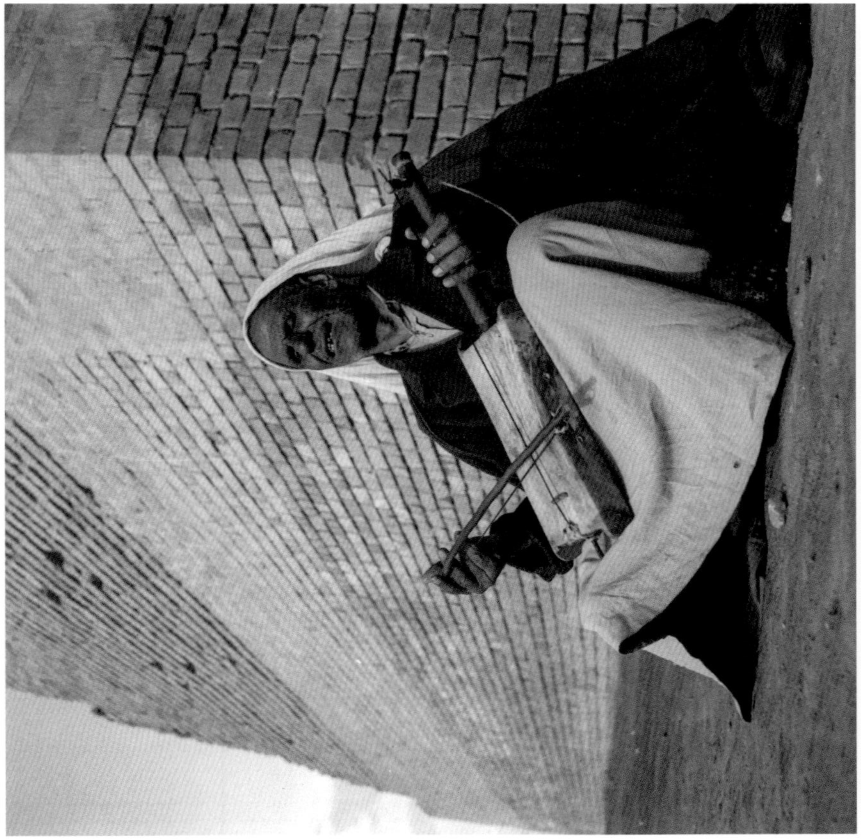

FIG. 3-5

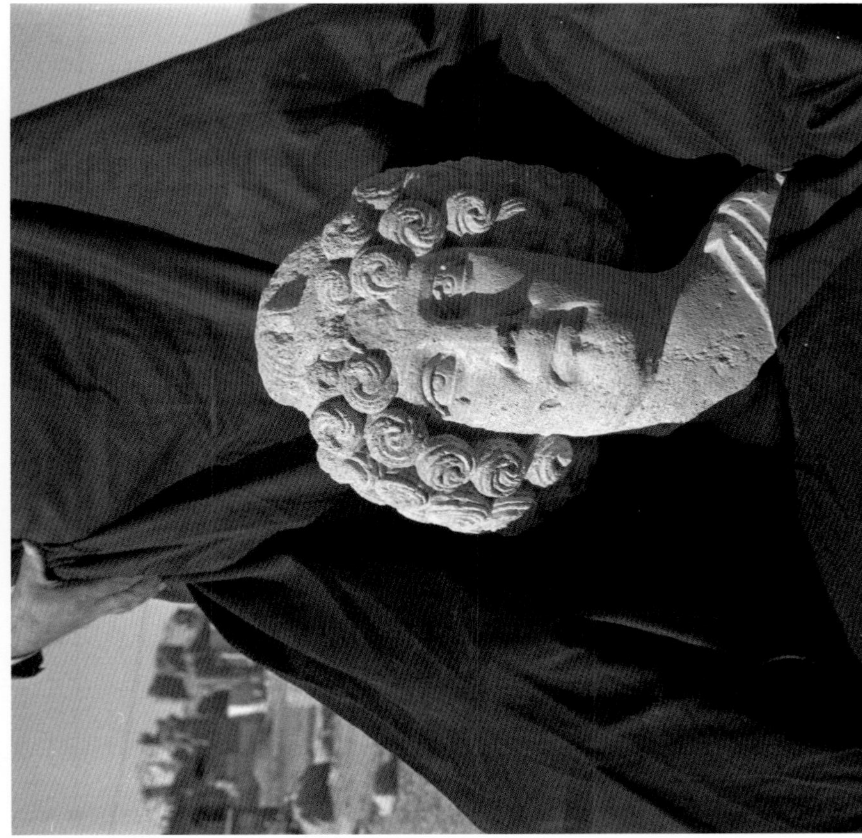

FIG. 3-6

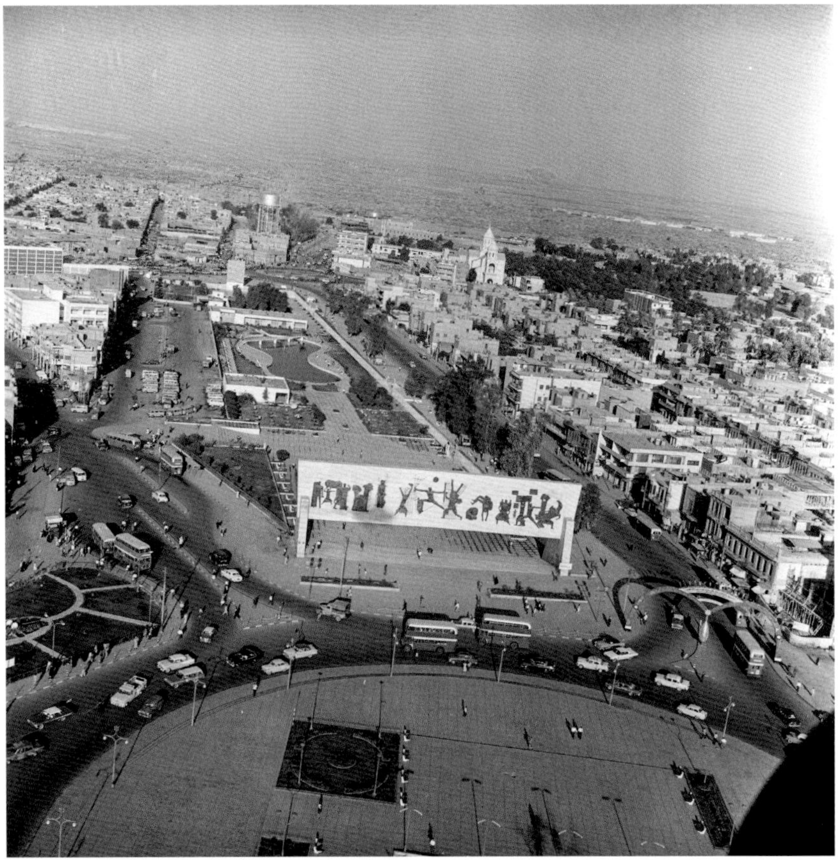

FIG. 3-7

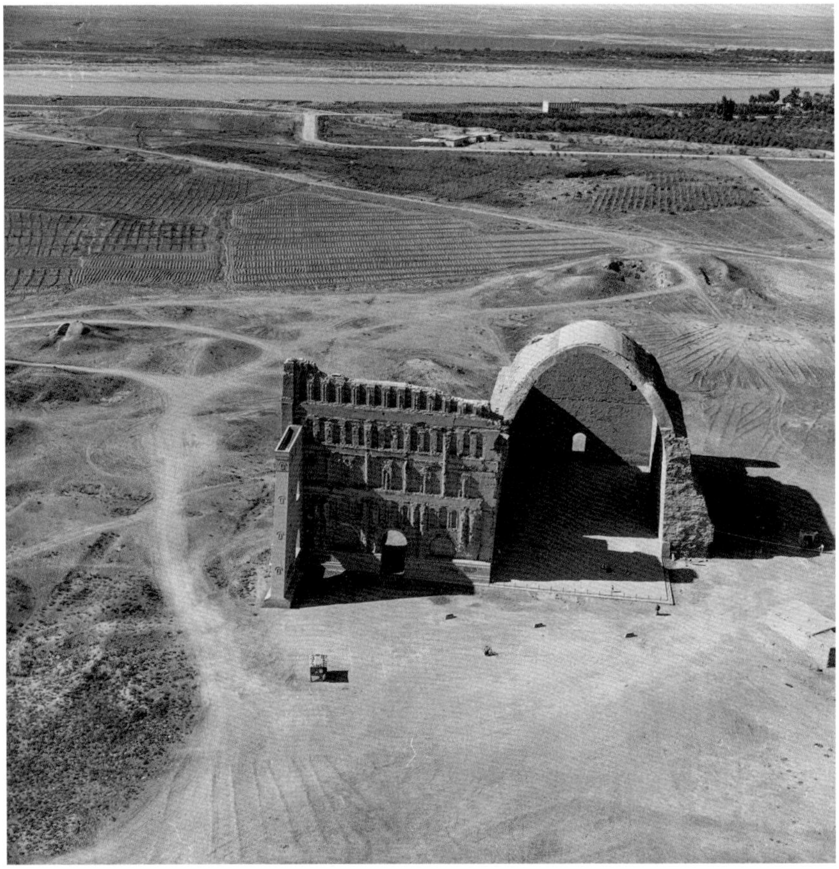

FIG. 3-8

sighted crude oil as he came across several seepages and natural tar pits during his travels in Iraq.[9] Another article explains cheekily that if it were not for oil Noah's ark would have sunk, as oil coating helped prevent ancient wooden ships from sinking.[10] It is easy to read an allusion to the redemptive power of "black gold" in twentieth-century Iraq: lifting the destiny of the country as it had rescued the ark from the deluge millennia earlier.

Ahl al-Naft also endeavored to impress upon its readers the continuity between Iraq's past and present by emphasizing the country's rich archaeological heritage as a feature of its productive subsoil. After all, antiquities were treasures "extracted"—like oil—from the guts of the earth. The magazine portrayed Iraq's ancient heritage in different visual modalities, juxtaposing perspectives from above, particularly aerial shots of archaeological and excavation sites, against close-up views of statues (**FIG. 3-9**), objects, and details of ancient bas-reliefs (**FIGS. 3-10** and **3-11**) and tablets. Amateur and professional artists, often employed by the company as illustrators, re-created Mesopotamian scenes and motifs to popularize images of heritage as the core of modern national culture. The cover of the June 1953 issue depicts female musicians riding in a Sumerian carriage mounted with a bull-headed lyre, the legendary musical instrument of Mesopotamia. The cover celebrated the procession displaying Iraq's ancient civilizations that was organized in Baghdad for the accession to the throne of King Faysal II. The caption on the back cover makes direct reference to the picture's connection with an archaeological object, specifying that the image replicated one of the scenes from Ur displayed in the Iraq Museum (**FIG. 3-12**). Inside the issue, a long feature article on the king's coronation included photographs of the procession alongside those of dignitaries and official events, a further example of how *Ahl al-Naft* crafted visual tropes that associated modernity and tradition.

The magazine also used the contrast between traditional and modern to naturalize the presence of the oil industry in Iraq's social and national life. Photographers and artists composed images that combined oil technology and modern infrastructure—from refineries to roads—with scenes from the Iraqi countryside to make acceptable the dramatic changes that were taking place around *Ahl al-Naft*'s readers. The cover of the second issue of the magazine featured a shepherd with an oil rig in the background (**FIG. 3-13**). The back cover of the November 1951 issue showcased the imposing Assyrian gate at the entrance of the Iraq Museum in Baghdad. The photo draws the viewers' attention toward the arch as the foremost symbol of Iraq's national heritage, set against the black car parked in front of it, one of the coveted symbols of Iraqi modernity. Designed by the British archaeologist and architect Seton Lloyd, who joined the Iraqi Directorate of Antiquities in 1939, the gate is described in the caption below the picture as an example of modern Iraqi architecture embellished by Assyrian decorative motifs (**FIG. 3-14**). Aerial photography was used to suggest the similarity of the traces left on the Iraqi landscape by archaeological excavations and those left by irrigation projects in an article that highlighted archaeology and hydraulic engineering as complementary in their scientific basis.[11]

Ahl al-Naft also promoted ideas of national culture, heritage, and development through powerful images that mixed antiquities and oil infrastructure with

OPPOSITE, TOP: FIG. 3-7 Latif Al Ani. Baghdad, Jewad Selim's *Freedom Monument* at Tahrir Square. Gelatin silver negative on cellulose acetate film. 1961. AIF: 0190an00047. Checklist no. 81.
OPPOSITE, BOTTOM: FIG. 3-8. Latif Al Ani. Ctesiphon, aerial view of the ruins of the Tāq Kasrā (Arch of Ctesiphon). Gelatin silver negative on cellulose acetate film. 1960. AIF: 190an00032. Checklist no. 47.

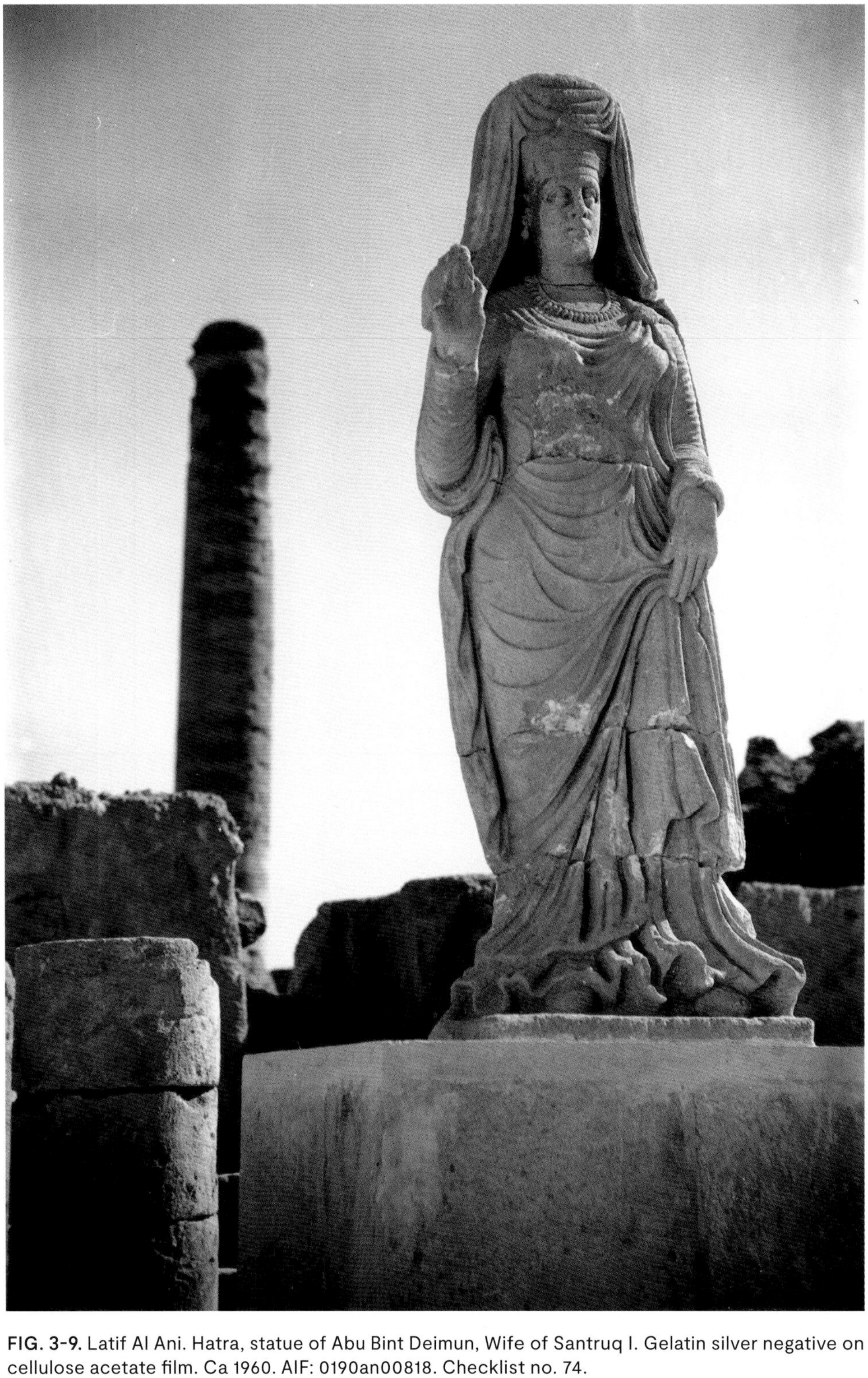

FIG. 3-9. Latif Al Ani. Hatra, statue of Abu Bint Deimun, Wife of Santruq I. Gelatin silver negative on cellulose acetate film. Ca 1960. AIF: 0190an00818. Checklist no. 74.

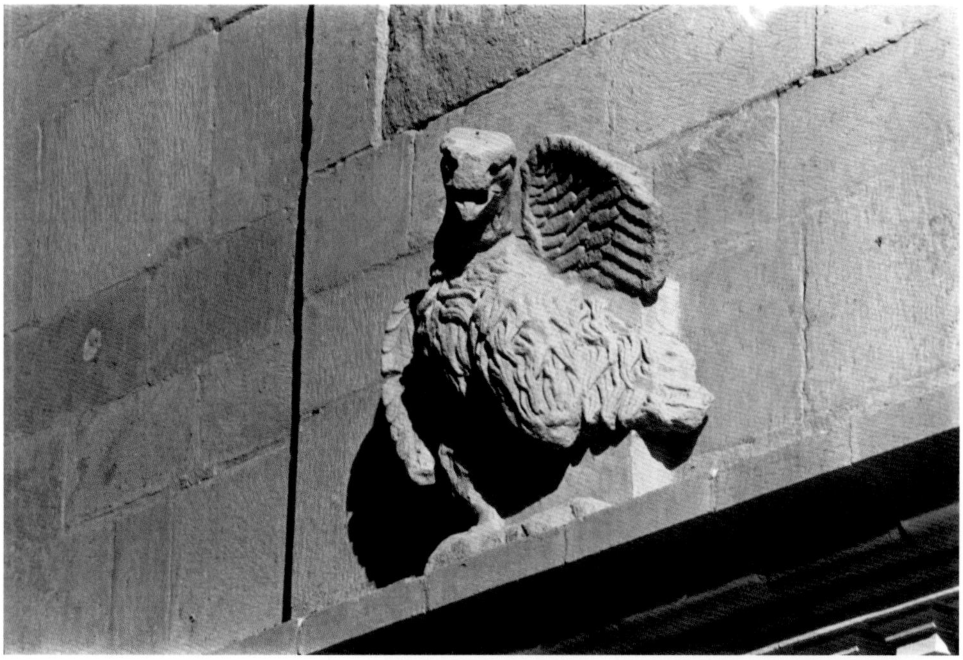

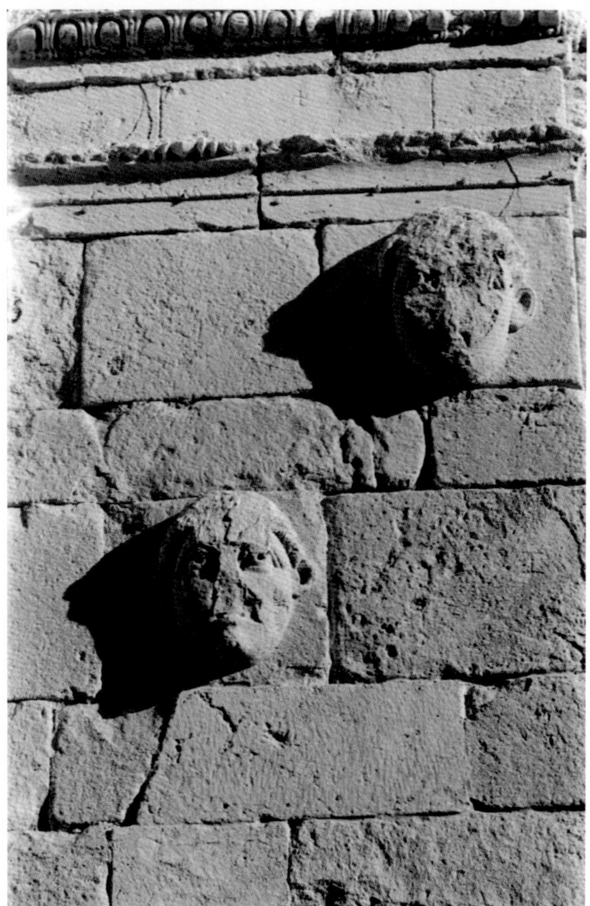

TOP: FIG. 3-10. Latif Al Ani. Hatra, South Iwan (Hall, No.12), eagle (architectural relief). Gelatin silver negative on cellulose acetate film. Ca. 1960. AIF: 0190an01776. Checklist no. 73. **BOTTOM: FIG. 3-11.** Latif Al Ani. Hatra, The Temple (Iwan) of Shamash, mask (architectural decorations). Gelatin silver negative on cellulose acetate film. Ca. 1960. AIF: 0190an01779. Checklist no. 72.

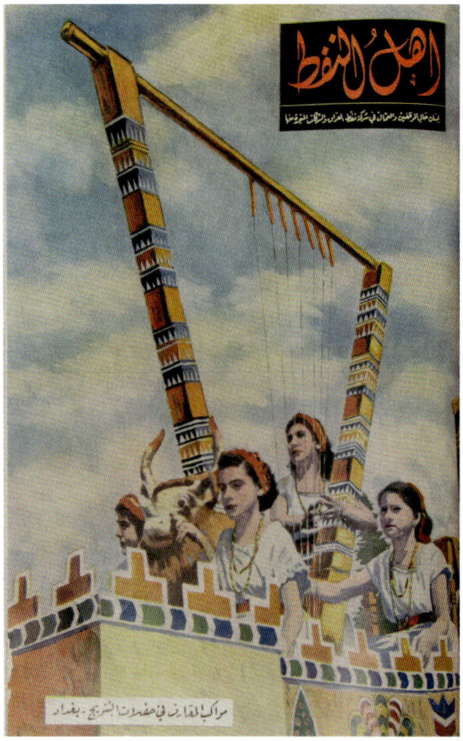

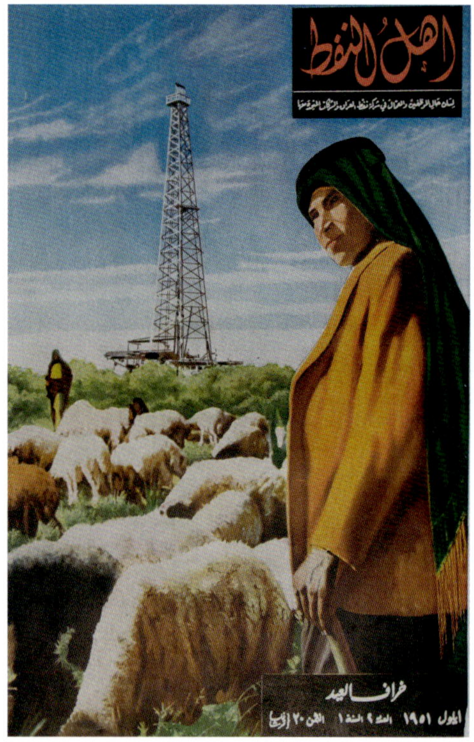

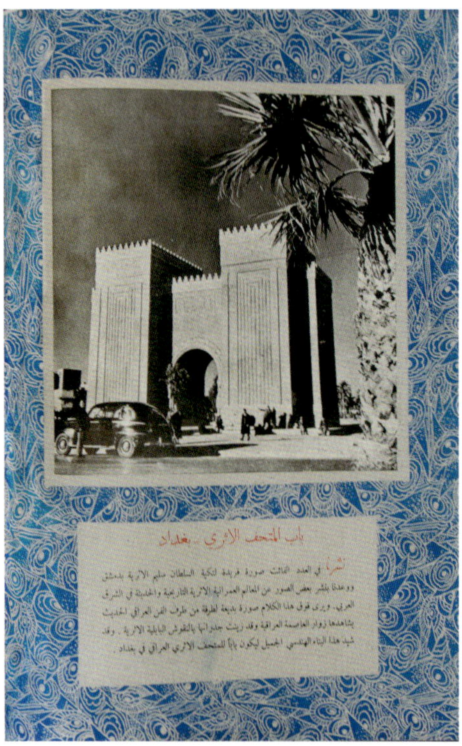

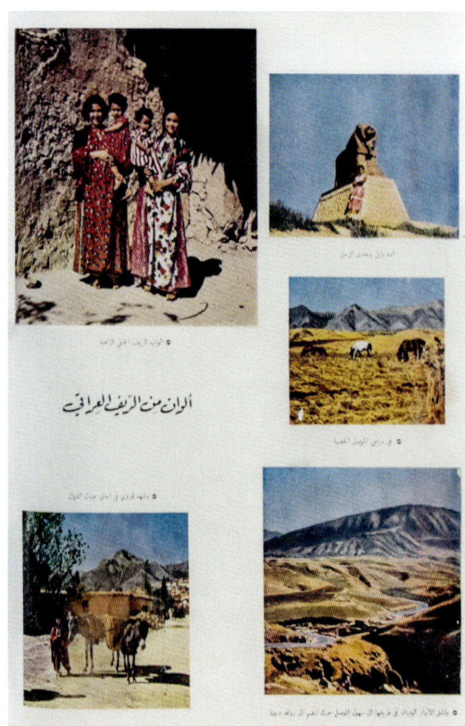

LEFT TOP: FIG. 3-12. *Ahl al-Naft*, no. 23 (June 1953): front cover. The caption on the back cover reads: "The Sumerian lyre: in the council of Sumerian kings in the ancient city of Ur. The picture is from one of the images kept in the Iraq Museum." **RIGHT TOP: FIG. 3-13.** *Ahl al-Naft*, no. 2 (September 1951): front cover. **LEFT BOTTOM: FIG. 3-14.** *Ahl al-Naft*, no. 4 (November 1951): back cover. **RIGHT BOTTOM: FIG. 3-15.** "The Colors of the Iraqi Countryside," *Ahl al-Naft*, no. 67 (March/April 1957): color plate, no page.

people and nature. The countryside of northern Iraq is presented as impregnated with history and popular traditions but in the process of being transformed by technology and modernity. The use of color plates in the magazine created a dazzling visual effect that blended human, natural, and technological elements. In one of the plates, nature appears colorful and confident, mirroring the traditional clothes of Kurdish village women (**FIG. 3-15**). Three Kurdish villagers in traditional dress are pictured in 1958 with the building site of the Dukan Dam in the background, the largest infrastructural project of the monarchy, completed after the Revolution. The photo—whose dark tones give the three men posing in front of the camera a somewhat menacing appearance—was published alongside an image of the Sarchinar cement factory, the first to be built in northern Iraq (**FIG. 3-16**).

—

From the beginning of its publication, one of *Ahl al Naft*'s objectives was to lift the veil of mystery that surrounded the oil industry. The magazine popularized IPC's technical operations—from petroleum extraction to production and distribution—with articles on engineers, geologists, and technicians, on Kirkuk's oil fields and its complex technical machinery, on the chemical processes at work in distillation plants, and on the construction and management of the pipelines that moved Kirkuk's oil to the Mediterranean. In the early years, features on national and international exhibitions showcased oil operations and the company's partnership with the Iraqi government, while promoting the visibility of the industry in Iraq and abroad. In 1954 the magazine published features on Basra's industrial exhibition, most likely one of Al Ani's first assignments as a trainee photographer. It also ran several articles on the IPC pavilion at the first Damascus International Fair, where the company

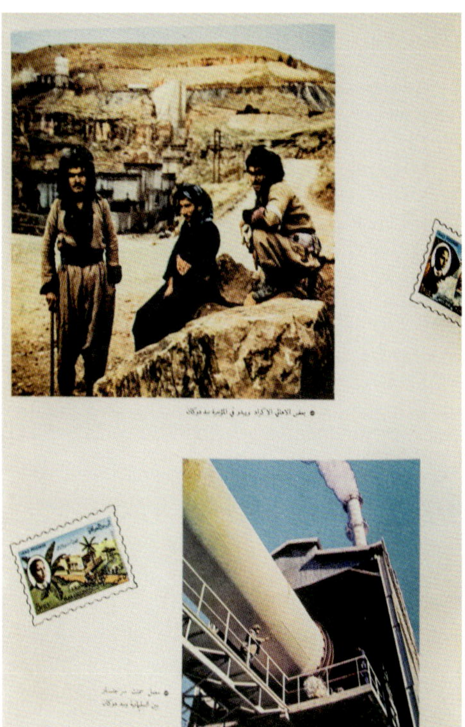

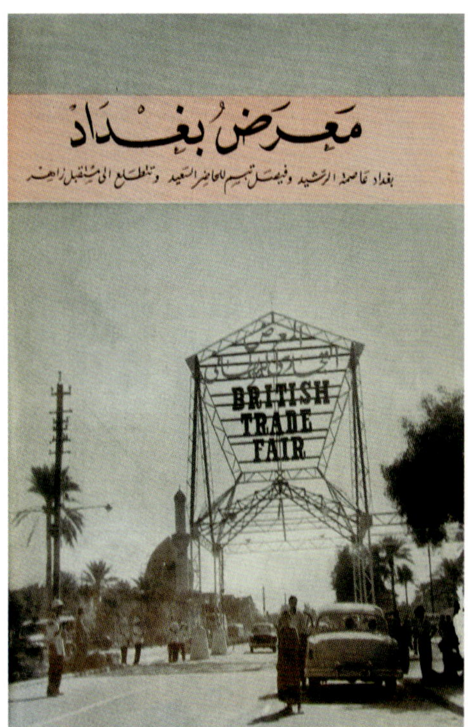

LEFT: FIG. 3-16. *Ahl al-Naft*, no. 80 (June 1958): color plate, no page. **RIGHT: FIG. 3-17.** "Baghdad's Fair," *Ahl al-Naft*, no. 41 (December 1954): 14.

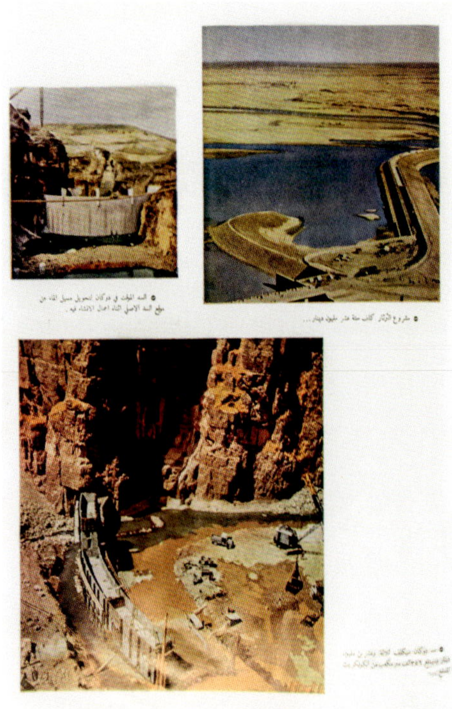

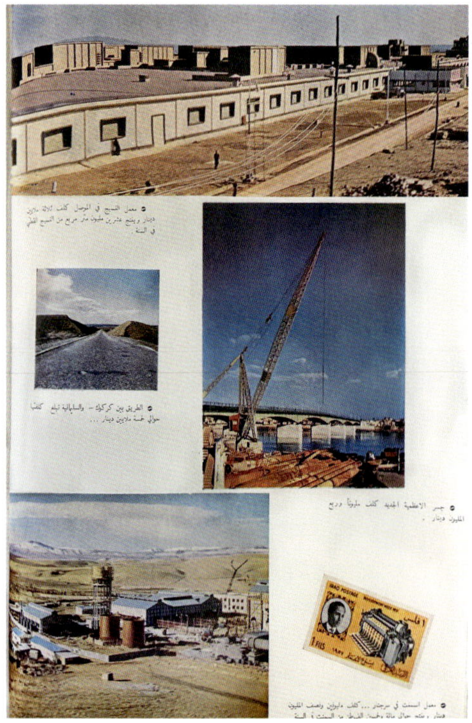

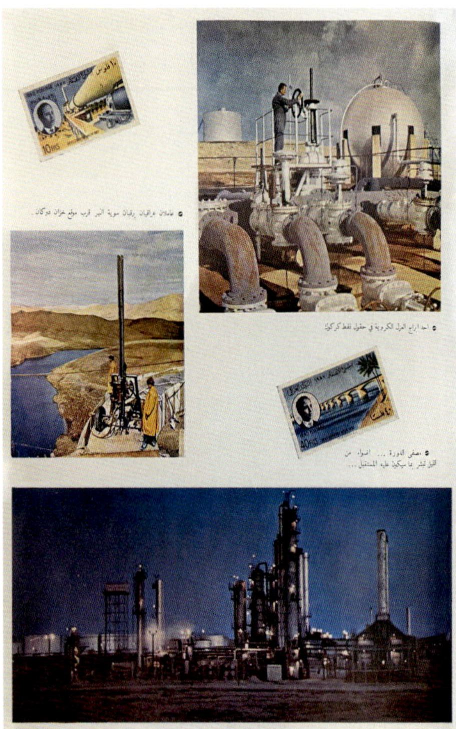

LEFT TOP: FIG. 3-18. "The six million dinar Tharthar project"; "The Dukan barrage that directs the water flow from its original location through the construction work"; "The Dukan Dam will cost 23 million dinars and will swallow 356,000 square meters of reinforced concrete." **RIGHT TOP: FIG. 3-19.** (from top counterclockwise) "The textile factory in Mosul cost three million dinar and produces twenty million square meters of cotton cloth per year"; "The road between Kirkuk and Sulaymaniya whose cost was approximately five million dinars"; "The two and a half million dinar cement factory in Sarchinar which produces one hundred and fifty thousand tons of cement per year"; "The new Azimiyya bridge which cost a million and a quarter dinars." **LEFT BOTTOM: FIG. 3-20** (from top right counterclockwise) "One of the spheroid isolation towers in the Kirkuk oil fields"; "Two Iraqi workers monitor the level of the river waters near the Dukan Dam"; "The al-Dawra refinery . . . the night lights herald the future." Translated by the author. All captions from *Ahl al-Naft*, no. 68 (May/June 1957).

emphasized the expansion of its operations as part of the success of industrial production in the Arab world. The British Trade Fair held in Baghdad also received prominent exposure in the magazine, with bright color images showing IPC exhibits with maps and interactive panels that claimed petroleum had served mankind for seven thousand years. The feature opens with a black-and-white photo of the fair's entrance gate, an iron structure reminiscent of the base of an oil derrick (**FIG. 3-17**).

Toward the end of the decade, *Ahl al-Naft* published increasing numbers of photographs of modern infrastructure as evidence that oil wealth was being put to work for the benefit of the Iraqi people. The construction site of the Dukan Dam—designed to provide water storage, irrigation, and eventually hydroelectricity—was one of the recurring images that popularized government plans for rural regeneration and agricultural development. A series of color plates published in the May/June 1957 issue during Iraq's Development Week brought together the iconic infrastructural and industrial projects of the late monarchical era: the Dukan Dam, the Sarchinar cement factory, Mosul's textile industrial unit, the newly built al-Dawra oil refinery (completed in 1955), and last but not least Kirkuk's oil fields (**FIGS. 3-18**; **3-19**; and **3-20**). The theme of the "city beautiful" was also an integral part of IPC's infrastructural propaganda as images of wide roads and modern architecture became the most recognizable symbol of Iraq's modernization. An article published in 1955 under the title "Baghdad in 1960" celebrated the glorious future of urbanization, anticipating the lavishly illustrated features published in *Iraq Petroleum* in the following years that praised the burgeoning modernist architecture of the Iraqi capital as original, bold, and ultramodern. Reminding readers that cement was Iraq's new builder, *Ahl al-Naft* relentlessly applauded Iraq's architectural and construction boom as a new renaissance.[12] As tarmac roads and cement bridges improved car mobility in and between Iraq's urban centers, they were presented as symbols of national achievement whose construction was rooted in the engineering tradition of Mesopotamian civilizations.[13]

—

Browsing *Ahl al-Naft* allows us to consider the lens of corporate propaganda and photography as instruments for the representation of the peoples, histories, and archaeological heritage of Iraq. The magazine is a powerful reminder of the intricate relationship between oil interests and Iraq's projected futures at a crucial juncture of the country's modernization. It brings into sharp focus the British political and cultural colonization of the country but also the transfer of technical skills that took place in the process, as exemplified by Al Ani's apprenticeship with IPC. *Ahl al-Naft* speaks to a painful present of the failed accomplishments of earlier promises of modernization, yet it prompts us to remember rather than forget Iraq's illustrious past.

*The author would like to thank Mohamed Al Mubarak for help with the research for this chapter, and Brad Bauer and Maria Chaves from Archives and Special Collections at NYU Abu Dhabi for assistance with the images.

1 Fuccaro 2023, 90–94.

2 *Ahl al-Naft*, August 1954, 16–17.

3 *Ahl al-Naft*, August 1951, 3.

4 Quotes from Chalabi 2017, 25–26 and 35.

5 Fuccaro 2023, 101.

6 Chalabi 2017, 26.

7 Nye 1994.

8 Fawzi 1951, 4–5.

9 Al-Majdhub 1951, 11.

10 *Ahl al-Naft*, December 1951, 13–14.

11 *Ahl al-Naft*, March 1959, 19–21.

12 For oil urbanism and urbanization in Kuwait and the Middle East, see: Fuccaro 2013; Al-Nakib 2013; *Ahl al Naft*, September 1955, 12–13; and *Ahl al-Naft*, June 1956, 42–43.

13 *Ahl al-Naft*, May/June 1957, 16–20.

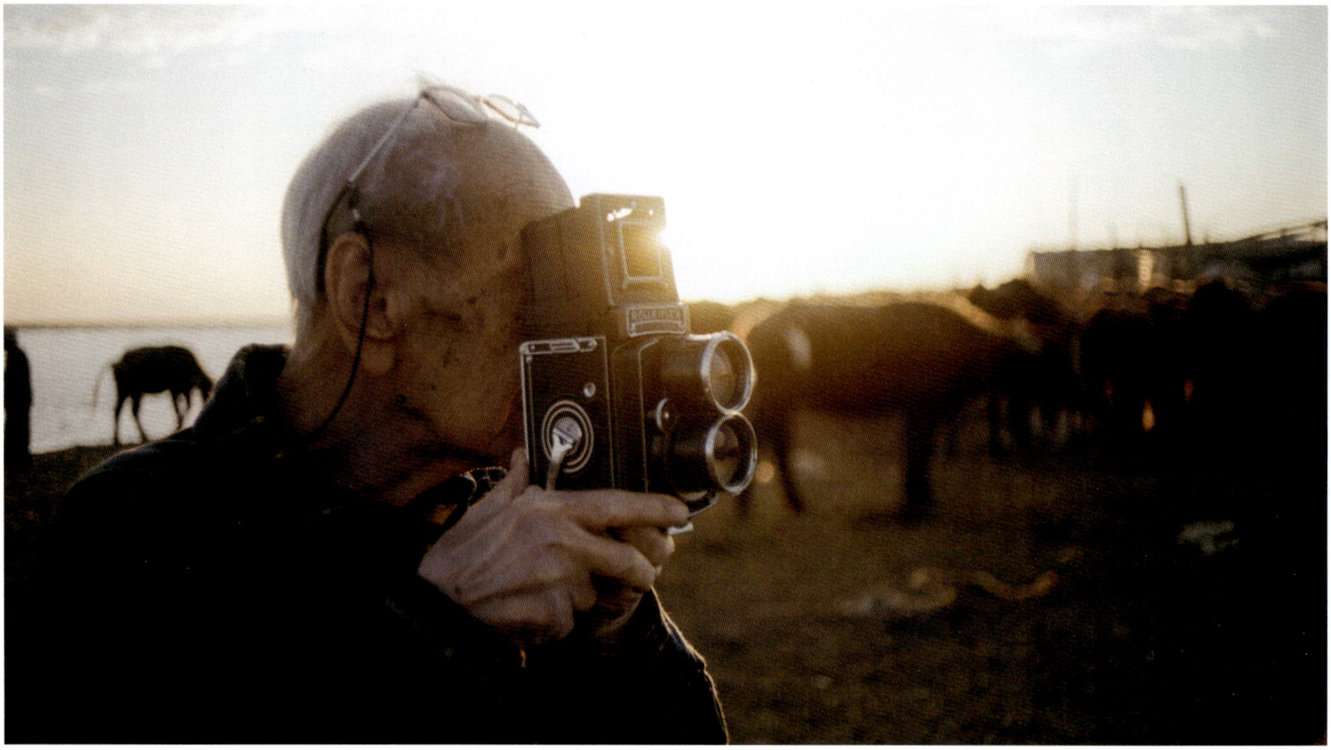

CHAPTER 4

A FORGOTTEN IRAQI PHOTOGRAPHER REDISCOVERED

Pedro Azara

The long and haunting documentary *Iraq's Invisible Beauty* (2022) is truly a revelation. It will be especially impactful for those, like me, who had not previously heard of Latif Al Ani (1932–2021, **FIG. 4-1**), a remarkable and relatively unknown Iraqi photographer. The film, by the Iraqi-Belgian filmmaker Salim Omar Kalifa and the Belgian producer Jurgen Buedts, is the first and only one about Latif Al Ani. Unfortunately, Al Ani died in November 2021 before the documentary was completed.

The first frames introduce Latif Al Ani as a tired, disillusioned old man traveling from the Kurdish mountains to the marshes, dragging himself through the remnants of his country, which was destroyed by Islamic State in Mosul and the Second Gulf War (**FIGS. 4-2** and **4-3**). These images heavily contrast with the early photographs of Latif Al Ani as a young man. In a still photograph, he is seen standing in a beautiful mountainous landscape—the same landscape depicted in the documentary. But here the scenery seems miraculously preserved. There is no destruction in sight, only a young photographer proudly holding a camera (**BACK COVER**). The documentary responds to this scene within its first minutes, showing the drastic changes endured by the surroundings.

Latif Al Ani was an exceptional photographer who was affected by the political conflict and war in Iraq. Unfortunately, due to the turmoil that surrounded him, he was only recognized quite late in his life for his contribution to photography. In 2015, following years of isolation due to political suppression, his photographs were exhibited in the Iraq Pavilion at the Venice Biennale—the first time his pictures had been shown publicly since the mid-sixties—which led to public praise but also some criticism. After this exhibition, Al Ani grew excited and hopeful for

FIG. 4-1. Sahim Omar Kalifa and Jurgen Buedts. Latif Al Ani. Digital still from *Iraq's Invisible Beauty*. 2010–14. Checklist no. 86.

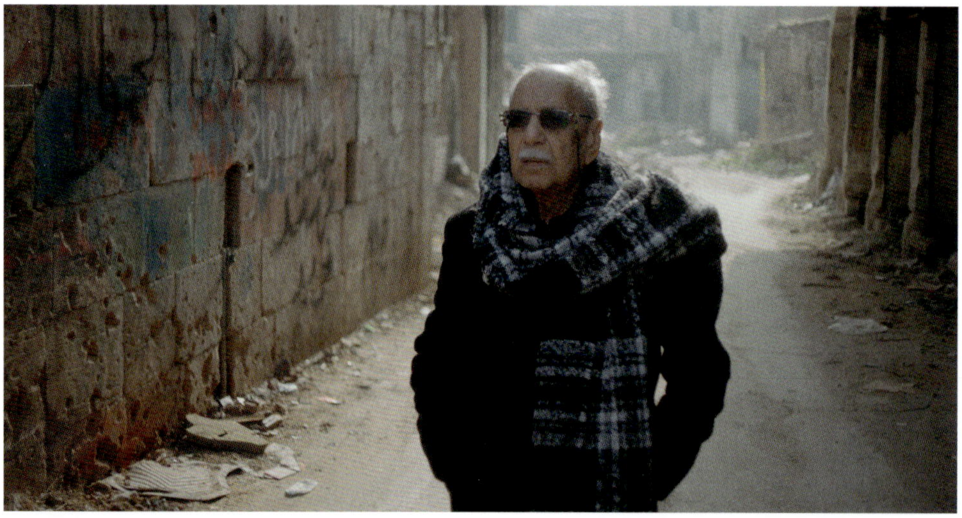

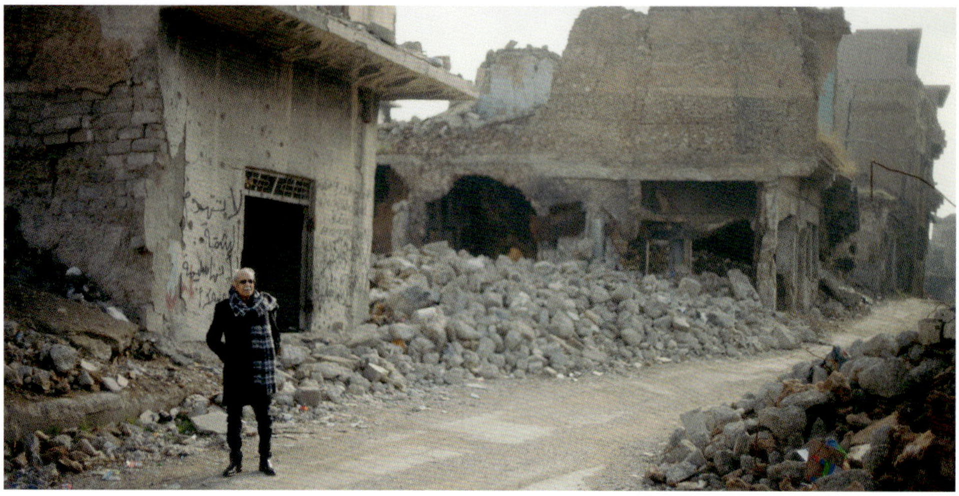

TOP: FIG. 4-2. Sahim Omar Kalifa and Jurgen Buedts. Latif Al Ani. Digital Still from *Iraq's Invisible Beauty*. 2010–14. Checklist no. 87. **BOTTOM: FIG. 4-3.** Sahim Omar Kalifa and Jurgen Buedts. Latif Al Ani. Digital Still from *Iraq's Invisible Beauty*. 2010–14. Checklist no. 88.

the future, looking forward to further exhibitions of his work in Europe, where his photography was eventually shown but without his presence. The recognition had arrived too late. By the time his work reached European viewers, he was eighty-three years old. He had long been silenced by Saddam Hussein's government, having been forbidden to take pictures and lacking freedom to move within Baghdad. After the tragic assassination of his uncle, Al Ani had to flee the country.

The wars in Iraq shattered Al Ani and his legacy. Almost all of his original prints disappeared, his personal archives were stolen or destroyed, and the national and municipal archives in Baghdad were sacked during the invasion by the North American army in 2003. Fortunately, there still remain negatives, given by the photographer himself to the Arab Image Foundation in Beirut in 2000.

—

Latif Al Ani was introduced to photography early on, as a teenager. His first camera was a Twin Lens Reflex Rolleiflex, gifted by his elder brother, which produced large square negatives. He kept this camera until his death, using it to shoot some of his last pictures (by then he was also taking photographs with a mobile phone). He found a photography teacher not far from where he lived—in a bazaar on Mutanabbi Street, in the heart of Baghdad—a Jewish photographer, of whom we have only the nickname "Nissan," provided by Al Ani in an interview.[1]

While Al Ani's brother and Nissan promoted Latif's passion and talent for photography, it was the role played by his friend Aziz Ajam, who worked at the cultural magazine *Ahl al-Naft* (People of Oil), published by the Iraqi Petroleum Company (IPC), that allowed him to gain fame and later to be discovered by the Westernized world. Thanks to Ajam, Latif was hired by *Ahl al-Naft*, which published its contents in Arabic, Kurdish, and English. The editor of the magazine, the British photographer Jack Percival, eventually gave Al Ani the opportunity to expand the themes of his photographs, which until then had been confined to still lifes.[2]

During his time at *Ahl al-Naft*, Al Ani was assigned to document the rapid industrial changes in Iraq and the country's accelerated modernization, which was understood in the 1950s and '60s as a tool for a bright future: the quick replacement of manmade tools and products with machine-made ones; arts and crafts supplanted by industrial design; handicraft of a few objects exchanged for mechanical and massive production with no artistic aura; plans for new urban development with unnecessarily straight, wide streets and avenues, articulated by large roundabouts; and, among other concepts, new cities or neighborhoods with few distinct housing typologies replacing the webs of lanes and decaying wooden dwellings to make room for dams, electric power plants, high-voltage towers, dense nets of cables crossing the sky, and all the equipment needed—large pipelines and oil refineries—to allow the largely agricultural country to enter the twentieth century.

While documenting the impending changes in the city and architecture around him, Al Ani turned his camera to buildings such as the El Rawaf and Awqaf (**FIG. 4-4**) and became friends with one of the great Iraqi modernist architects at the time, Hisham Munir (b. 1930), who was responsible for the two buildings mentioned (**FIGS. 4-5** through **4-8**).[3] Al Ani was also a friend of Jewad Selim, a fellow Iraqi artist. One of Selim's most renowned pieces, the spectacular *Freedom Monument* (*Nasb al-Hurriyah*; 1958–1961)—designed in collaboration with the architect Rifat Chadirji (1926–2020)—can be found in the center of Baghdad (**FIG. 4-9**). Its horizontal composition of figures and scenes sculpted in iron, displayed in a single row, was inspired by Mesopotamian cylinder seals and proudly stands in Tahrir Square.

Following the dismantlement of the Ottoman Empire at the end of World War I, and the British Mandate of Mesopotamia (1920–1932), Iraq gained its independence. But it was not until July 14, 1958, when a bloody coup d´état tore down the monarchy and replaced it with a military dictatorship, that the British influence—which had remained visible, for instance, in the colonial architecture—began to slowly vanish. Three years after the coup, in 1961, IPC—still a British enterprise in spite of its name—left Iraq with all of its archives, including Al Ani´s photographic negatives and records. At this point, if they have not been lost or destroyed, they might be untraceable due to political instability and disorganization.

OVERLEAF, LEFT TOP: FIG. 4-4. Latif Al Ani. Baghdad, Hisham Munir's Endowment Office. Gelatin silver negative on cellulose acetate film. 1960. AIF: 0190an00145. Checklist no. 3. **LEFT BOTTOM: FIG. 4-5.** Latif Al Ani. Hisham Munir´s El Rawaf Building. Gelatin silver negative on cellulose acetate film. 1971. AIF: 0190an01216. Checklist no. 4. **RIGHT TOP: FIG. 4-6.** Latif Al Ani. Baghdad, Hisham Munir's Villa. Gelatin silver negative on cellulose acetate film. 1960. AIF: 0190an00253. Checklist no. 9. **RIGHT BOTTOM: FIG. 4-7.** Latif Al Ani, Baghdad, Hisham Munir's Villa. Gelatin silver negative on cellulose acetate film. 1960. AIF: 0190an00269. Checklist no. 10.

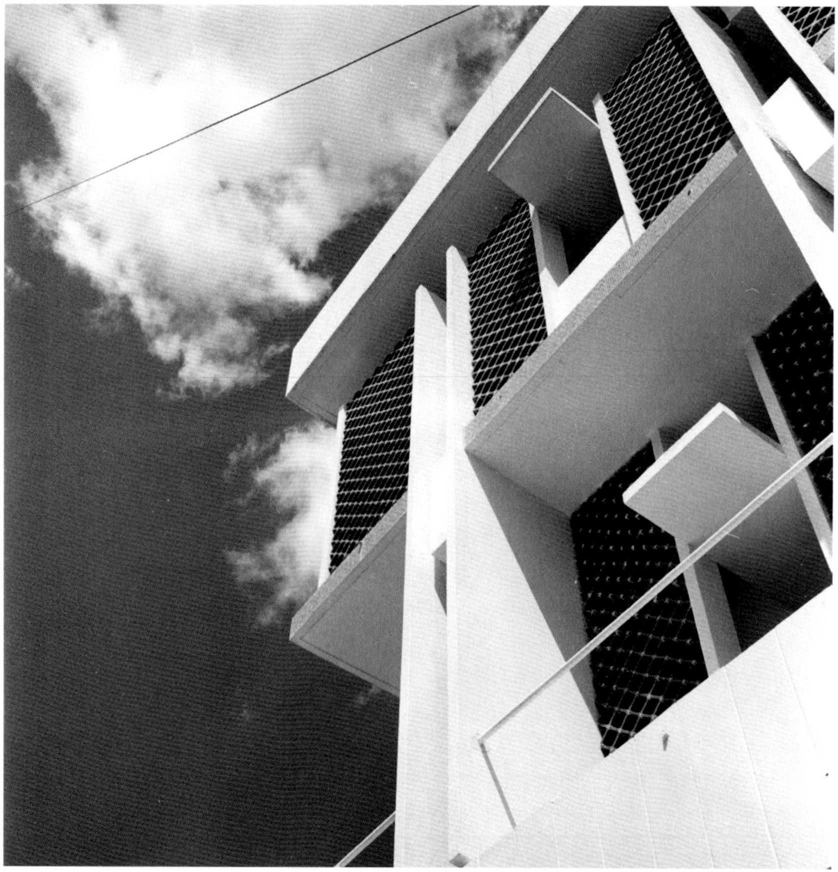

FIG. 4-4

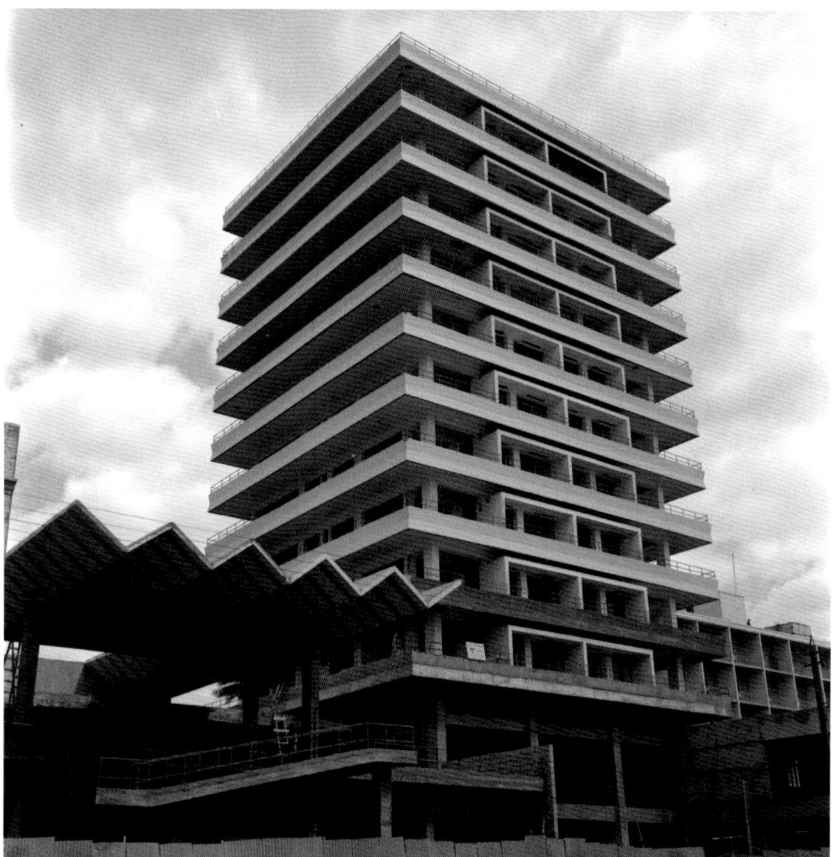

FIG. 4-5

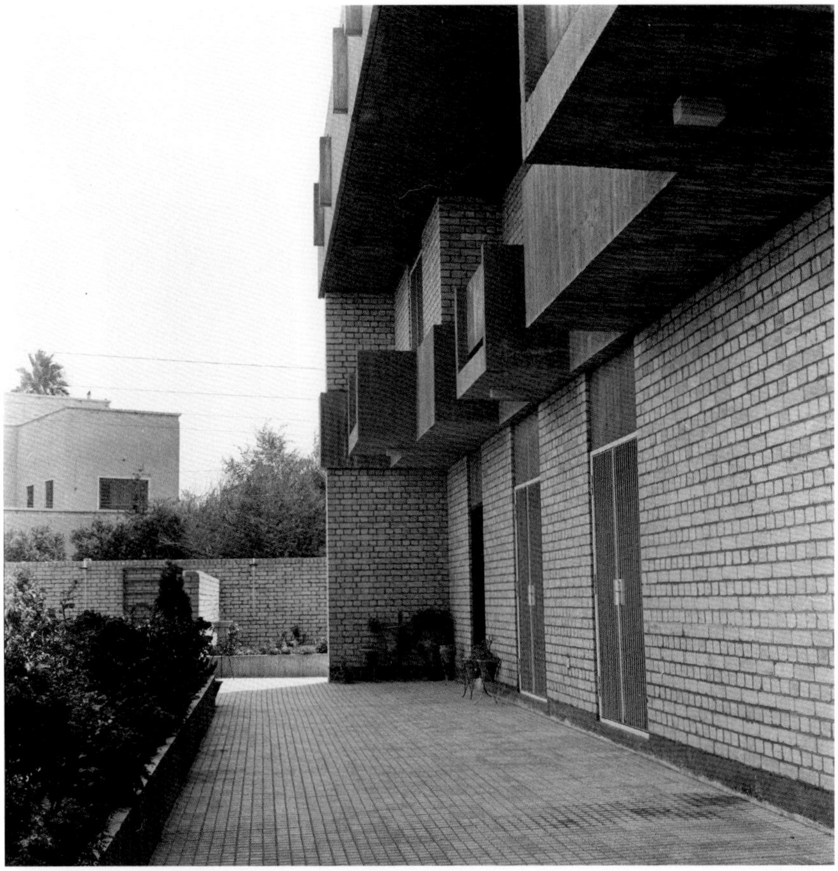

FIG. 4-6

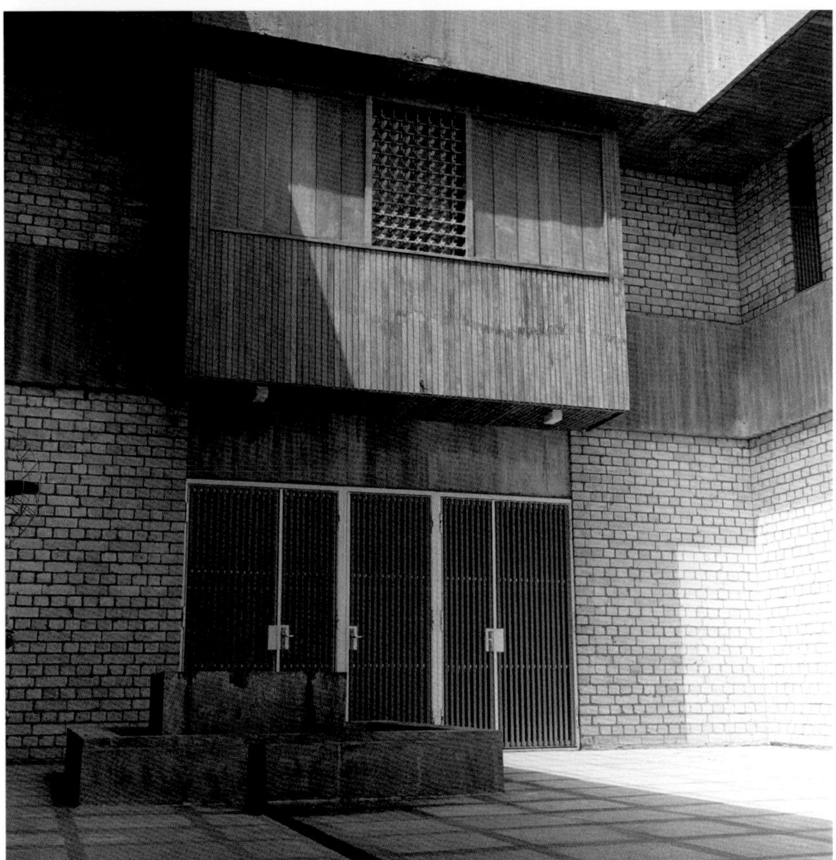

FIG. 4-7

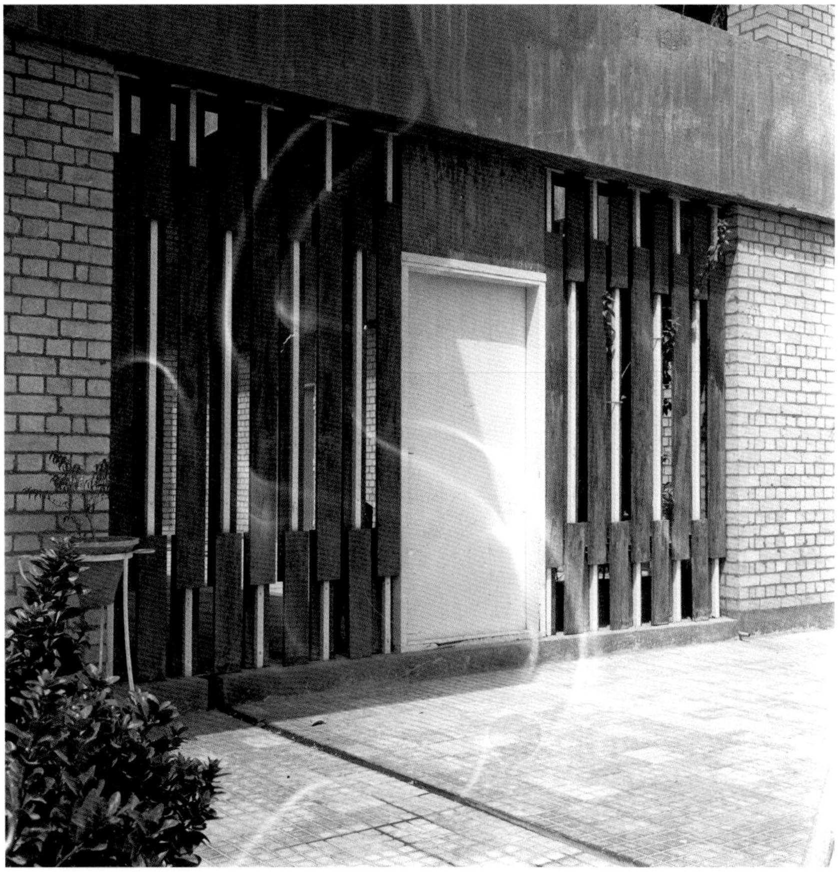

FIG. 4-8

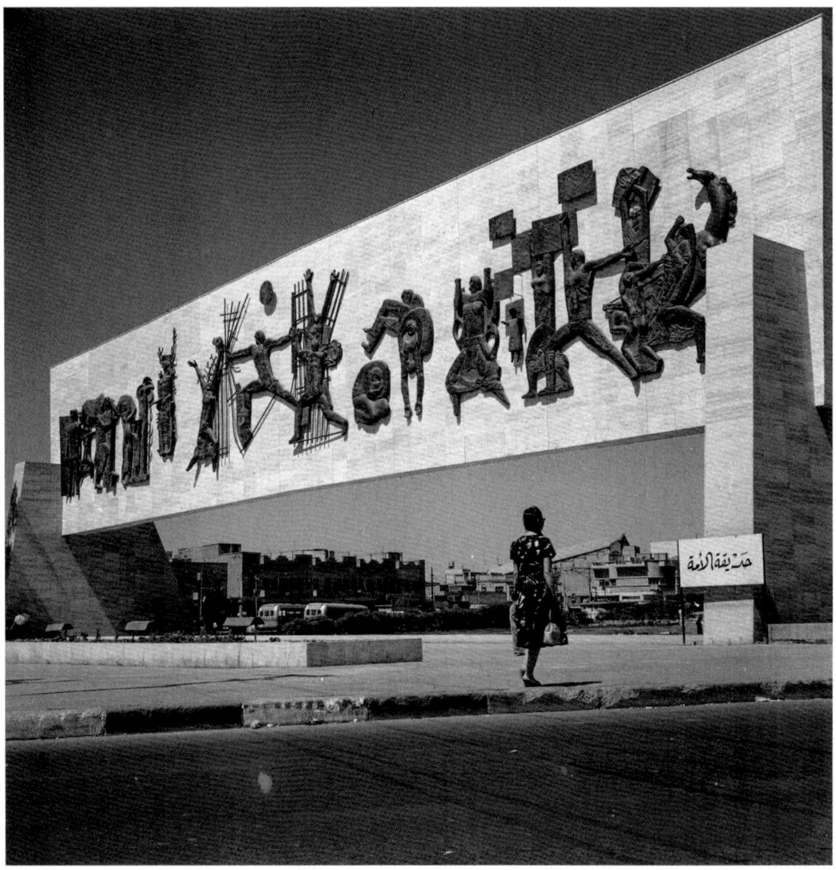

FIG. 4-9

As the monarchy crumbled and the military dictatorship took its place, the image and condition of Iraq quickly changed and speedily converted to Western standards. For countries not aligned with the Soviet Union, Western standards were "a dream come true."

Without a trace of British influence, modernization took over the country—the cities and the countryside changed with it, adapting themselves with force and speed to Western aesthetics (**FIG. 4-10**). The transformations in the landscape and the urban fabric paralleled social and moral changes. (Unveiled) women began to play economic, cultural, political, and social roles outside the domestic space as they worked and socialized (**FIGS. 4-11** to **4-13**). The image of the Iraqi population became almost indistinguishable from that in Western countries.

These were the themes that Latif Al Ani documented through his photographs. He captured with urgency the historical transition of a country leaving behind almost a thousand years of inertness under the control of the Ottoman Empire. Iraq was transformed forever, with no possibility or desire to go back to its past.

—

Archaeology and photography are historically interconnected. The first need for photography in places such as Mosul may have been due to Western archaeological missions during the early 1920s. Mosul, like Erbil, was at the center of a large territory in northern Iraq where a number of well-known biblical or Neo-Assyrian archaeological sites were located. Photographs were taken not necessarily to capture the work undertaken in these archaeological missions, but rather to immortalize the discoveries themselves.[4]

More than once, Al Ani looked to the past with longing. He experienced and attentively observed how archaeological sites were being "discovered" and exploited by Western missions. In fact, local populations had been aware of the historical sites before the arrival of foreign archaeologists in the mid-nineteenth century. Financed by European, and later North American, museums, Western archaeologists fought, using all kinds of treachery, to collect and export Neo-Assyrian and Babylonian sculptures and relics, for the glory and pride of the museums financing the expeditions.

The word *expedition*—which originates from the Latin "to make ready"—plays a significant role in military vocabulary. It is not surprising that archaeology, religion, and military affairs were closely connected during the first archaeological missions and that some of the first Western archaeologists were members of the military. Early expeditions were treasure hunts: European archaeologists

OPPOSITE, TOP: FIG. 4-8. Latif Al Ani. Baghdad, Hisham Munir's Villa. Gelatin silver negative on cellulose acetate film. 1960. AIF: 0190an00268. Checklist no. 11. **BOTTOM: FIG. 4-9.** Latif Al Ani. Baghdad, Jewad Selim's *Freedom Monument* at Tahrir Square. Gelatin silver negative on cellulose acetate film. 1961. AIF: 0190an00044. Checklist no. 84. **OVERLEAF, LEFT TOP: FIG. 4-10.** Latif Al Ani. Baghdad, Mathaf Square: Khaled Al-Rahal Maquette. Gelatin silver negative on cellulose acetate film. 1961. AIF: 0190an00558. Checklist no. 83. **LEFT BOTTOM: FIG. 4-11.** Latif Al Ani. Ctesiphon, tourist in front of the ruins of the Tāq Kasrā (Arch of Ctesiphon). Gelatin silver negative on cellulose acetate film. 1964. AIF: 0190an00977. Checklist no. 51. **RIGHT TOP: FIG. 4-12.** Latif Al Ani. Ctesiphon, tourist in front of the ruins of the Tāq Kasrā (Arch of Ctesiphon). Gelatin silver negative on cellulose acetate film. 1964. AIF: 0190an00978. Checklist no. 53. **RIGHT BOTTOM: FIG. 4-13.** Latif Al Ani. Hatra, tourist in front of the statue of Abu Bint Deimun, wife of Santruq I. Gelatin silver negative on cellulose acetate film. 1960. AIF: 0190an00648. Checklist no. 69.

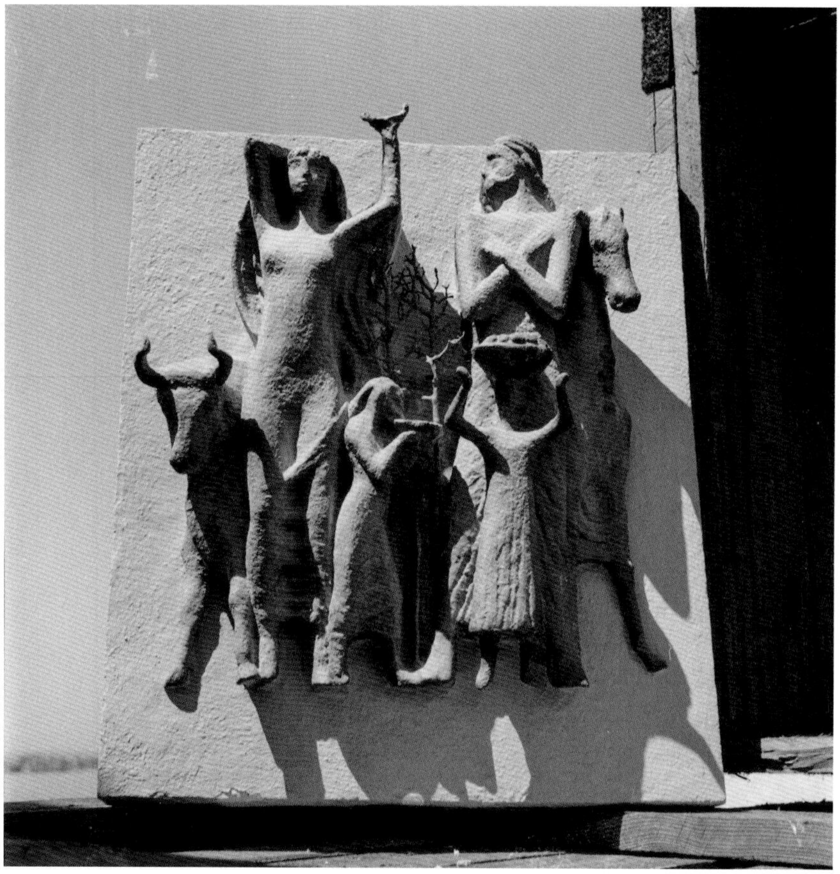

FIG. 4-10

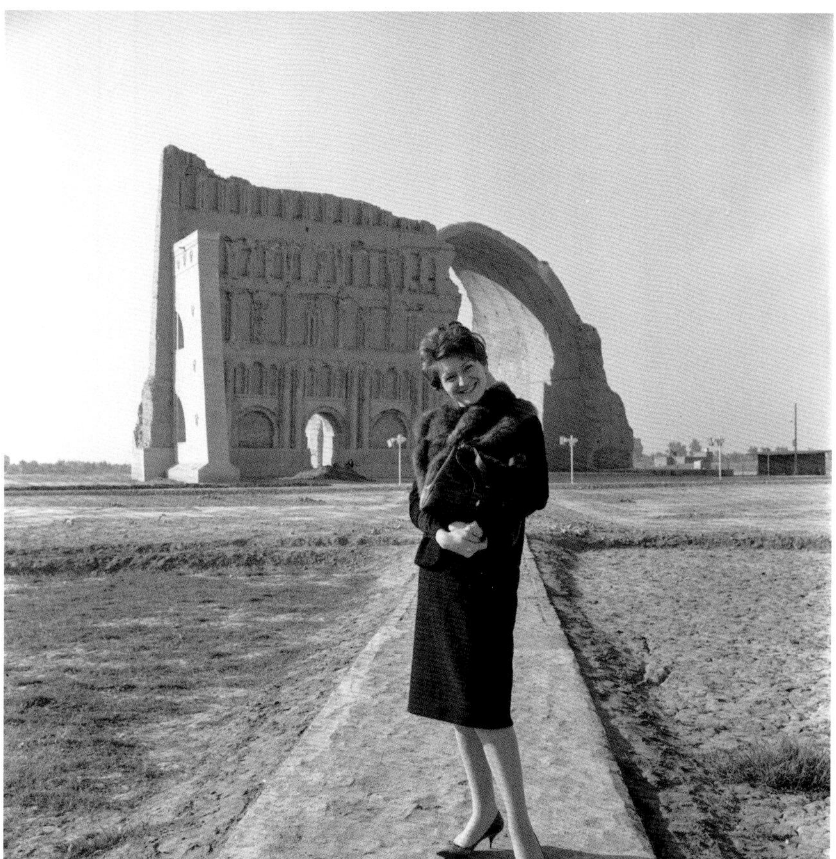

FIG. 4-11

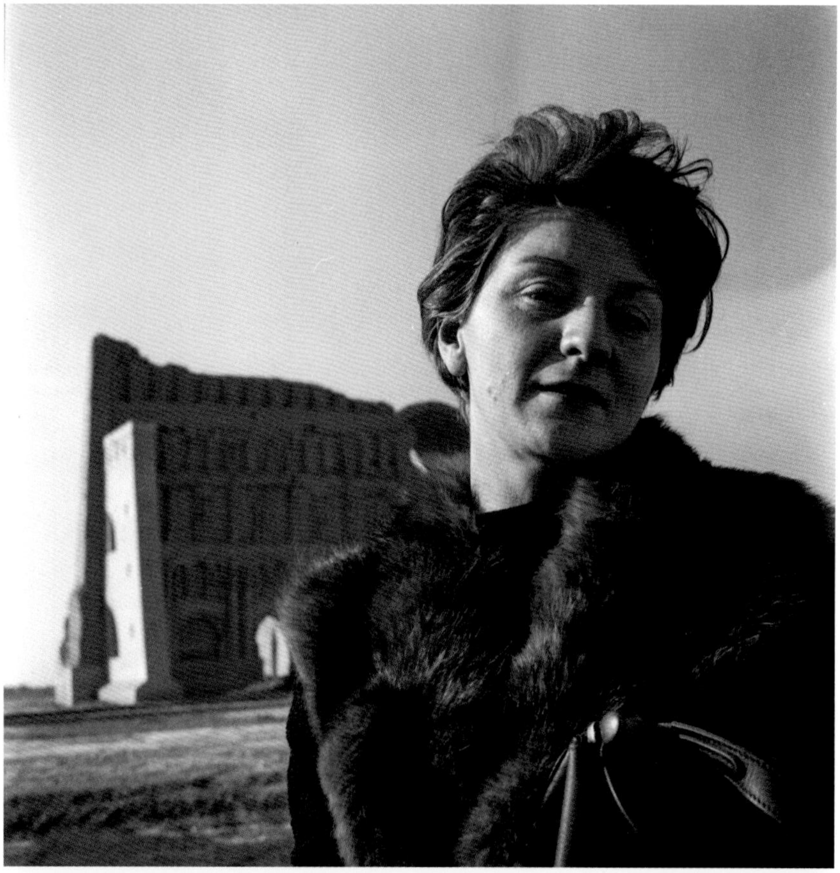

FIG. 4-12

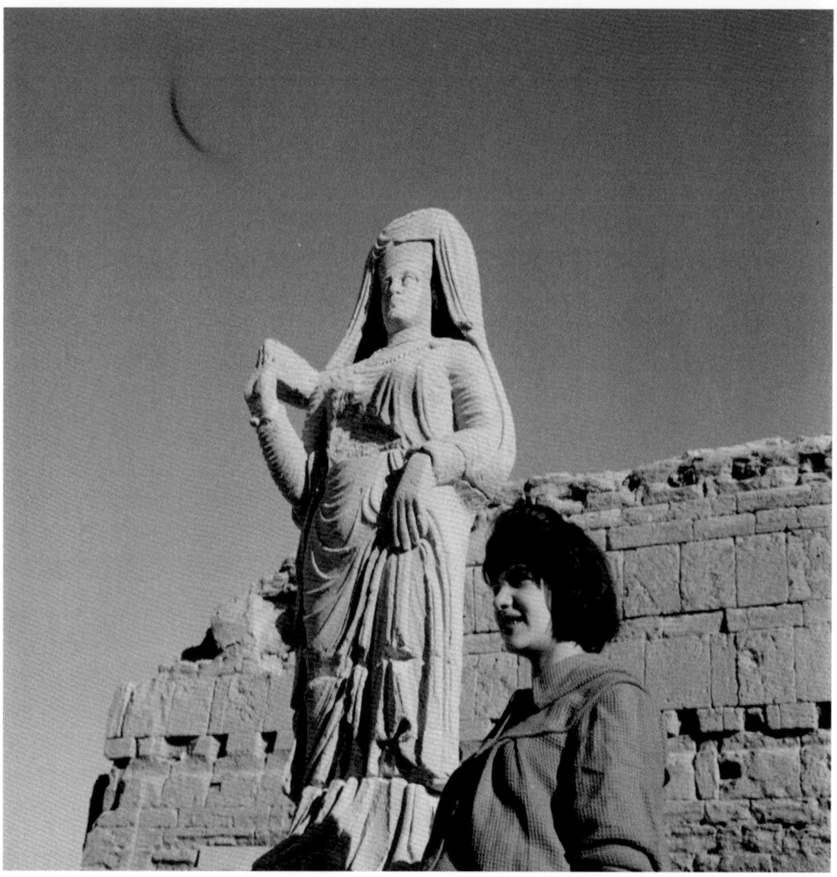

FIG. 4-13

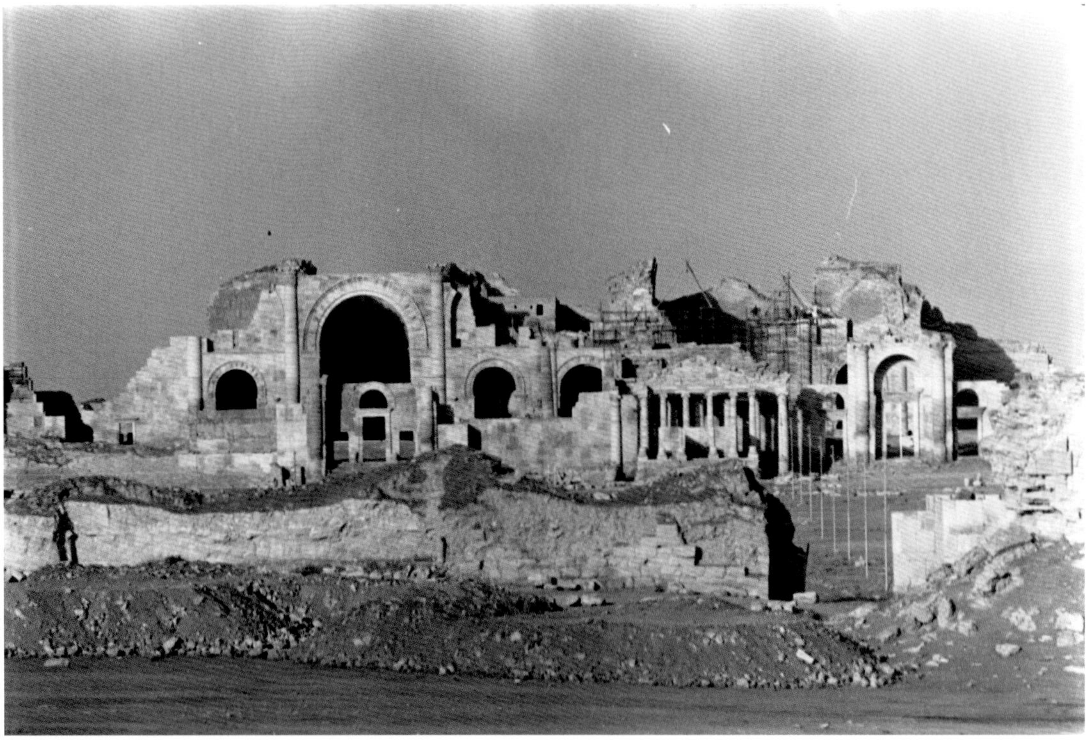

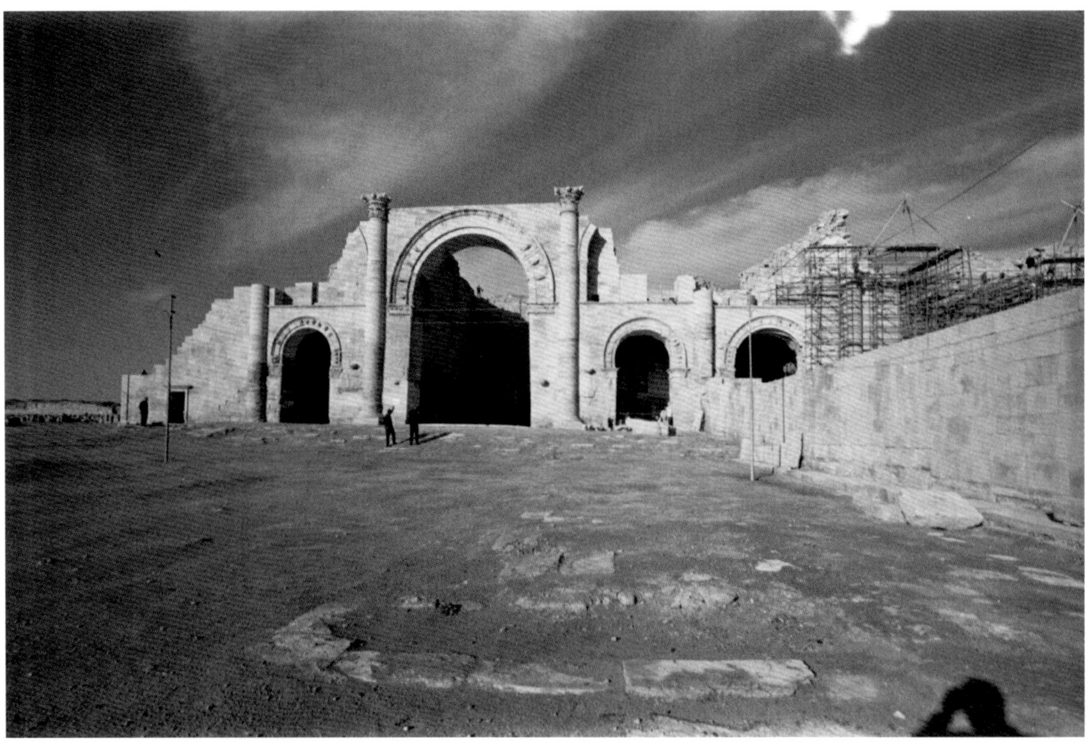

TOP: FIG. 4-14. Latif Al Ani. Hatra, The Great Iwans. Gelatin silver negative on cellulose acetate film. 1960. AIF: 0190an01784. Checklist no. 65. **BOTTOM: FIG. 4-15.** Latif Al Ani. Hatra, The Great Iwans. Gelatin silver negative on cellulose acetate film. 1960. AIF: 0190an01788. Checklist no. 66.

rushed to the ruins, competitively and ruthlessly, in order to gain the supremacy of their national museums. Western cultures saw their roots in a biblical Eden, and archaeologists saw themselves as "returning" to the Near East to recover what they considered relics of Western civilization. In the process, like bulls in a china shop, archaeologists displaced the Ottoman and Arab populations from their ancestry, sabotaging and erasing their relationship with the finds in their territories. Following World War I, this archaeological treasure hunt was facilitated by the colonization of a large part of the Middle East.[5]

—

Most of Al Ani's photographs from the 1950s and 1960s—like most early and mid-twentieth-century images of archaeological sites—are black and white.[6] They offer more than what they show at first glance. Al Ani pictured ancient sites like the Arab Samarra, the Mesopotamian sites of Hatra (**FIGS. 4-14** and **4-15**), Ctesiphon (**FIGS. 4-16** and **4-17**), and Babylon, and the ziggurat of Dur-Kurigalzu in the Baghdad periphery. He also photographed the Baalbek temple in Lebanon and the Giza pyramids in Egypt.

As an artistic technique, photography was still quite modern in 1940s and '50s Iraq. While modernization began to revolutionize the country in the subsequent decades, Al Ani was able to capture it with his camera. At the same time, he was able to bring a modern and unique point of view to the shots. Some of his images of cities, archaeological sites, and landscape are aerial views (**FIGS. 4-18** and **4-19**). Taking advantage of the IPC planes used to survey oil fields, he was able to shoot never-before-seen images of architecture and ruins covering Iraq. He reached beyond the established limitations of human vision, and his images transcend the relationships between nature and culture, buildings and cities, cities and the countryside. These pioneering aerial views showed how everyday changes in terms of building, living, and relating to the surroundings in Iraq were also happening on a larger scale. Changes took place everywhere, and the eye from far above was better able to perceive and communicate them.

Al Ani's photographs of ruins were not meant to be historical documents. While the whole archaeological site was never pictured, his choice of views is telling: the ruins are not alone. They do not seem to be the main element in the composition, but rather a sort of theatrical scenery (**FIG. 4-20**), sometimes far behind, almost invisible, or partially hidden by a few visitors.

We might hypothesize that the photographs represent what visitors saw, that the camera acted as the visitor's eye, but this is not the case. The reason that the ruins as a whole are not pictured is because no one in the photograph is really looking at them. The visitors do not recognize the ruins as having a character of their own or as remarkable entities or as survivors from the past—the Iraqi past, worthy of being seen—but rather as trophies, something to pose in front of. Most

OVERLEAF, LEFT TOP: FIG. 4-16. Latif Al Ani. Ctesiphon, view of the site. Gelatin silver negative on cellulose acetate film. 1964. AIF: 0190an01595. Checklist no. 48. **LEFT BOTTOM: FIG. 4-17.** Latif Al Ani. Ctesiphon, the ruins of the Tāq Kasrā (Arch of Ctesiphon) from a Bedouin tent; a dallah in the foreground. Chromogenic process film negative on cellulose acetate film. 1965. AIF: 0190an00980. Checklist no. 50. **RIGHT TOP: FIG. 4-18.** Latif Al Ani. Baghdad, Jewad Selim's *Freedom Monument* at Tahrir Square. Gelatin silver negative on cellulose acetate film. 1961. AIF: 0190an00070. Checklist no. 82. **RIGHT BOTTOM: FIG. 4-19.** Latif Al Ani. Ziggurat of Dur-Kurigalzu (Agargouf) as seen from a plane. Gelatin silver negative on cellulose acetate film. 1960. AIF: 0190an00008b. Checklist no. 2.

FIG. 4-16

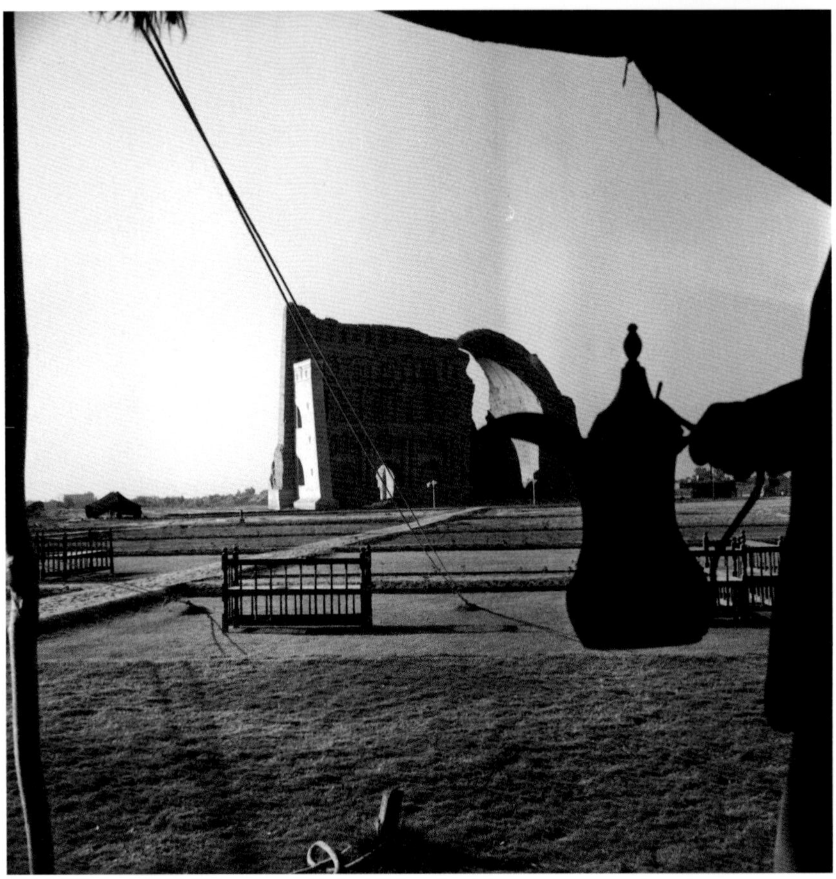

FIG. 4-17

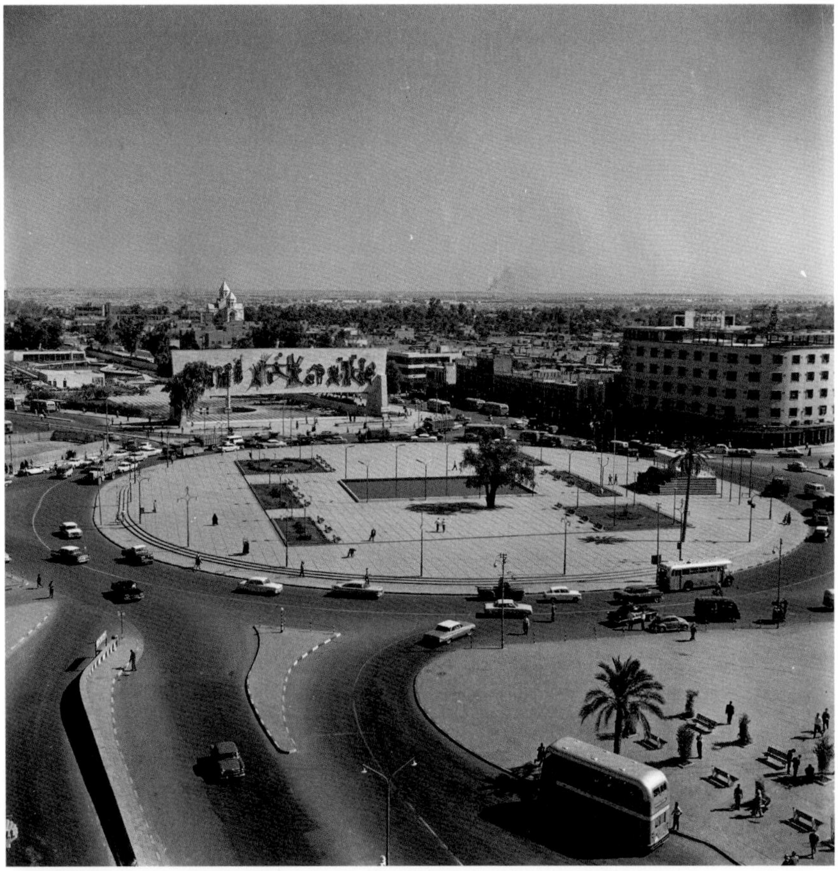

FIG. 4-18

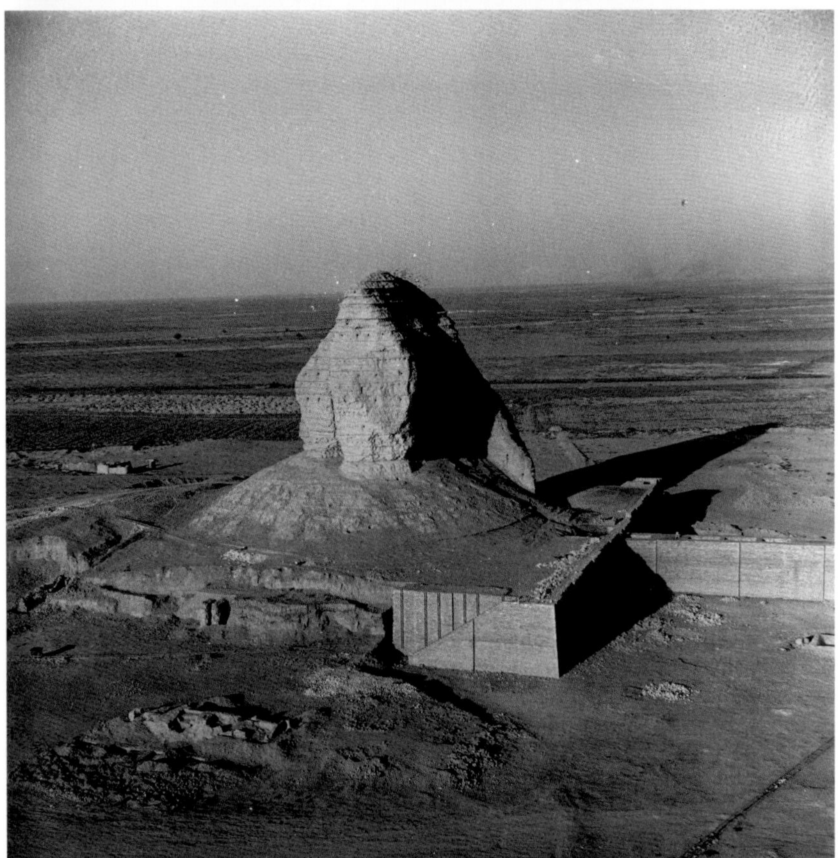

FIG. 4-19

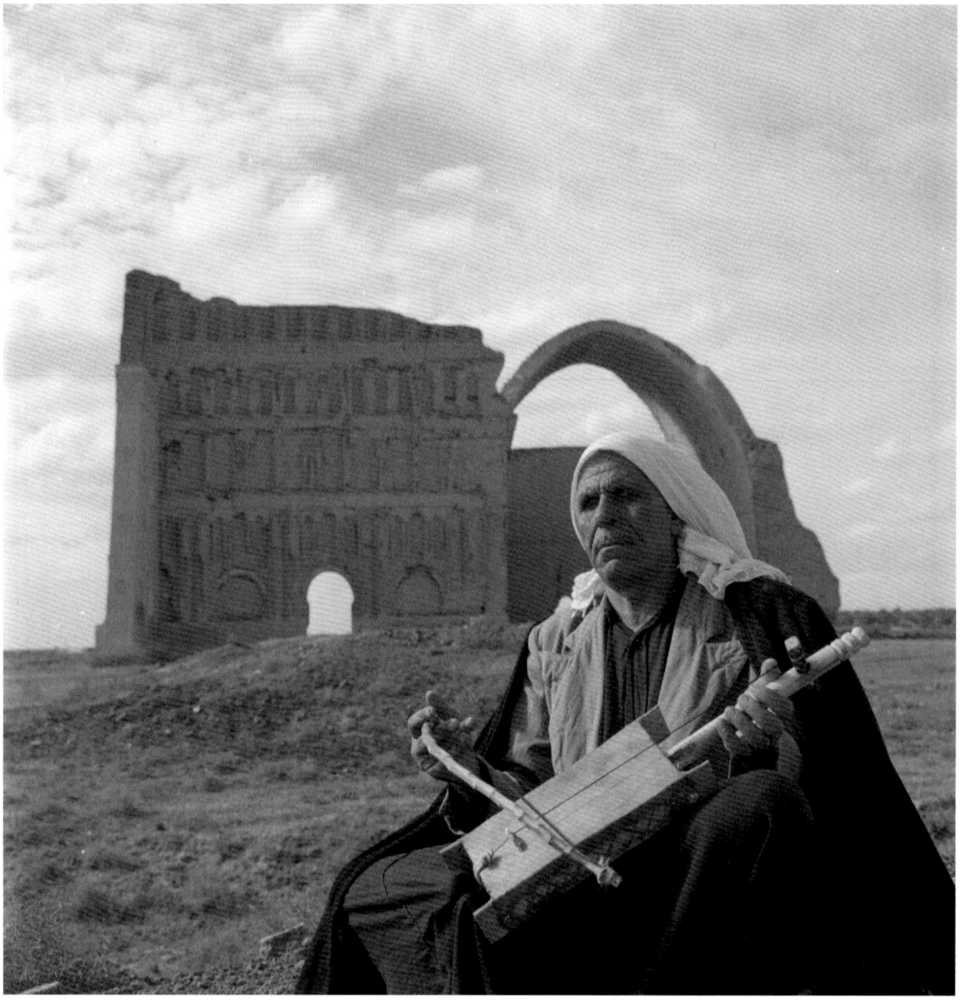

FIG. 4-20. Latif Al Ani. Ctesiphon, ruins of the Tāq Kasrā (Arch of Ctesiphon) with musician playing the rebab. Gelatin silver negative on cellulose acetate film. 1964. AIF: 0190an00560. Checklist no. 46.

visitors, as Al Ani corroborated in a 2017 interview, were wealthy foreigners, generally North American tourists. He noted with dismay: "Newcomers came. Pandora's box was opened."[7]

The foreign tourists pose in elegant yet inappropriate outfits, in front of the ruins. They do not seem interested in the history behind them; their only concern is to be photographed at these "spots"—for a historical selfie long before the plague of banal selfies. The ruins form part of an exotic scenario in the middle of a desert or an arid land. The visitors wear "costumes" and use the ruins as a backdrop for their show. The ruins could have been modern replicas, and it would not have mattered at all.

Until the 1970s, Rasheed Street, Baghdad's central avenue, was the most elegant thoroughfare in the city. Latif Al Ani took photographs of the tourists who dressed glamorously in chic urban fashions. Yet, their stylish tastes clash with common sense, as men wear long-sleeve t-shirts and ties in scorching temperatures,[8] and women wear cocktail dresses and stiletto shoes to walk in the desert. Moreover, they are not walking anywhere, they are just posing, indifferent to the place, unaffected by what is surrounding them (**FIG. 4-21**).

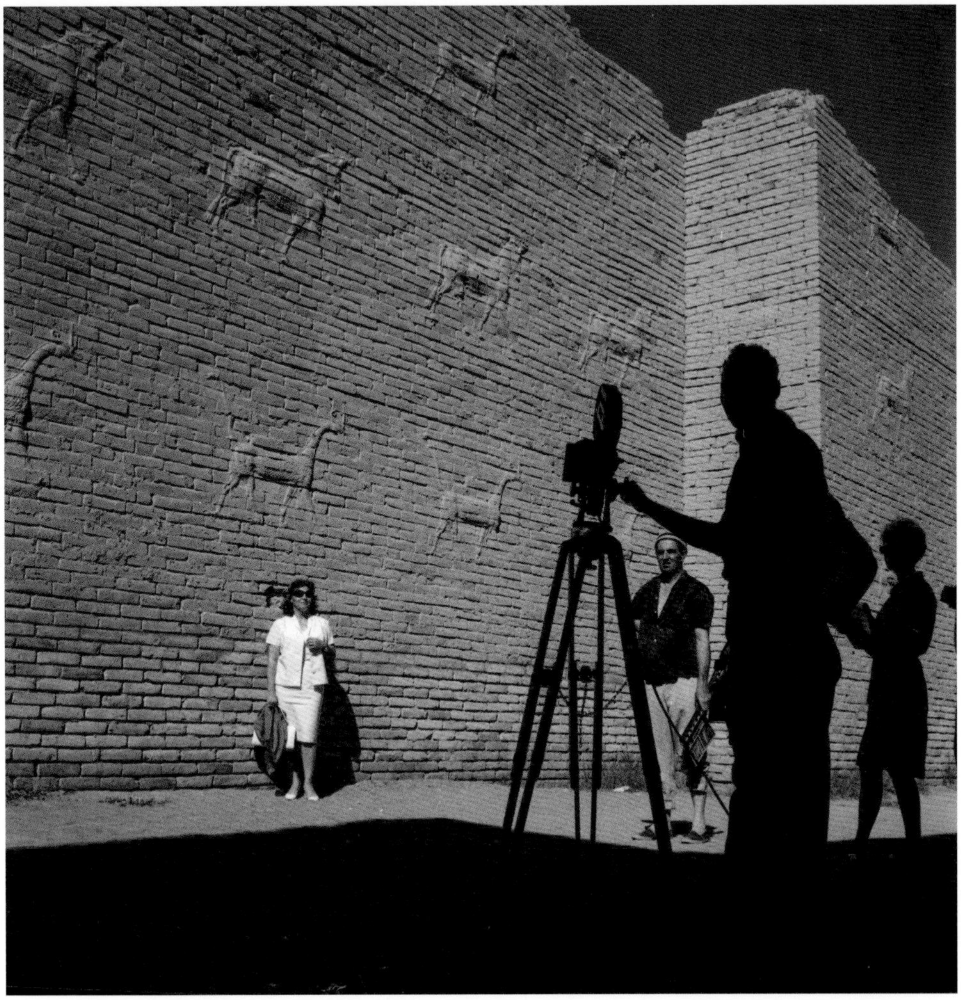

FIG. 4-21. Latif Al Ani. Babylon, Babel Films shooting an ad for Arab tourism in front of the wall of sacred bulls and mušḫuššu dragons at the Ishtar Gate. Gelatin silver negative on cellulose acetate film. 1961. AIF: 0190an00067. Checklist no. 20.

In some cases, visitors briefly "embraced" the culture, in festive parties. They dressed in Bedouin "costumes" with a new *djellaba* and a *keffiyeh*, but wearing their Western clothes underneath. Their Bedouin costumes were just for fun, worn ironically for the photographs. Visitors smiled, turning their backs to the magnificent ruins, uninterested in them and the culture and history surrounding them. In effect, they wanted to be seen and photographed precisely in these places that served as "Orientalist" scenarios. Local people helped them into their costumes and served them. In the background, a "real" Bedouin, perhaps blind, would be sitting in the dust, playing a rebab (similar to a fiddle) for the tourists.

Observing and analyzing the photographs of the ruins, we can ask, Was Latif Al Ani taking photographs to promote the beauty and safety of the archaeological site? These images were certainly taken for IPC or *Ahl al-Naft*, and thus we can assume that they were not meant to ridicule foreign tourists. Yet the photos seem to actively caricature the culture. The scenes were similar to a "face in the hole" board of a fun fair, except that visitors themselves really dressed like "natives"—as some British colonial writers often described the Iraqi people.

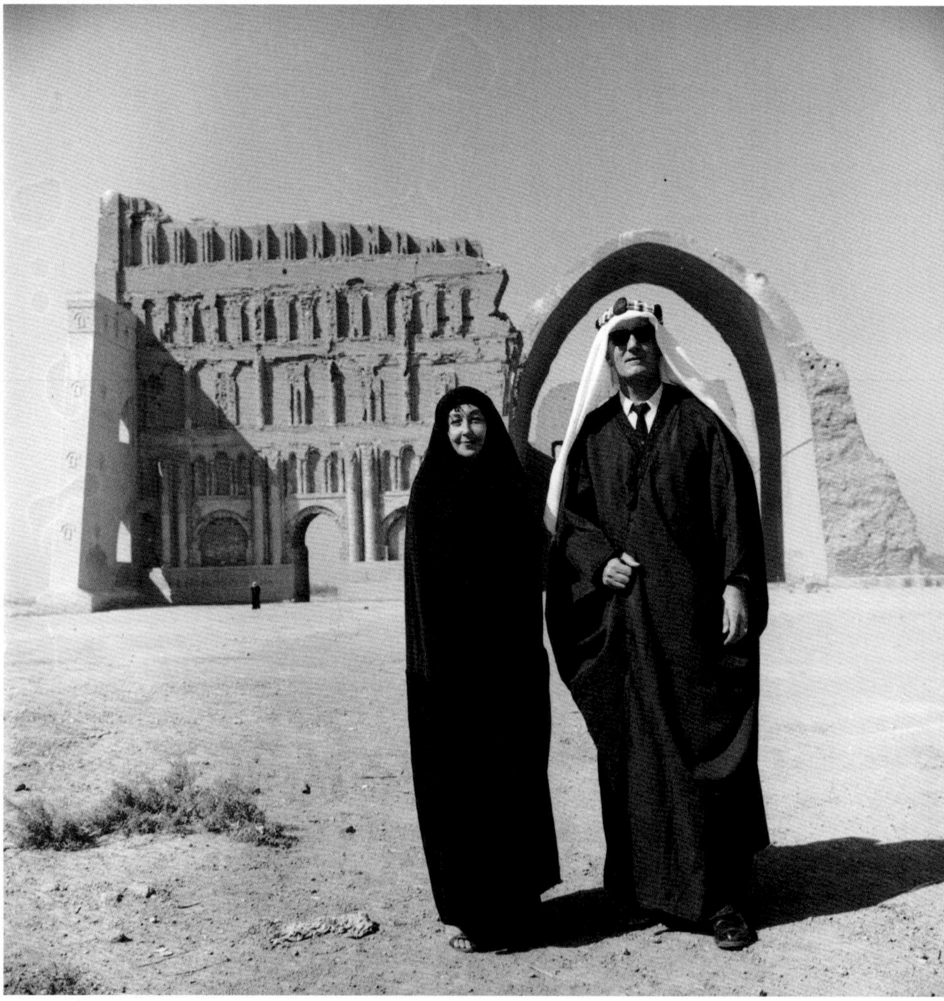

FIG. 4-22. Latif Al Ani. Ctesiphon, tourists in front of the ruins of the Tāq Kasrā (Arch of Ctesiphon). Gelatin silver negative on cellulose acetate film. 1964. AIF: 0190an01266. Checklist no. 43.

Or, was Al Ani trying to bring an implicit critical view to these scenes? He was undoubtedly asked to present the image of a modern and open Iraq. His goal was, as he explained in interviews, to show the beauty—not always obvious—of Iraq.[9] But he was also aware that the country's beauty was fading. Changes in Iraq, in Baghdad especially, were happening quickly; the transformation of the country was severe and not all the changes were beneficial. Al Ani´s vision was neither innocent nor deceptive, even though he was working for a large British oil company. Through his photographs, he offered an affectionate but not exalted transcription of reality, sometimes humorous and ironic—for instance how the incongruity of a scene or the ridiculous poses of the foreign visitors in front of the archaeological ruins can be perceived subtlety. He was not taking a political stance, even if his photographs were widely promoted abroad, especially in embassies. It is difficult to determine how these wealthy visitors, acting as if they were Lawrence of Arabia or on an American urban avenue, were judged by Al Ani. But photographs are not neutral: when a photographer shoots a scene, the image resulting from it denotes how the scene was perceived and communicated. Cameras can either enhance or deface the people and places they

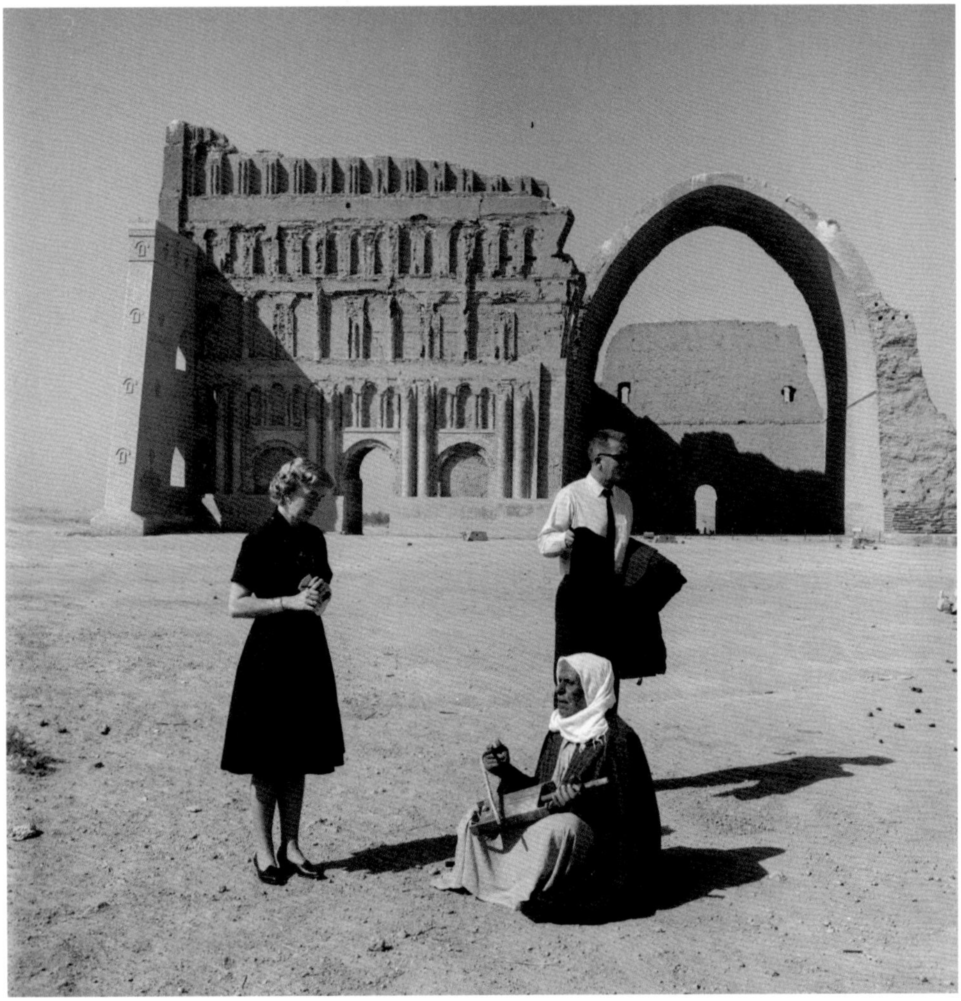

FIG. 4-23. Latif Al Ani. Ctesiphon, tourists in front of the ruins of the Tāq Kasrā (Arch of Ctesiphon) with musician playing the rebab. Gelatin silver negative on cellulose acetate film. 1964. AIF: 0190an01178. Checklist no. 38.

capture. There is a subtle distortion, an accent punctuating reality, detaching and extracting the photographed scene from its surroundings. The photograph singles out a moment, which adheres to a bigger picture, and this emphasized instant acquires a meaning of its own.

Would Latif Al Ani wish to have displayed a single iconic photograph from all those taken on a particular day or at a particular scene? By looking at his photographic archives in Beirut, it is not unreasonable to consider that some photographs were intended to be images in a series, rather than individual shots. The photographs we have retained resemble stills from a film, meant to be seen all together, one after the other. They constitute a sequence and tell a story.

The series of photographs taken in front of Ctesiphon shows this clearly (**FIGS. 4-22** and **4-23**). The tourists in each picture seem to be related to each other. They are couples, siblings, or families, appearing in a single photograph, but their presence also relates to other, similar images, as in a sequence of film frames. To fully appreciate the photographs, the viewer must look at them not as independent images but instead as a series that does not reproduce the world but rather creates a world of its own, inevitably inviting a special and complex view. We may

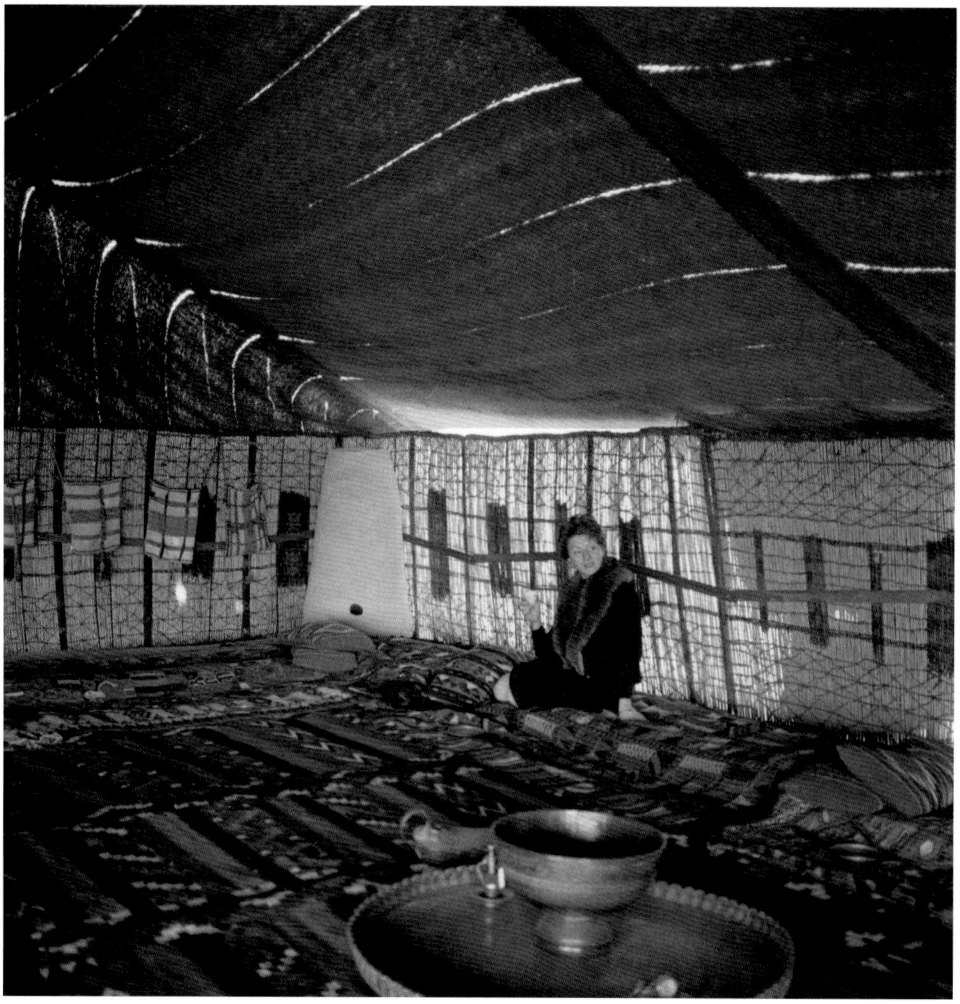

FIG. 4-24. Latif Al Ani. Ctesiphon, tourist in a Bedouin tent in front of the ruins of the Tāq Kasrā (Arch of Ctesiphon). Gelatin silver negative on cellulose acetate film. 1964. AIF: 0190an01593. Checklist no. 52.

consider that Latif Al Ani was challenging the notion of photography as used by the photographer Henri Cartier-Bresson, who saw photography as an attempt to capture a "decisive" moment, whereas Al Ani's vision may have been more experimental or "avant-garde." He was not acting as a "classical" photographer, but as a visual artist using the photographic medium, and producing not a single, perfect image of a scene, but rather a series of images, as in a film. Some Latif Al Ani photographs are to be appreciated as part of a whole series, where differences between images are subtle but visually important.

Latif Al Ani also captured the work of modest workers and artisans—a seamstress, a mechanic, a metalworker in a bazaar— focusing on people alone, carefully taking notes of all the details displayed in front of him. Yet, he avoided photographing the slums surrounding Baghdad and the inhumane conditions of the residences. Due to droughts and the lack of housing improvements in southern Iraq, whole families were obliged to leave the marshes and go to the capital to live in extreme poverty and unsanitary conditions. People in the slums lived with animals among mud and dirt, fighting starvation and disease. Ethically, Al Ani could not have found beauty in such conditions. As he did not want to frame the slums and their inhabitants in any way that differed from the emotionally and visually painful reality, he preferred not to photograph them at all.

Even though we cannot be certain how Al Ani would have printed the images from the negatives in the archives, we have clues where he circled or marked some of them, giving us an insight into his vision. What we have now is a sort of draft of what we believe Al Ani would have wanted to show in his photographs. In view of the uncertainty of final compositions, and to avoid guessing and altering Al Ani's vision, modern prints of his negatives show the entire image, even if there are parts within the negatives that are not perfectly focused or might seem extraneous to the final frame. Latif Al Ani pursued the perfect image in a perfect print, but his meticulous vision has vanished. We must therefore simply accept the remnants that have endured.

—

After IPC left Iraq in 1961, Latif Al Ani began to work at the Ministry of Culture, where he founded the first photographic department[10] and where he was in charge of a cultural magazine titled *New Iraq*. The magazine was published in five languages (Arabic, Kurdish, English, French, and German) and regularly included Al Ani's own photographs.

In the 1970s, he began a journalistic period, when he joined the Iraqi News Agency. During this time, Al Ani's photographs were made to record and capture moments in time and not, as before, to search for permanent beauty within the mutability of time. There were public, official institutions that would not have allowed him to show certain brutal images of the misery of Iraq. But Latif Al Ani's work was not censored, as his images never showed the country as inhuman or devastated. Rather, he showed the positive and negative consequences of the inevitable changes.

Iraq's majestic archaeological remains were the only aspect of reality that lingered as a sort of immortal image of the country. They stood as a life raft so as not to get lost in the waves of transformation and modernism. The ruins were physically and spiritually far from buzzing city life and the constant rattle of Iraq's growing industrialization. Archaeological sites seemed out of time and only offered a glimpse of the present when foreign tourists visited. They remained forever associated with tradition and the daily rituals that were disappearing in cities like Baghdad (**FIG. 4-24**). They stood tall, with their dust and a hint of nostalgia, evoking the beauty of a past time.

The 1960s were the international decade for Latif Al Ani. His photographs were shown not only in Iraq, but also in Paris, Berlin, San Francisco, Chicago, and Washington. Throughout 1963 he had a traveling exhibition in the United States, and in 1965 he was invited to East Berlin for a solo show. His colored photographs made in the 1970s were political journalistic documents, more than artistic views.

Due to a series of planned assassinations, Saddam Hussein rose to power as vice president of Iraq in 1969, before becoming president after a palace coup in 1979. Latif Al Ani was then no longer authorized to work as a photographer in the public space. He slowly disappeared from the public eye, vanishing from memory.[11] It was not until forty years later that scholars brought him back into view. Fortunately, during the last few years of his life, Al Ani was able to see how his popularity and recognition had grown.

Latif Al Ani's photographs cause a certain emotional shock, as they display an aura of nostalgia: nostalgia for a time of urban freedom. Even if he did not want to show physical and moral ugliness, such as the misery related to colonialism and dictatorship, the extension of slums, and the consequences of military violence inside Iraq's Ba'ath party, his photographs remind us of these changes and realities. His early photographs reveal an image of Iraq that is perhaps partial but nevertheless real, and far different from the country Al Ani saw for the last time in 2021. *Iraq's Invisible Beauty* shows this contrast at its beginning, when the photographer as an old man walks through a devastated city like Mosul. Scenes from the documentary show a dilapidated country where oil and dirt, corruption and violence are intertwined. The photographs taken by a young Al Ani show us what has been lost since the 1950s, and especially since the 1990s—due to the Iran-Iraq war, the First Gulf War, the 1973 oil embargo, the Second Gulf War, Iraq's Civil War, and the devastation and extreme violence caused by ISIS and similar organized groups. For a brief moment, these photographs also help us forget the current day-to-day difficulties unfolding in a shattered country. What remains in Latif Al Ani's photographs are images of a lost Iraq, and of a brilliant archaeological past—still standing in spite of wars, destructions, and looting—a past that may help us regain a certain hope in the future, a future still out of reach and difficult to picture.

*Text revised and corrected by Kalima Amber Vico Gerard, to whom I am most grateful.

1 Chalabi and Van Cauteren 2015.

2 Chalabi, Montazami, and Taba 2017, 25–26.

3 Hisham Munir studied architecture in the United States and worked for Walter Gropius at the Baghdad University project starting in 1957. He was a practitioner of brutalist architecture, especially at the campus of Mosul University, completed in 1966, and at the Baghdad municipality building, completed in 1975. The former's exceptionally large library was burned by ISIS in 2015. The portfolio of early Hisham Munir projects can be consulted at https://www.archnet.org/publications/10401 (last consultation: June 28, 2023).

4 Contrary to popular belief, Iraq—then a country with Jewish, Christian, and Muslim populations coexisting without any major concerns—was not affected by any Protestant, Jewish, or Sunni ban on naturalistic images or photographs (especially in Mosul, a mostly Christian city).

5 See Azara 2012, 311–17.

6 Al Ani's use of black-and-white photography seems to have been a stylistic choice, but it is true that he used color in the 1960s and '70s, especially as a photojournalist when he was working for the Iraqi News Agency. It is important to note that he attended theoretical and practical classes at the Gevacolor School in Mortsel-Antwerp (Belgium) to learn how to develop, print, and enlarge films made with the Gevacolor process (introduced by Agfa-Gevaert in 1947), and he received a certificate on July 3, 1964.

7 Chalabi, Montazami, and Taba 2017.

8 While we do not know exactly when the photographs were taken, the lack of jackets and winter attire seems to point toward summer.

9 Rigamonti di Cutò 2018. This interview was published on the occasion of the Latif Al Ani exhibition organized by the Ruya Foundation at the Coningsby Gallery in London, December 4–16, 2017.

10 Sikorski 2019.

11 A common Iraqi 25,000-dinar red bill includes on one side an engraving based on Al Ani's photograph of a young peasant. It was used without his permission after Saddam Hussein's fall. The original photograph has disappeared. Few people know that they have had a reproduction of a Latif Al Ani photograph in their hands, as he was generally forgotten until quite recently.

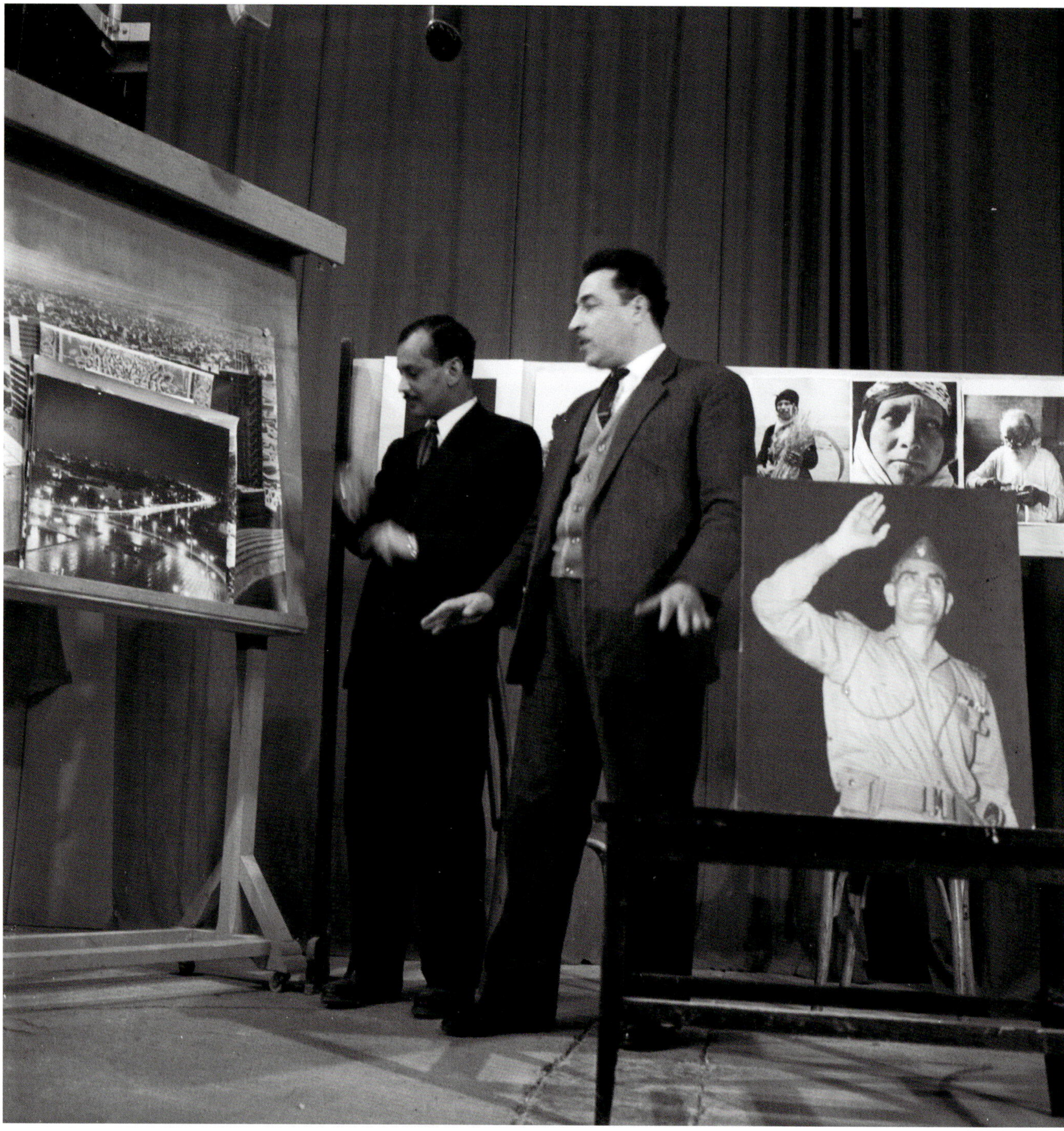

CHAPTER 5

AL AMILOON FIL NAFT: IMAGING OIL THROUGH ART

Ala Younis

Between 1961 and 1972, the magazine *Al Amiloon Fil Naft* (Oil Workers) played a significant role as a cultural space that showcased and supported Iraq's creative scene (**FIG. 5-1**). Initially established as an internal monthly publication for the workers and employees of the Iraq Petroleum Company (IPC) in Baghdad, Mosul, and Basra, *Al Amiloon Fil Naft* nevertheless provided a platform for both established and emerging talent, extending its content beyond the oil industry. The magazine took pride in being the first to feature the works of many writers who, within a few years, became prominent figures among Iraqi writers and poets of the time. While one can detect a disparity between IPC and the magazine's literary and artistic content regarding the presentation of knowledge and the ownership of technological images, the oil-industry content in *Al Amiloon Fil Naft* also made space for parallel reflections on the social and political status and situations related to heritage-based art. I would argue that the heritage-inspired art stirred active reading of the technical content from which it seems detached, and, further, that active reading of the paired content on the pages of *Al Amiloon Fil Naft* compensated for the seeming absence of a relationship between technology and the art published in its pages.

Every issue of *Al Amiloon Fil Naft* featured two covers, one in English and one in Arabic, each potentially showcasing different images (**FIG. 5-2**). While the English covers often featured images of oil fields, workers, or industrial elements, the Arabic covers generally reproduced works by renowned and emerging artists. Notable artists whose works appeared included Jewad Selim, Kadhim Haidar, Hafidh al-Droubi, Faeq Hassan, Jabra Ibrahim Jabra, Nuri al-Rawi, Nuha al-Radi, Dia al-Azzawi, Rafa Nasiri, Suad Attar, Layla Attar, Ismail al-Chekhli, Hashim

FIG. 5-1. Photographer unknown. Television Studio Baghdad, Latif Al Ani and Nuri al-Rawi. Gelatin silver negative on cellulose acetate film. Undated. AIF: 0190an00657.

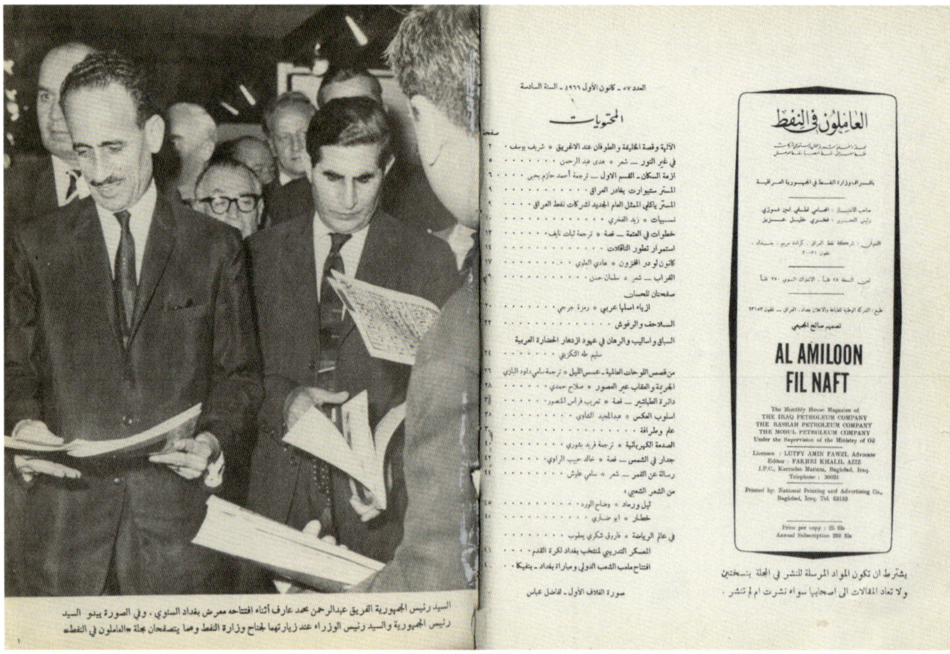

FIG. 5-2. President Abdul Salam Arif checks issues of the magazine at the Oil Ministry Booth at Baghdad Annual Exhibition. *Al Amiloon Fil Naft*, no. 57, December 1966. With the magazine published in two languages, readers could choose to read the magazine from right to left (in Arabic) or from left to right for English articles.

Samarchi, among others. The subjects varied, primarily reflecting scenes from Iraq's heritage, rural or religious landscapes, traditional practices, and occasionally abstraction, but also included works that were in solidarity with the Palestinian cause (as explained further below). Except for limited instances, the content or forms of these works did not touch on the topic of oil in its broadest context—its technology or the modernity this national wealth might have brought to the cityscape or areas near the oil fields.

At the same time, the photographs from IPC that appeared on the English covers depicted employees installing pipes in the oil fields, undergoing training abroad, or playing in teams in football tournaments. Primarily published uncredited and undated, the photos also showcased oil refineries, structures in the oil fields, and oil machinery and silos. As the documentary photos on the magazine's English covers were paired with paintings on the Arabic covers, the effect was an artistic intervention that exposed the latent educational potential that the didactic materials may have carried.

—

Writers and artists frequently visited IPC's headquarters in Karadat Maryam, Baghdad, to submit copies of their work to Jabra Ibrahim Jabra (1919–1994), a poet, novelist, painter, translator, and literary critic, who worked at the oil company's public relations office in Iraq. While Jabra significantly influenced the materials selected for publication, his name never appeared as part of the editorial team, and yet *Al Amiloon Fil Naft* is never mentioned without reference to him. Jabra offered a substantial fee of 5 Iraqi dinars for each published text, which enticed more writers to send their materials by mail to the editorial office in Baghdad. A disclaimer in each issue stated that submissions had to be in two copies, neither of which would be returned to the author, regardless of whether the material was published. Writers followed up on their submissions by contacting the office or enlisting acquaintances to advocate for their work, hoping to see their creations featured in the increasingly significant magazine.

Al Amiloon Fil Naft aimed to diversify its content to suit its readers, whose preferences were vast and varied. It was not a purely literary magazine, nor could it publish all the stories and poems it received, making it imperative to carefully select the content based on its quality, significance, and suitability for publication. As one issue stated:

> We publish . . . stories and poems, sometimes more in a single issue than what dedicated literary magazines publish. It is important to reiterate that all submitted materials receive thorough attention, even though the magazine is not obliged to prioritize one writer over another or present specific pieces unless they meet the earlier criteria. Furthermore, esteemed writers are kindly requested to refrain from persistently inquiring or personally visiting the office to inquire about the publication date or protest the non-publication of their work. The magazine values the creativity of its contributors, and any oversight or delay in publication, as mentioned before, cannot be resolved through insistence or review.[1]

Feeling pressured by the many inquiries, the magazine editors often published their relationship with the submitted materials. They repeatedly reminded readers that *Al Amiloon Fil Naft* was an oil community, not a literary magazine. The editors compiled an index of materials published between May 1966 and April 1967 and published it on three pages of issue 114 in December 1971. The list included eleven articles related to women's interests, thirteen on sports, thirteen on renowned intellectuals or scientists, sixteen on history, and nineteen on scientific topics. In fact, the published literary and art content was far more extensive, comprising fifteen articles on artists, eighteen translated stories, twenty-five short stories, thirty-five literary and social themes, and sixty poems. The oil-related content included five articles focused on IPC departments, training, and archaeological works, as well as fifteen articles that covered the increase in oil production, oil field fires, development in oil tanker design (including Japan's outstanding oil tanker market), reports on oil reserves worldwide, news from laboratory research on oil products, oil streams in Europe, and proceedings from the sixth annual conference of Arab oil.

In that same issue, the editors announced the titles of three accepted entries but noted that they had rejected twenty-six. To soothe the anxieties of writers anticipating publication, in the final issues of the magazine the editors began including lists of accepted and rejected submissions, disclosing only the titles of the submitted works. This opacity was respectful and resourceful, as it protected the authors' reputations and allowed them space for the potential reworking of their texts if they wanted to submit to other publishers under new titles.

The editors also featured snippets from readers' letters that contained a question about a submission or a line or two from a poem. The editors were competent to fall these too on the pages of *Al Amiloon Fil Naft*, as in these lines that appeared in a reader's letter:

All what I own, my love, is a hut
Yes, a very humble hut
I cover its floor with a straw mat,
not a carpet made in Shiraz or Tabriz
You yearn for things sold on River Street,
I can't afford them with a thousand loans
drawn from the bank of mortgages or from my wedding loan that would never be enough
I, my precious one, do not possess anything but my offered love and loyalty[2]

This poem is notable for the stark contrast it poses to the prosperous conditions illustrated by the promises of the oil company that published the magazine. Coupled with the desperate desire to be published, the letters at times also communicated a general feeling of powerlessness. While the enthusiasm for literary texts and works of art featured in the magazine were related to creative practice and personal ambition, it also reflects how publication provided a footing for rising literary figures who pursued literature as a career that would provide them a living.

The magazine circulated approximately eight thousand copies per issue, either distributed to IPC staff along with their salaries or sold to the public for 25 Iraqi fils per issue, or 250 fils for an annual subscription, paid in cash or stamps.[3] *Al Amiloon Fil Naft* had a print run significantly smaller than IPC's earlier magazine, *Ahl al-Naft* (People of Oil), which published forty thousand copies in the 1950s.

After Abd al-Karim Qasim (1914–1963) overthrew the monarchy and established the Republic of Iraq in July 1958, nationalizing IPC became his goal. However, his plan did not materialize due to a shortage of local expertise capable of running the company and its operations. Iraq first needed to cultivate a generation of knowledgeable citizens who could assume control over the company upon its nationalization in 1972 by Saddam Hussein, who was then the deputy of President Ahmed Hassan al-Bakr (1914–1982). In the 1970s, the oil company's magazine played a role in this cultivation, perhaps literally. It served as a literary and editorial space where words and images reflected or aggregated local sentiments, sometimes even expressing hostility toward entities similar to IPC's foreign administration or its legacy as a remnant of colonial exploitation and the displacement of national assets.

Given the tense publishing environment in Baghdad during that period, characterized by male dominance, class divisions, and political conflicts, writers eagerly awaited the lists of articles to be published, wrote further letters to the editors upon rejection, and explored other possibilities for publication. The magazine's pages devoted to IPC were, in general, politically neutral— except when a general sentiment prevailed in Iraqi society. For instance, issues published in the aftermath of the 1967 War voiced feelings of loss, anger, and lamentation through both imagery and commentary in *Al Amiloon Fil Naft*. As a displaced Palestinian, Jabra regularly injected the magazine with materials on the Palestinian cause and the conditions of its refugees. It also published celebratory content every July, to mark the anniversary of the 1958 revolution; highlighted socialist ideas when members of a community paved a street in their neighborhood; mourned the passing of soldiers; and, as in later issues, openly voiced support for the Ba'ath ruling party. Publishing in the magazine was a safety measure, an indication of political correctness, for individuals who were aware of the scrutinizing eyes of the regime's informants.

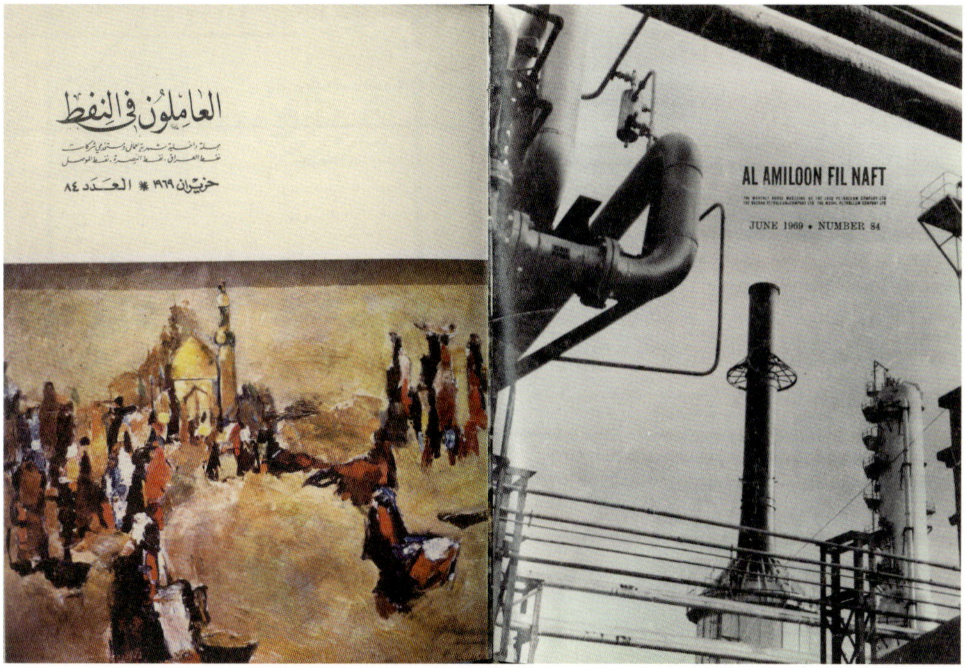

FIG. 5-3. (Left) Ismail al-Cheikhli's *Mazar* (Shrine). (Right) Photographer unknown. *Al Amiloon Fil Naft*, no. 84, June 1969.

—

The curation of the magazine's art content must have been subject to a different logic. Art that was featured on the cover was likely taken from photographic slides of the works. Due to the technologies of the time, which required a camera device and a film strip of twenty-four or thirty-six pictures before the film negatives or slides could be processed or printed, it might be safe to assume that not all artists could present photographic imagery of their latest work. To a great extent, the magazine's editors had to work from what was available, but also from their knowledge of contemporary art and the need to diversify the names of artists that were featured on the covers. Extensive effort was put into interviewing, writing, reporting, and sampling the IPC content, whereas literary works were relatively easy to publish. The selection of art could not have undergone the same attention as the IPC text, nor could the choices have been made as easily as decisions on literary works. The reproduction of artworks also required color printing and precision in production, all of which was dependent on printing facilities available in Baghdad and knowledge about how any concerns would affect the time required for production.

The Arabic cover of *Al Amiloon Fil Naft's* eighty-fourth issue, published in June 1969, features a reproduction of a painting by Ismail al-Cheikhli (1924–2002) titled *Mazar* (Shrine). The image takes up the lower half of the page, while the top is a beige strip with the magazine's name and issue number (**FIG. 5-3**). The painting's center is a golden-domed shrine with a large door and a high minaret. The shrine sits in the background, and human figures with flowing traditional dresses cluster on the sides of an empty unpaved road. No other architecture or nature is present; the scene is bare but focused. An air of pilgrimage fills the emptiness that surrounds the holy shrine. Al-Cheikhli painted multiple works on the religious shrines that dot Iraq's southern and eastern towns. A similar work, dated 1971 and featured on a religious website that analyzes the population of women in al-Cheikhli's shrine scenes, notes that during certain political eras men were not allowed to visit shrines, so most of the people appearing in any of these landscapes would be women.[4] Inspecting the cover further allows us to see details in the human figures, perhaps of women carrying offerings on their heads as they march toward the shrine.

An empty sky engulfs the minaret and the domed shrine, allowing the structure to stand out. The shrine's minaret relates visually to a cylinder in a photo used on the English cover of the same issue. Shot in one of the oil fields in Kirkuk, the image features long, thin, cylindrical structures that resemble the minaret but are assumed to be elements of the oil refinery. As the structures are unspecified in the image's caption, I inspected online diagrams of oil refineries to understand the function of these two cylinders: one is a fired heater; the other is a distillation tower.

Distillation towers are pressure vessels that heat crude oil in a pressurized environment to separate it into different components, each vaporizing at another boiling point.[5] The separate petroleum components are called fractions; the lightest, such as gasoline and liquefied refinery gases, evaporate and rise to the top of the distillation tower, a process that condenses them back into liquids. Medium-weight liquids, such as kerosene and distillates, stay in the tower's middle, while the heavy gas oils remain below. The heaviest fractions with the highest boiling points settle at the bottom of the tower before they transform into lighter liquids, such as gasoline.[6] These heavy liquids are sent to the fired heater so that their vapor and liquid mixtures return to the distillation tower. That is why we see both cylindrical towers close to each other in the picture.

As in the painting, an empty sky surrounds the towers in the photo. Both images allude to the monumentality of their featured structures and the distillation and purification operations inside. People visit the shrine to deposit prayers, shed tears, and make offerings before they leave lighter and purified. The offerings, and perhaps the prayers, circulate in subsequent cycles, transforming (invisibly) into other energies. Upon leaving the shrine depicted in the painting, which itself is devoid of the appearance of any technology, people will travel back home in vehicles running on extracted fuels like those produced in the towers.

To my knowledge, there is no documentation that the editors consciously linked the two covers. But the magazine created a space for interpretation that allowed for meaningful links between starkly different depictions of Iraq on the pages of the same magazine and as a creative product of the engaged art scene.

The two covers of issue 110, from August 1971, depict two different logics yet have inspiring similarities (**FIG. 5-4**). The Arabic cover reproduces an abstract painting by Qutaiba al-Sheikh Nouri (1922–1979), who was a trained Kurdish physician from Baghdad but also a self-taught artist who participated in a large number of foundational art shows in Baghdad from the 1950s until 1979, when he passed away at age fifty-seven. The cover artwork is unnamed but features a constellation of circles and semicircles that intersect each other in spiral forms. The artist painted circles in shades of blue overlaid on a beige background. Neat and geometric, the rings can also be seen as top or side views of the oil structures featured on the back cover, where two large cylindrical tanks stand with pipes and valves entering and exiting the structures. They appear too small to be storage silos, but the image caption tells us that they are part of the oil company's fire-extinguishing foam-generating machines. That means the structures also have level monitors,

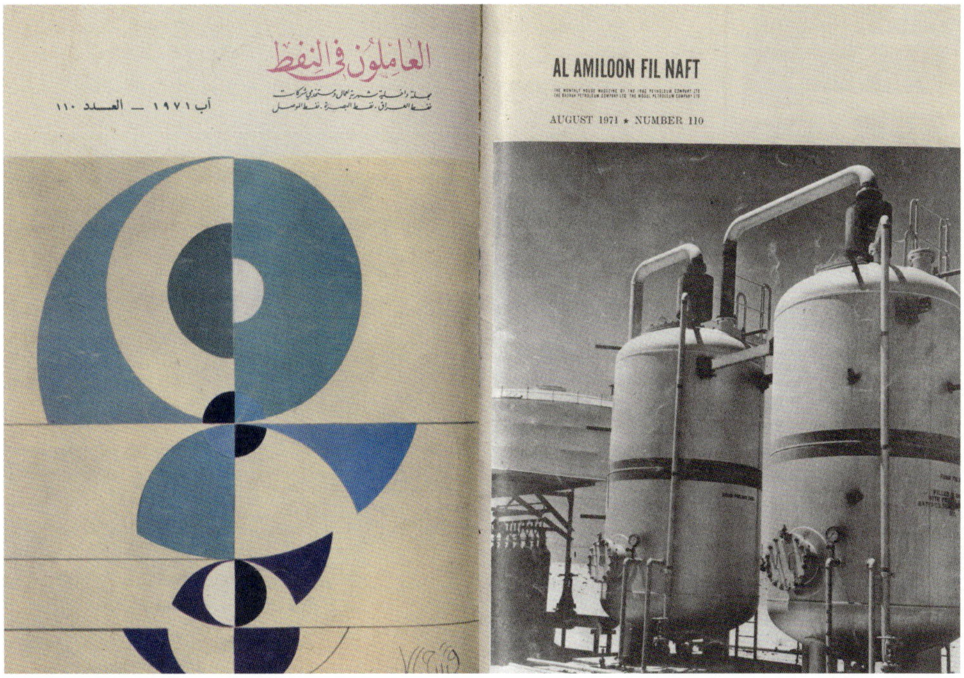

FIG. 5-4. (Left) Qutaiba al-Sheikh Nouri. Title unknown. (Right) Photographer unknown. *Al Amiloon Fil Naft*, no. 110, August 1971.

nozzles for water, foam, electricity, and more, valves and connectors, couplings, diaphragms, pressure regulators, hydrants, barrels, chambers, generators, alarm valve systems, spray heads, chemical systems, gaseous extinguishing systems, and other special equipment—all invisible in the picture.[7]

Here, I am as fascinated by the resemblances between the cylinders and Nouri's circles and the spirals of ejected foam imagined from the substance inside these structures, as by the unnamed/invisible systems that make the oil industry function. These latent meanings and elements of invisibility resemble the conscious relations between the knowledge that must have been (at least partly) present in the oil industry and the art paired with it in the magazine's pages. In this case, the art and literary content must be considered as indistinguishable from the oil realms that the magazine promoted and about which it hoped to cultivate knowledge. We can further understand this from an art statement by Nouri:

> I am a man of science and have developed an artistic sensitivity over the past five years toward the circle. It has provoked in me an interest in form and philosophy. I see it is always present in all visuals, in lines and surfaces, in the subliminal meanings of life, and I found in the Arabic letters so much of circular visions, arc flow, and musical rhythm. There is a deep connection between life and heritage when I bring letters into my art.[8]

It is fascinating to observe the connection between paintings and photographs, where they occasionally echo each other or show visual correspondences. For instance, abstract or geometric paintings containing circles may contrast with photographs featuring cylindrical tanks. Nouri connects "visuals," including his circles, to the use of language. In his view, Arabic letters have circular visions and

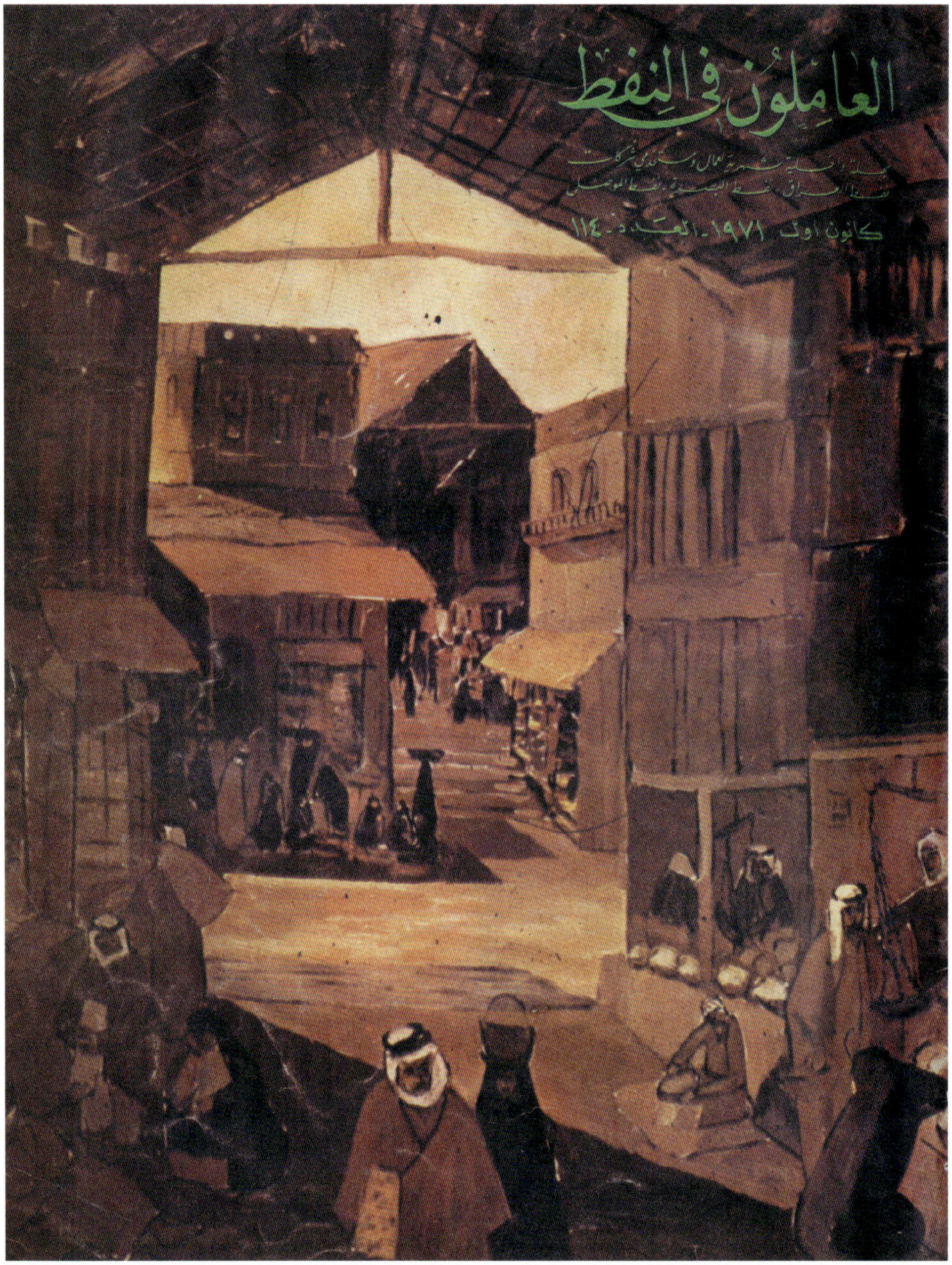

FIG. 5-5. Artist and title unknown. *Al Amiloon Fil Naft*, no. 114, December 1971.

rhythms, and one way to understand life is to break the letters down into forms that relate to each other. He does not limit this to the interpretation of everyday aspects but also to how to connect that to heritage, a dominant theme on the covers and in the pages of *Al Amiloon Fil Naft*. The circles that exist in these two cover images from the same issue are diagrams of or guides to interpreting, to assisting recognition of—or perhaps insisting on—a link between the two worlds, painting and photography, art and oil, workers and the oil company, language and technology, and art and technology. While the distance between the two realms might seem vast on the magazine's pages, they are brought closer by these active efforts to find meaning. The concerted engagement with images is part of what the magazine could offer its readers without a limitation on time.

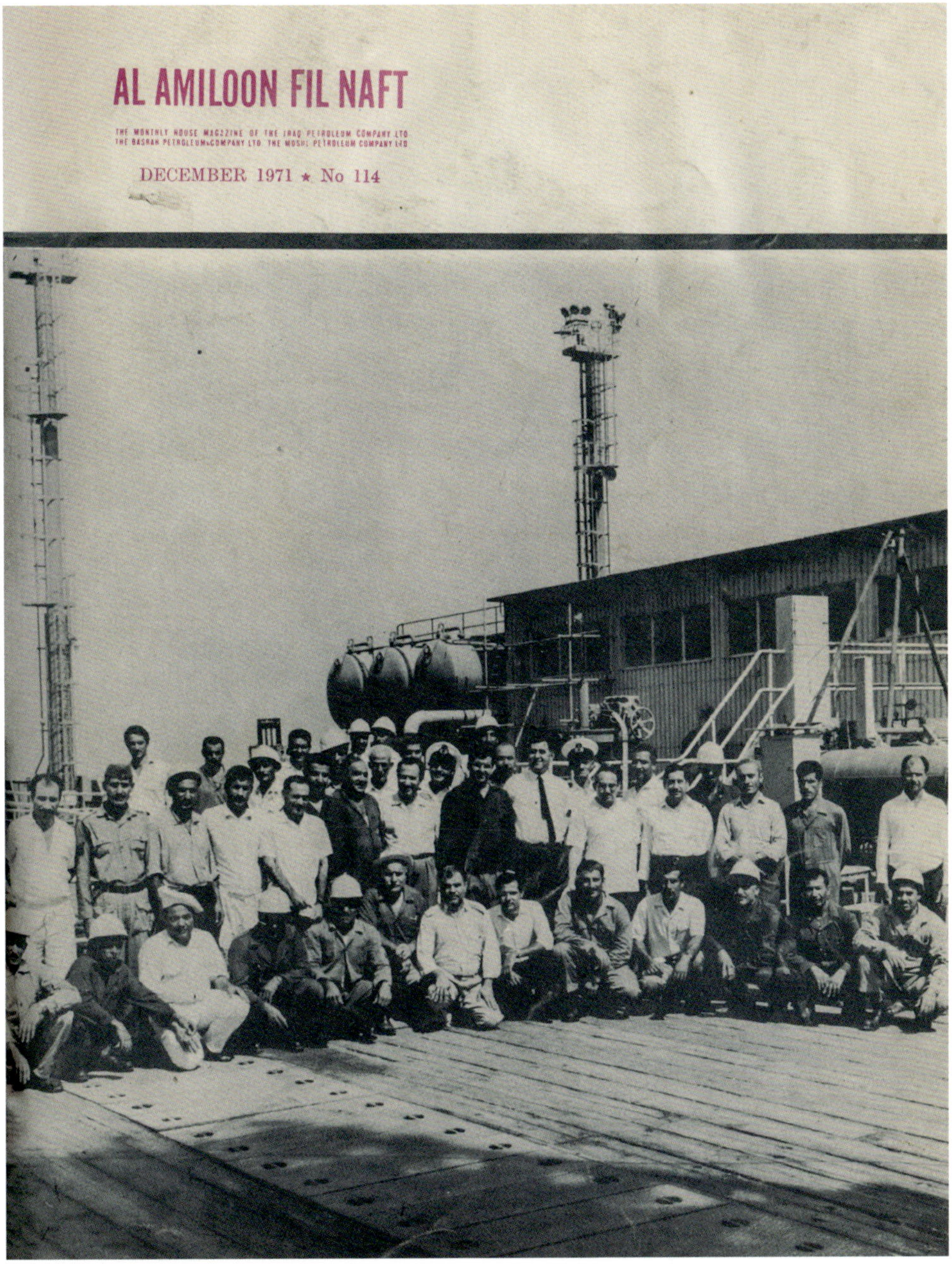

FIG. 5-6. Photographer unknown. *Al Amiloon Fil Naft*, no. 114, December 1971.

—

On the cover of issue 114, from December 1971, is a painting of a souk in the sacred city of Karbala, tinting the magazine cover with hues of red and orange (**FIG. 5-5**). The painter is unnamed, and the artwork is undated. Under the shade of a high triangular ceiling, merchants sit on the two sides of a pathway that leads to other parts of the souk. Buildings are from medieval times and built in three stories.[9] A man and a woman are in the foreground; he wears a travel pocket on top of his traditional garments, while the woman is covered in black except for her face and has set a basket on her head. Other men and women sit or stand on the souk grounds engaging in commerce while perspective deepens our understanding of the market size, architecture, and hustle.

The same structures are seen from a similar perspective in an old photograph posted on Facebook. The post claims that the market is the old gold souk that led to the merchants' souk, dismantled in the late 1970s to expand the area for the religious mosques on both sides of the holy city of Karbala. A comment was posted that one of the goldsmiths made gold crowns for teeth, while another added that the goldsmith wore the traditional headdress and his lawyer son helped him in the shop. A third person recalled frequenting a clinic run by a female doctor with his mother. As a teenager, he used to look through the clinic's window onto the souk, but only with care as the zinc roofs extending out of the windows were too fragile to withstand pressure. This description matches the zinc roofs that appear in the drawings, and thus suggests the painter's vantage point in the nearby textile market, which in the 1970s was one of the Karbala's public transport stops that brought pilgrims onboard buses.[10]

Issue 114 included forty-eight pages featuring various content, including nineteen different texts: short stories, poems, documentary reports, scientific articles, pieces on traditional practices, and sports-related coverage. The back cover showed a group photo of forty-four oil workers posing together on the Khor Al Amaya Oil Terminal docks, thirty-five kilometers southeast of Iraq's waterway in the Arabian Gulf. The image showcases the workers' diverse attire: some wear overalls, others don white shirts, one sports a tie, another is dressed in a guard's uniform, and one wears a captain's cap (**FIG. 5-6**). The background reveals two tall poles with stairs, rails, and telecommunication reception plates. Adjacent to these are three interconnected fuel tanks, pathways, valves, and an office station constructed from zinc sheets.

A quick online search provides further insights into the construction of this oil terminal, revealing that it consists of multiple docks interconnected by narrow pathways. A 42-inch sea export line supplies the terminal from the pump station on the Al Faw peninsula southeast of Iraq.[11] The terminal comprises two rectangular main platforms, with berths on the west platform's north and south ends. These platforms are steel-piled structures featuring steel decks, and walkways connect them. Each berth on the west platform has four loading arms used to transfer oil to tankers. Additionally, a larger platform for utilities and living accommodations is between the two loading platforms.[12]

The oil terminals are storage depots for oil, other fuels, and petrochemical products. This type of structure is most commonly found at ports and other harbor facilities to handle the transfer of oil products from inland oil sources that transport fuels via pipelines or from ships and oil tankers that berth at the port. For the former, these pipelines present a cheap method of importing oil to the ports, from where they are consolidated and regularly used to replenish outbound tankers. They also supply the fuel used to run these ships. Constructed in 1961 and operated by IPC's southern division, this terminal provided platforms from which Basra exported its crude oil.

Water is calm near the Khor terminal, making it easier for tankers to load[13] oil in the Arabian Gulf's turquoise waters. However, the photo published on the back cover of this issue is black and white. In contrast, on the English cover of issue 62, from May 1967, a color photograph shows three oil workers handling the valves of the oil-stained pipe as it is lifted by a crane to be fixed on a tanker. In dark-blue stained overalls, the workers' bodies animate the gestures of the operation, surrounded by the white-painted metal structures of the terminal. The image allows

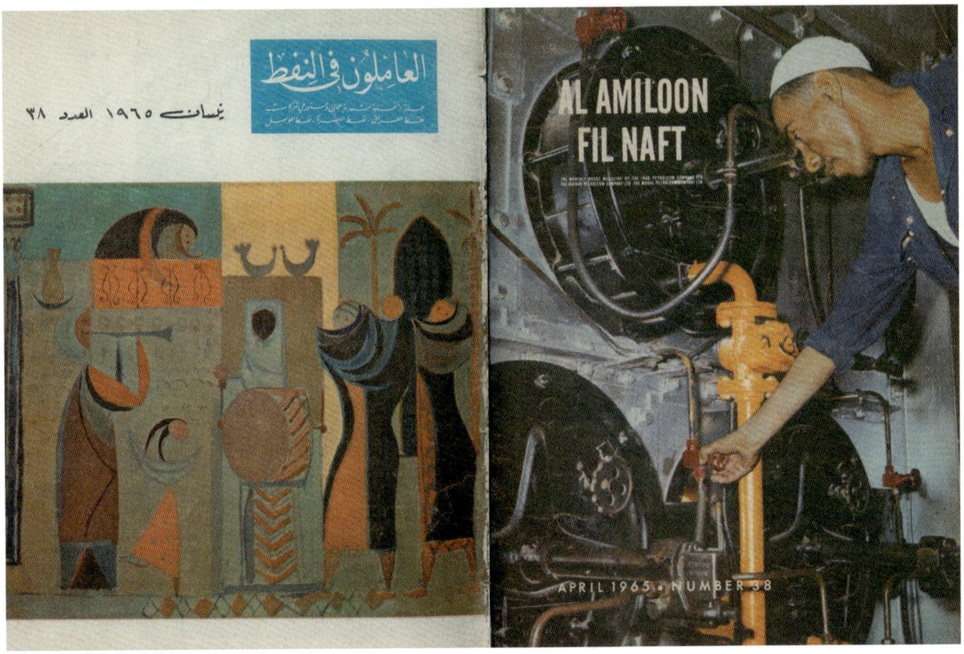

FIG. 5-7. Jewad Selim's *Street Musicians* (at left), reproduced in *Al Amiloon Fil Naft*, no. 38, April 1965.

us to imagine how complex, dangerous, heavy, hot, smelly, and noisy the life of oil workers must have been.

One can discern a link between these photographs of the Khor and the painting of the souk in Karbala, possibly created by the magazine's editors. Both are sites for loading and unloading, selling and trading, exchanging and passing through. Throughout the 1970s and early 1980s, the province of Karbala witnessed a flourishing gold trade. The Central Bank of Iraq supplied goldsmiths with monthly allowances of 3 to 5 kilograms of gold pieces in varying quantities, based on the capacity and importance of each goldsmith's workshop. This economic upturn and the thriving gold trade in Karbala made the city famous as an Islamic tourist destination. Consequently, several specialized artistic workshops for goldsmithing and wholesale trading emerged.[14] Similarly, Khor was a strategic port for half of Iraq's exports of oil, but both locations, through their own logic, faced a drastic decline in income when wars erupted in Iraq from 1980, and they became subject to assaults or redistribution of assets.

—

Returning to the aspect of language that Qutaiba al-Sheikh Nouri referred to when he articulated ways to simplify the forms in the structures that surround us so that we detect the links to our meanings and heritage, I would like to conclude with a discussion of the covers of *Al Amiloon Fil Naft*'s issue 38, published in April 1965. The Arabic cover bore a reproduction of a painting by Jewad Selim (1921–1961) titled *Street Musicians*, which dates to the 1950s (**FIG. 5-7**). Selim was a close friend of Jabra, who published the artist's works in a separate volume[15] following his sudden passing in 1961. The painting features two standing musicians playing on a drum and flute, respectively. A girl dances between the two men, while women in their traditional black garments, with colorful dresses spilling out from below, watch the performers. One woman watches from the roof of her house. Almost all of the elements in this work are geometrical shapes of circles, crescents, and rectangles, but they also flow in dynamic yet rhythmic constellations, interwoven with the architecture of the city to which they belong. They are painted in muted (possibly due to printing) shades of primary colors—blue, green, yellow, and red.

On the English cover is a color photograph of a worker from the Basra Oil Company, adjusting the burner in the boiler house at the Zubair Power Station. He wears blue overalls and a white traditional cap, whose form resembles the crescents in Selim's painting. The worker turns a red valve in the burner, and through the tanned skin of his arm we almost feel the temperature of the yellow pipe centimeters away. All of the pipes and valves connect to the burner, with its circular front and numerous small parts, in colors but also functions that connect and fade within each other. The vibrant colors of this photograph are fresh and alluring; here is a local man—whose community members enjoy the music performed spontaneously on their streets—diligently fulfilling his key role within the complex operations of the oil industry. He is demonstrating to the viewers his oil education and professional knowledge, while members of his community enjoy their heritage in an environment of art mixed with life. Knowledge and art are nonphysical, but they become visible in the oil field and in the city, and accessible on the pages of *Al Amiloon Fil Naft*.

Al Amiloon Fil Naft primarily published artworks on the Arabic covers, which open from right to left. The majority of the magazine content was also in Arabic, but when the publication was read from left to right, readers found a few English articles focused on oil. The English cover usually had a photograph from the sites of IPC and its companies in Mosul and Basra. While the oil content in *Al Amiloon Fil Naft* therefore provided a framework for reflections on the political context, the publication had the capacity to neighbor this content with contemporary literature and art focused on heritage that might seem neither political nor technological. The escape to, or grounding in, heritage-based art nevertheless stirred active reading of the technical content. I have demonstrated only a few avenues for such active reading. Revisiting the potential of invisible yet existing content, I would propose a rethinking of invisibility, imagination of intentions hidden within or behind language, linking structures by breaking their appearance into basic forms, and self-informing about technology to assume the depth of knowledge the editors partially masked. These approaches can serve as tools to read some of *Al Amiloon Fil Naft*'s editorial strategies with regard to the literary, art, and oil content in the magazine's attractive space of resourcefulness.

1 *Al Amiloon Fil Naft* November, 1969, 1. Translated by the author.

2 Translated from Arabic by the author.

3 One Iraqi dinar is equal to 1,000 fils, and its value was pegged at USD 2.80 until 1971, when the conversion rate rose to USD 3.3778. Therefore, the price of any issue would have been around USD 0.07.

4 Imam Hussein Holy Shrine website, https://imamhussain.org/arabic/7568.

5 Forged Components Inc. 2023.

6 U.S. Energy Information Administration, 2023.

7 Shilla Fire Co., 2019.

8 Ibrahimi Collection, n.d.

9 "Heritage Markets in Karbala," *Markaz Turath Karbala* (Karbala Heritage Center), April 22, 2018. https://www.mk.iq/view.php?id=2796.

10 "Karbala Old Days" page, Facebook, posted April 25, 2019, https://m.facebook.com/owl990shoat/posts/2186792581416329.

11 Al Faw is a town on the right bank of the Shatt al-Arab, Iraq's gateway to the Arabian Gulf. Al Faw was one of the primary battle sites during the Iran-Iraq war (1980–88).

12 Office of the Special Inspector General for Iraq Reconstruction 2007.

13 Stanley 2003.

14 Al-Saadi, n.d. The article concerns jewelry making, including goldsmithing, for beautification and ornamentation.

15 Jabra Ibrahim Jabra, Jewad Selim *wa Nasb al-Hurriya (Liberty Monument or Freedom Monument*), Baghdad: Ministry of Information, 1974.

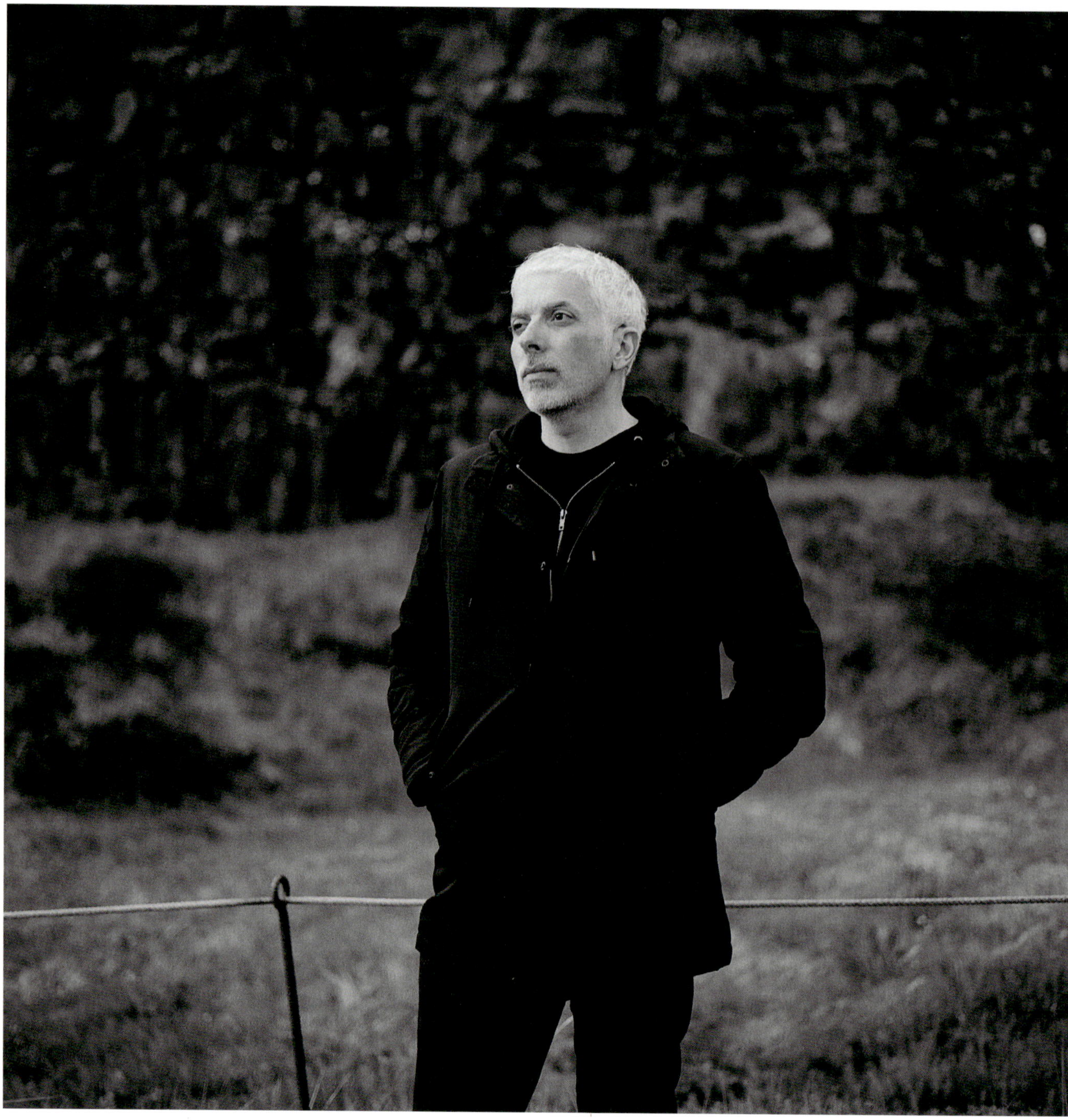

CHAPTER 6

DEBRIS: THE VISUAL TAPESTRY OF SHI'ITE IRAQ

Adel Abidin

Through years of closely observing the tumultuous state of my country, Iraq, I have witnessed the harrowing descent into an unending sectarian war that has resulted in targeted killings based solely on one's identity. As the conflict escalated, it became increasingly evident that checkpoints scattered across the nation had transformed into haunting institutions, issuing death sentences based on the mere mention of a person's name. This blatant disregard for human life and the blind adherence to inherited beliefs have made individuals alarmingly susceptible to manipulation and exploitation.

As an artist, it is not my intention to align myself with any particular side in this complex and deeply rooted conflict. Instead, I recognize my responsibility to conduct an insightful analysis that delves deeper into the intricacies of the situation, utilizing the powerful language of visual expression. In undertaking this research, I have made a deliberate choice to focus on exploring the Shi'ite perspective rather than the Sunni viewpoint, not because I consider the Sunni perspective to be conservative or uninteresting, but because I have found the Shi'ite aspect to be particularly vibrant, captivating, and worthy of examination. This choice is rooted in my personal investigation and artistic inspiration, and it in no way seeks to undermine or diminish the significance of the Sunni narrative.

The core of my research centers around visual aspects and their profound impact on daily life. I find it fascinating to explore how visual representations can shape and influence social perceptions and behaviors. It is within this context that I have embarked on an exploration of the historical and contemporary significance of iconic paintings and their lasting effects on our collective consciousness (**FIG. 6-2**).

FIG. 6-1. Thana Faroq. Adel Abidin, portrait, 2023.

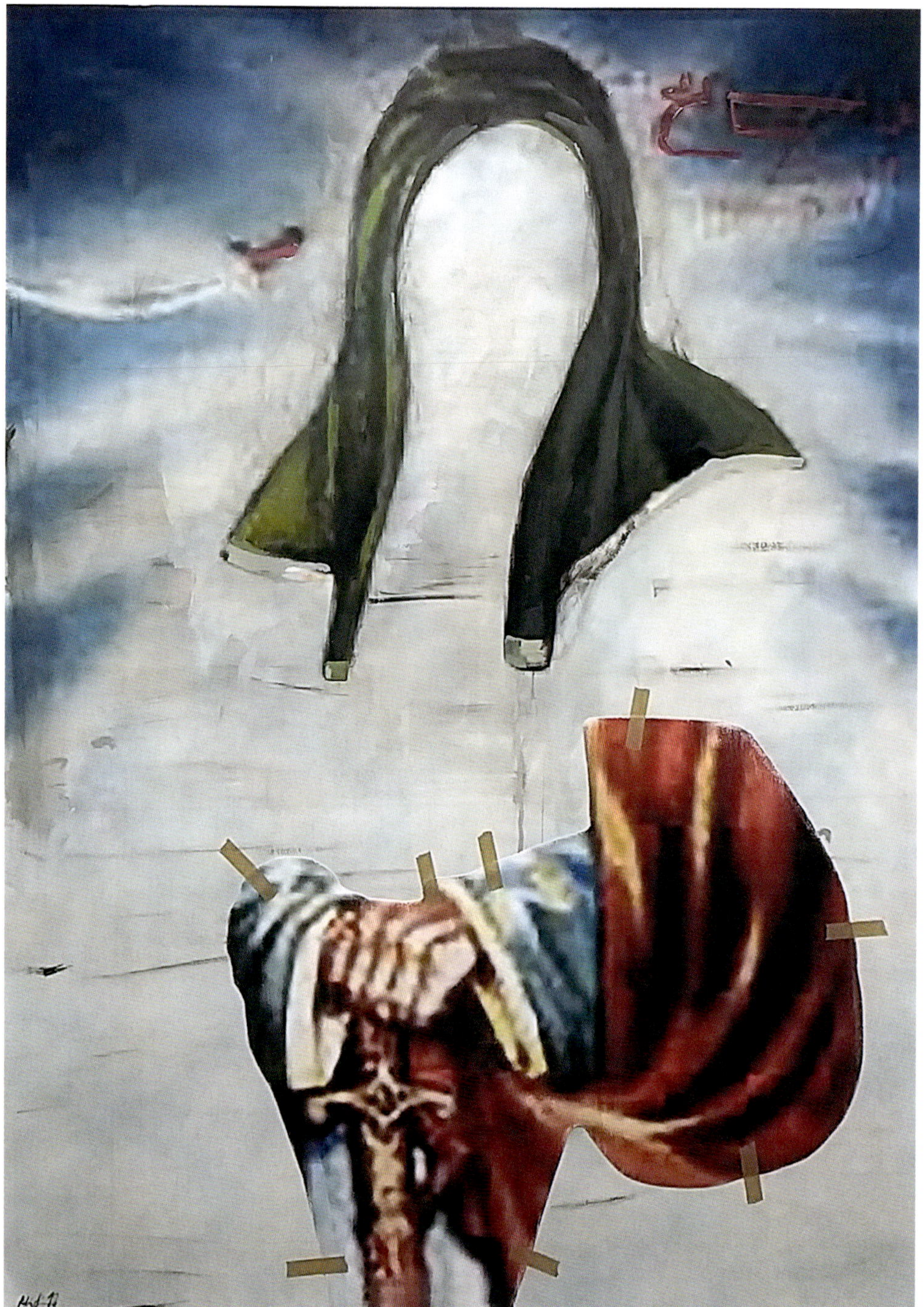

FIG. 6-2. Adel Abidin. "Ghostly Icon" from *CUT OUTS*. Mixed media and print on paper. H. 150 cm; W. 110 cm. 2019.

Christian missionaries, in their fervent travels around the world, have long sought to spread their beliefs and teachings. They have utilized a variety of means to convey the profound suffering of Christ, employing not only words but also powerful visual tools—iconic paintings that capture the true essence of his pain. These depictions, portraying a fellow human being subjected to torment, unimaginable torture, and crucifixion, have struck a deep chord within the hearts of many, including myself. The resonance these images have found among diverse audiences is a testament to their ability to visually communicate the shared experience of human suffering, transcending cultural, linguistic, and religious boundaries.

When Christian missionaries arrived in Persia (Iran), they brought with them their visual depictions of Jesus's torment, propagated through iconic images. It is here that the Shi'ites in Iran found a profound resonance between the agonizing suffering of Jesus and the plight of Imam Al-Hussain, the revered grandson of the Prophet Muhammad. The betrayal, torture, and ultimate martyrdom of Imam Al-Hussain in 680 CE, which occurred during one of the most ignominious battles in Islamic history, serves as a poignant parallel to the sufferings of Jesus. The Shi'ites, moved by this powerful connection, embraced the visual language of pain and torment as a means to express their own anguish. They began creating their own visual depictions, akin to advertisements of pain, in order to evoke empathy and engage the masses in a manner similar to the strategies of Christian proselytizers. These visual representations played a pivotal role in cementing the collective memory of the Shi'ite community, serving as a reminder of the immense sacrifices made by their beloved imam and his followers.

It is important to note that the depiction of Imam Al-Hussain was not initially uniform or standardized. As Persia, open to influences from East Asia, absorbed various artistic traditions, early representations of the imam exhibited striking features (**FIG. 6-3**). However, over time a consensus was reached within the Shi'ite community regarding his most appropriate visual representation. Drawing from rich oral traditions and historical accounts passed down through generations, artists converged on a specific depiction that best embodied the characteristics and aura associated with the revered imam. While variations still exist, a general agreement has been established, enabling individuals to readily identify Al-Hussain through visual cues and accompanying written identifiers.

Ironically, the historical narrative of Shi'ism revolves around a series of imams who met tragic fates, falling victim to swords, poison, betrayal, and disappearance. The model initially chosen to represent Imam Al-Hussain inadvertently became the template for subsequent depictions of the Twelve Imams (the divinely inspired descendants of Muhammad), with minor modifications to their accessories and

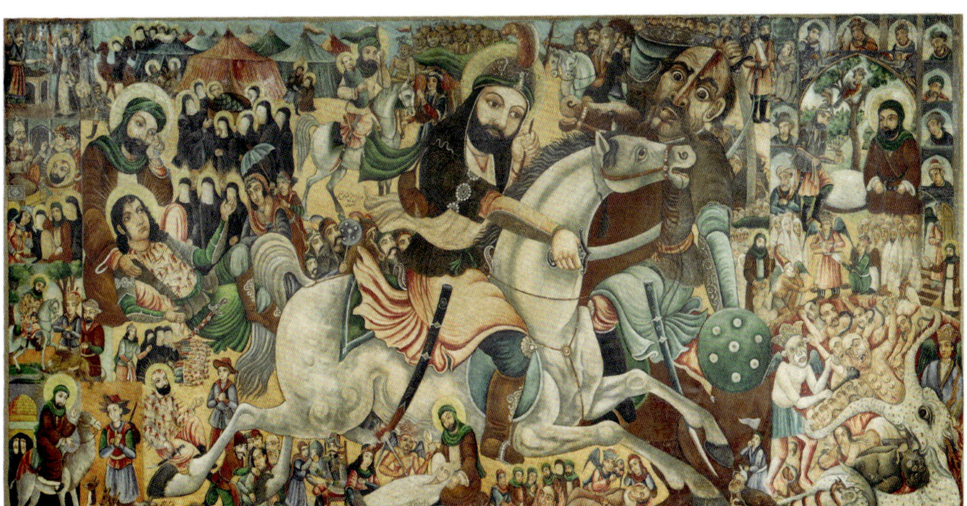

FIG. 6-3. Abbas Al-Musavi. *Battle of Karbala*. Oil on canvas. H. 175.4 cm; W. 341.6 cm; D. 5.7 cm. Late 19th–early 20th century. Brooklyn Museum, Gift of K. Thomas Elghanayan in honor of Nourollah Elghanayan, 2002.6.

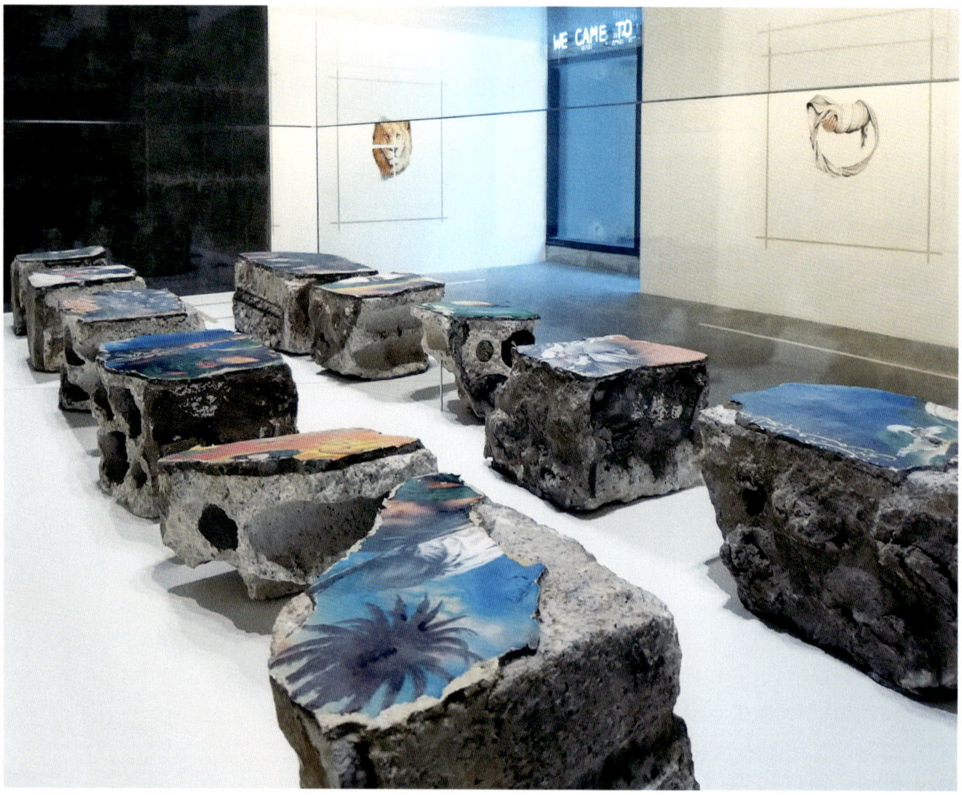

FIG. 6-4. Installation view of Adel Abidin's *Debris* at Galerie Tanit, Beirut. Digital image. 2019. Checklist no. 8.

attire serving as the primary means of differentiation. This necessitated the inclusion of labels on each image, underscoring the potential confusion arising from their striking visual similarities.

In recent years, visual representations of the imams have taken the form of colorful printed posters that have found their way into the urban fabric of Iraqi cities (see **FIG. 6-12**). These posters, emerging predominantly during the anniversary commemorations of Imam Al-Hussain's death, adorn fences, towering walls, billboards, and other public spaces. They share two common features: the model representing all the imams and the ubiquitous word *Ya* (يا), meaning an appeal to a person or even a divine figure. As a result, they can differentiate between the same model and identify him with the specific imam in each poster. The widespread presence aims to raise awareness and reshape the perception of these cities. Yet, beneath the surface, a complex interplay of historical wounds, guilt, and political agendas unfolds, impacting individual and collective experiences.

Within the broader context of my artistic exploration, I have long been fascinated by humanity's innate desire to seek idols and symbols of inspiration. This search often extends to religious figures or prominent personalities that embody qualities worthy of admiration, dependence, and support. In creating my work titled *Debris* (**FIG. 6-4**), I sought to shed light on the glorification of historical wounds and the utilization of these wounds to manipulate emotions and shape the political agendas that permeate our daily lives.

One element of my installation titled *Ya!*—a large, suspended roll of glossy paper and a pile of posters—aligns with the global devaluation of humans, ideals, and religion (**FIGS. 6-5** and **6-6**). By unraveling a large roll of white posters from the

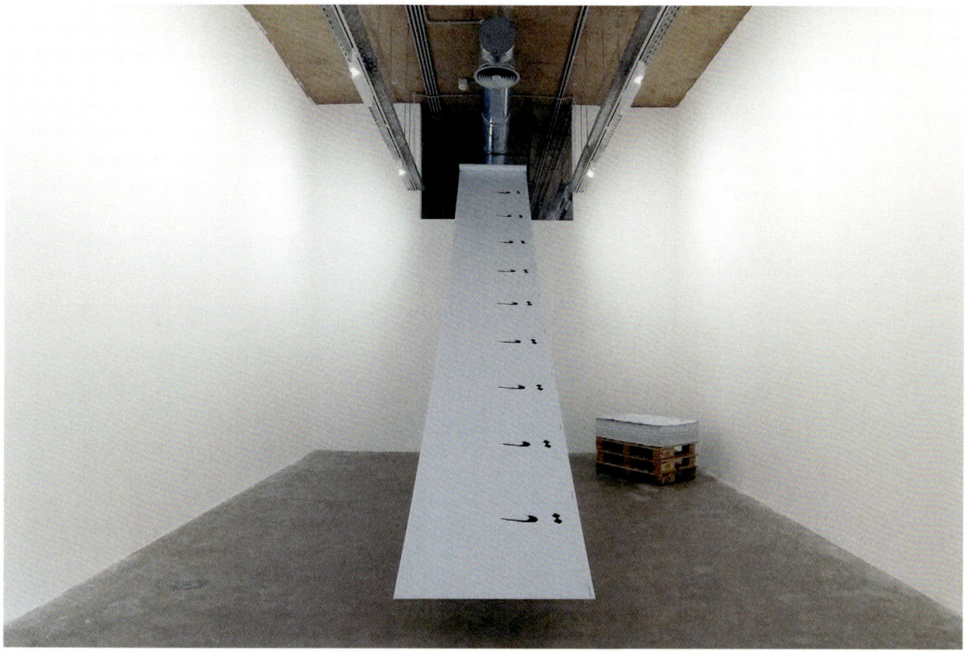

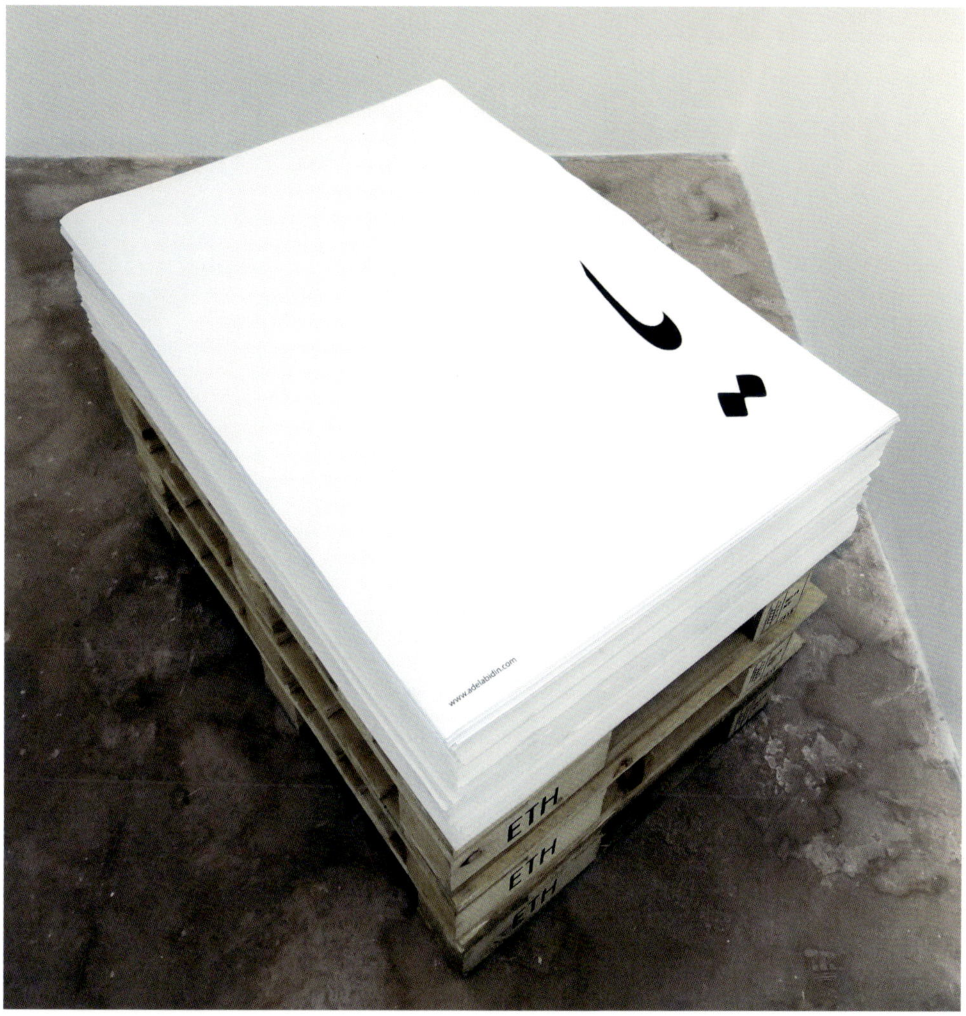

FIGS. 6-5 AND 6-6. Adel Abidin. *Ya!* Metal structure and paper roll. Installation view at Galerie Tanit, Beirut. Digital image. 2019.

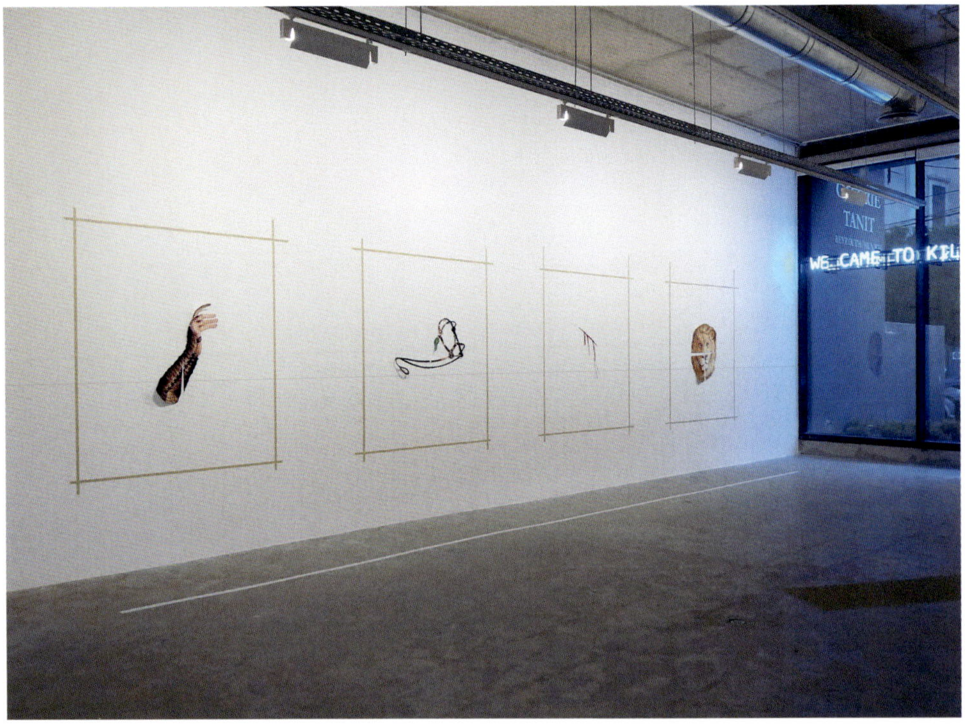

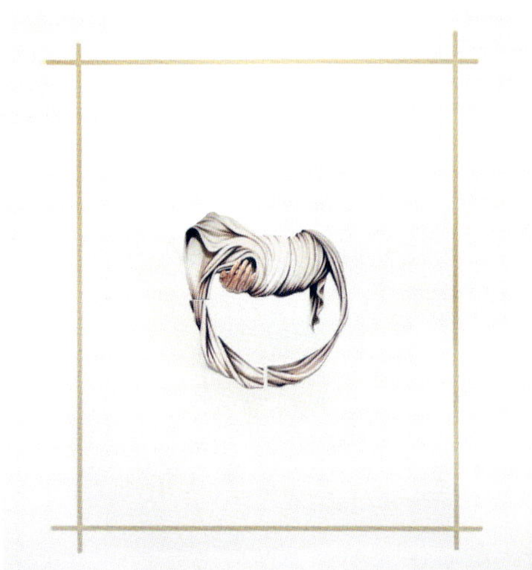

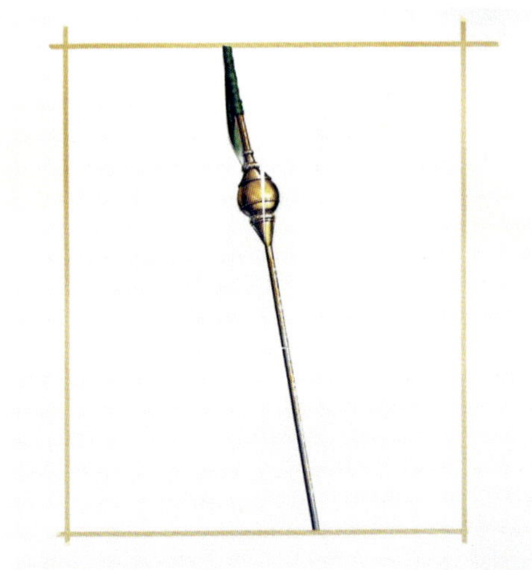

TOP: FIG. 6-7. Adel Abidin. *CUT OUTS*. Installation view at Galerie Tanit, Beirut. Digital image. 2019. **LEFT BOTTOM: FIG. 6-8.** Adel Abidin. "Baby" from *CUT OUTS*. Inkjet print on stainless steel metal cut-outs and masking tape. H. 170 cm; W. 142 cm. 2019. **RIGHT BOTTOM: FIG. 6-9**. Adel Abidin. "Pole" from *CUT OUTS*. Inkjet print on stainless steel metal cut-outs and masking tape. H. 170 cm; W. 142 cm. 2019.

ceiling, I sought to create an immersive experience whereby viewers find themselves suspended between the "sky" and the ground, caught between ethereal realms. The roll, filled with blank posters, serves as a metaphorical representation of the production of meaninglessness, where the only printed word is a resounding call: *Ya!* This evocative Arabic term leaves viewers pondering its significance and contemplating the state of our sacred idols and the erosion of their once unquestionable values.

The second part of my work, titled *CUT OUTS*, draws inspiration from a study of Iranian sectarian paintings that have been adapted by Iraqi artists (**FIG. 6-7**). These paintings depict the Shi'ite imams and have gradually evolved into outdoor billboards and advertisements scattered throughout the city of Baghdad, assuming characteristics reminiscent of pop culture representations. What struck me during my study was the consistent use of a single model to represent the Twelve Imams across different paintings, with only minor adjustments made to differentiate each figure. This realization prompted me to explore the significance of the surrounding elements and accessories within these compositions.

In my endeavor to isolate and examine the essential elements, I began meticulously cutting out these objects from reproductions of the Iranian paintings, recognizing their profound significance within the overall context. By printing these cut-outs directly onto 1-millimeter stainless steel, I transformed them into independent visual components that can now function autonomously. Some of the cut-outs, when separated from their original environments, took on a ghostly appearance (**FIG. 6-8**), while others became alluring or seemingly insignificant objects (**FIG. 6-9**). Through this process, I sought to highlight the inherent value and meaning present within these isolated elements, independent of their original context.

As I conducted my research, the Web became my primary source of visual material, and I chose to preserve the cut-outs in their original forms, maintaining their resolution quality and visual aesthetics. This decision adds a layer of authenticity to my exploration, capturing the nuances and imperfections of the digital realm that has become integral to our contemporary visual landscape.

In conclusion, my artistic research delves into the rich tapestry of sectarian conflicts in Iraq, specifically examining the Shi'ite perspective and the visual language employed to convey pain, memory, and collective identity. Through an analysis of historical influences, the ubiquity of visual representations, and the deconstruction of iconic imagery, I seek to inspire contemplation and spark dialogue regarding the role of art in shaping perceptions, memory, and the intricate dynamics of society. By intertwining historical narratives with contemporary artistic expressions, my aim is to contribute to a deeper understanding of the complexities that define us as individuals and communities.

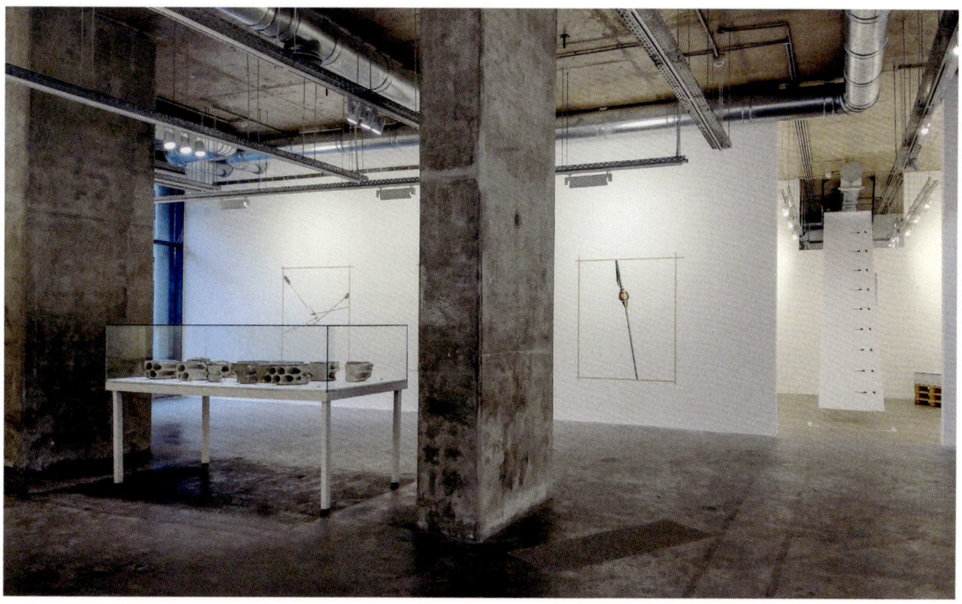

FIG. 6-10. Adel Abidin. *Debris*. Installation view from the artist's solo exhibition *Ya!* at Galerie Tanit, Beirut. Digital image. 2019.

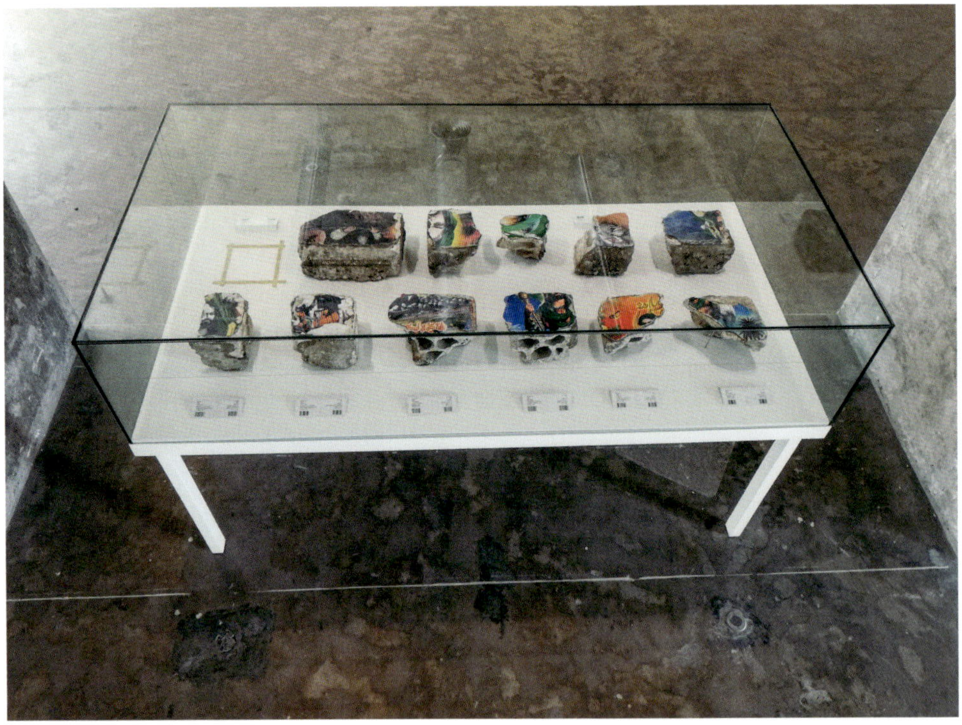

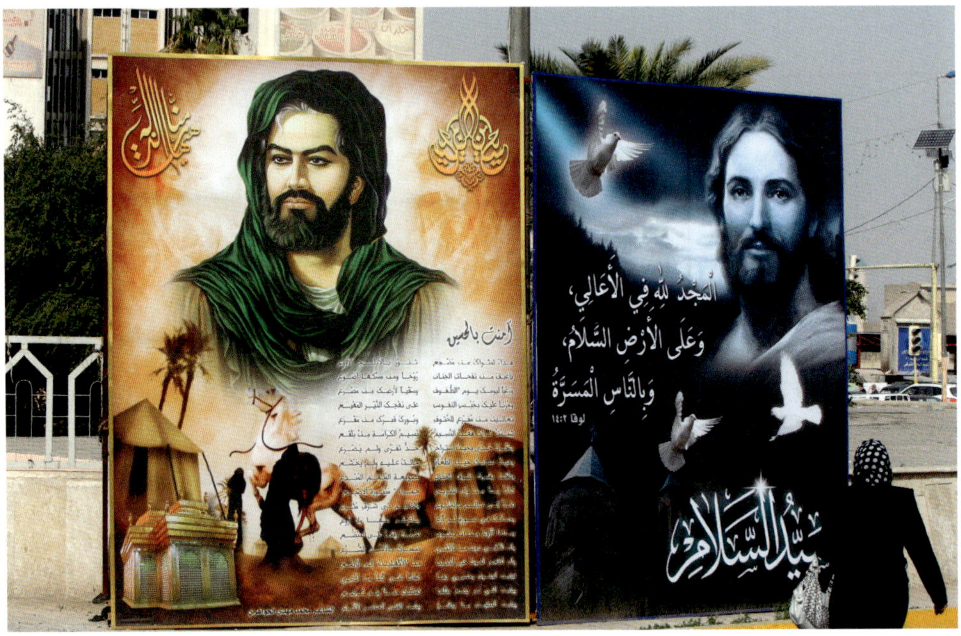

TOP: FIG. 6-11. Adel Abidin. *Debris*. Installation view at Galerie Tanit, Beirut. Digital image. 2019. Checklist no. 8. **BOTTOM: FIG. 6-12**. Iraqi woman walks past the posters of Jesus Christ and Shi'ite Imam Al-Hussain. Baghdad, January 27, 2011. ALI AL-SAADI/AFP via Getty Images.

The work in this exhibition, *Debris: Unveiling the Fragments of Shi'ite Identity in Iraq*, represents the scattered remnants and rubble of demolished walls and sites across multiple cities in Iraq (**FIG. 6-10**). These structures were once adorned with posters displaying the images of the Twelve Imams, taken directly from Iranian depictions. The posters adorned the façades of public buildings and urban walls, particularly during the memorial commemorations of the imams' deaths. In some areas, the walls were repeatedly torn down and rebuilt, reflecting the volatile nature of the environment.

The posters themselves were affixed to the walls, reminiscent of ubiquitous marketing billboards or propaganda posters.

This art installation consists of the salvaged debris, which serves as a visual representation of the remaining fragments of eleven imam posters (**FIG. 6-11**). The twelfth imam, Al-Mahdi, disappeared in the city of Samara in Iraq, and according to belief he will reappear as a sign of the end of the world, akin to the Messiah (**FIG. 6-12**). The collected debris includes fragments of walls still partially adorned with glued posters. These poignant remnants are displayed on a large glass-boxed pedestal/table, accompanied by labels indicating the precise locations from which the debris was retrieved.

By presenting these shattered reflections of Shi'ite identity, *Debris* invites contemplation of the transient nature of symbols and the enduring impact of collective memory within a complex sociopolitical landscape.

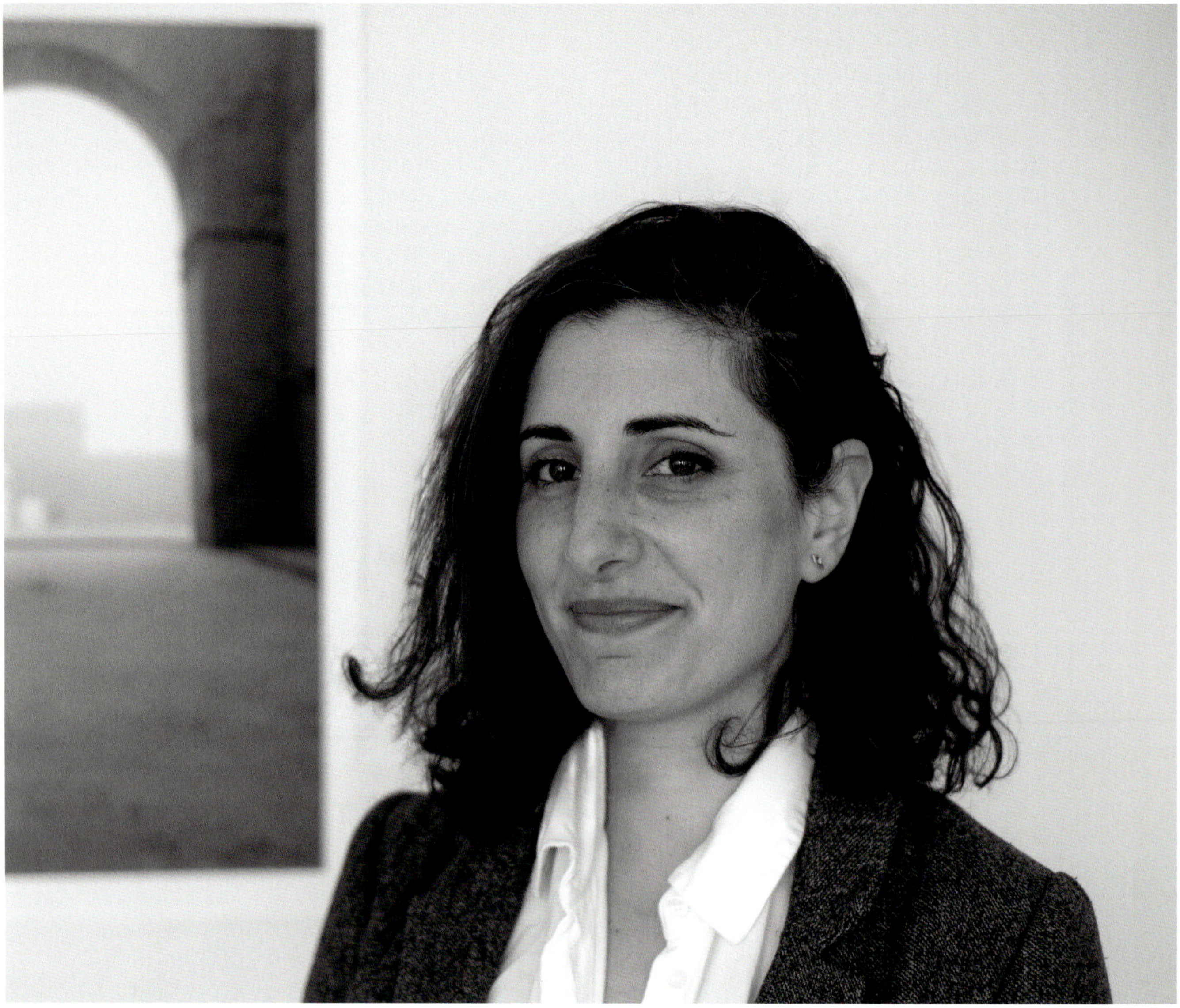

CHAPTER 7

SHADOWS

Nadine Hattom

It is one thing to learn about one's own heritage through family memories and anecdotes, and another to experience it through an occupation of its archives past and present.

I set out to visit Iraq through Anbar Province from the west, crossing the border into Iraq from Jordan. I also knew full well that it was unlikely that I would get there. It was the early 2010s and there was an illusion that perhaps the situation in Iraq under the US occupation was stabilizing. However, I had heard that Anbar Province in Iraq's west was full of bandits and it was unsafe to travel through there. Add to that being from Iraq's Mandaean ethnic minority, which became increasingly threatened since the 2003 invasion, and it was a fool's errand to even entertain such a thought as a return visit to Iraq.

Still, such is the displaced heart. I planned my visit to Jordan, and hired a taxi to take me through the Syrian desert in Jordan in the direction of Iraq (**FIG. 7-2**).

Before my trip, I searched online for images of Anbar Province and Lake Habbaniyah. I knew little about them or what they looked like. Perhaps my parents had visited the lake on a school excursion. My searches returned an overwhelming number of high-resolution, public-domain images of US military missions taken in Anbar Province and beyond. I continued searching for more sites. Googling the Hatra ruins in Nineveh. The Wikipedia article shows US soldiers at the site. The images were breathtaking. Bathed in a golden hue with the dust-filled rays of the sun. I wanted to soak up the palette and textures. The sand. The stone. The warmth emanating from them. The sun-washed shrubbery. I was born from those very colors one hot summer's day in Baghdad.

I felt an injustice that the predominantly available documentation of the sites of my cultural heritage should capture camouflaged US soldiers with weapons.

FIG. 7-1. Portrait of Nadine Hattom, 2023.

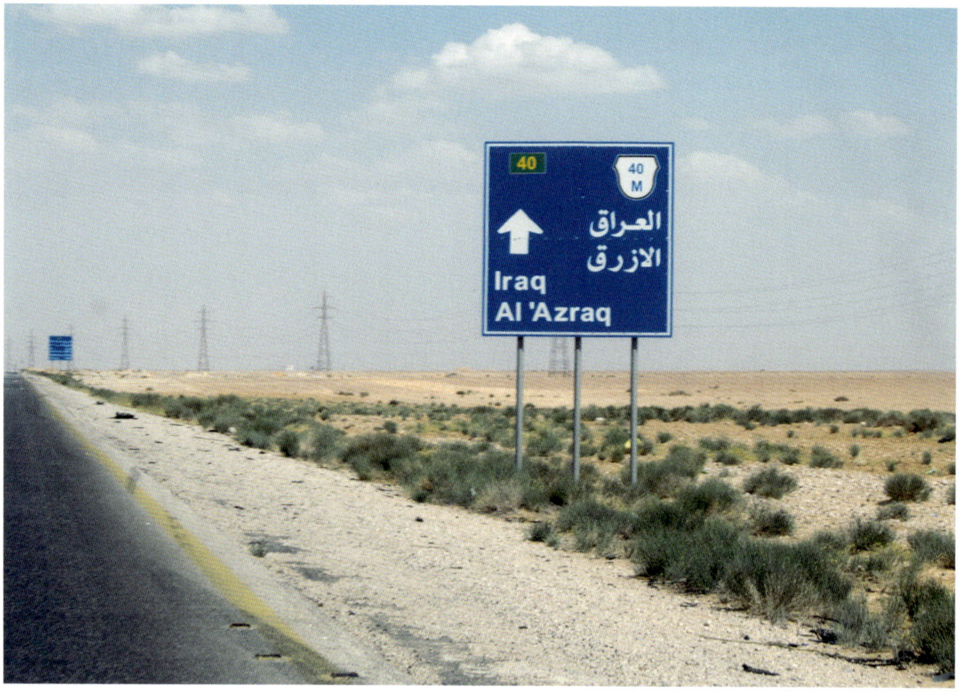

FIG. 7-2. Nadine Hattom. Syrian Desert, Jordan. May 10, 2013. Digital image.

Sites that draw a line back through my ancestry and the land they settled on. Sites I'd never seen with my own eyes.

What were the soldiers really doing there, I wondered? One image on the Wikipedia article (sourced from the US Department of Defense) for Hatra had the following caption:

> *After an early morning Key Leader Engagement, soldiers from Crazy Troop, 3-7 Cavalry, 2HBCT, 3ID, take a small detour to Al Hatra, an ancient ruined city located southwest of Mosul in the Al-Jazarah region and do a little site seeing* [sic] *before heading back on a three hour convoy to Contingency Operating Site Marez, Sept 18.*

Another image showed a lone soldier looking up at the ancient structure (**FIG. 7-3**). Dwarfed by its magnificence. Dressed for combat but juxtaposed against a backdrop of the ancient city.

The image carried the following caption:

> *A U.S. Marine with a ground combat element assigned to Delta Company, 2nd Light Armored Reconnaissance Battalion, Task Force Mechanized, Multi-National Force-West walks through the Hatra Ruins in the Jazeerah Desert in Iraq on July 20, 2008. The task force is conducting disruption operations in the area to deny the enemy sanctuary and prevent foreign fighters from accessing the area. DoD photo by Lance Cpl. Albert F. Hunt, U.S. Marine Corps.*

Why couldn't that be me standing there gazing at the Hatra ruins? Would I ever have the chance to see them? The chance to engage with my own cultural heritage on its own

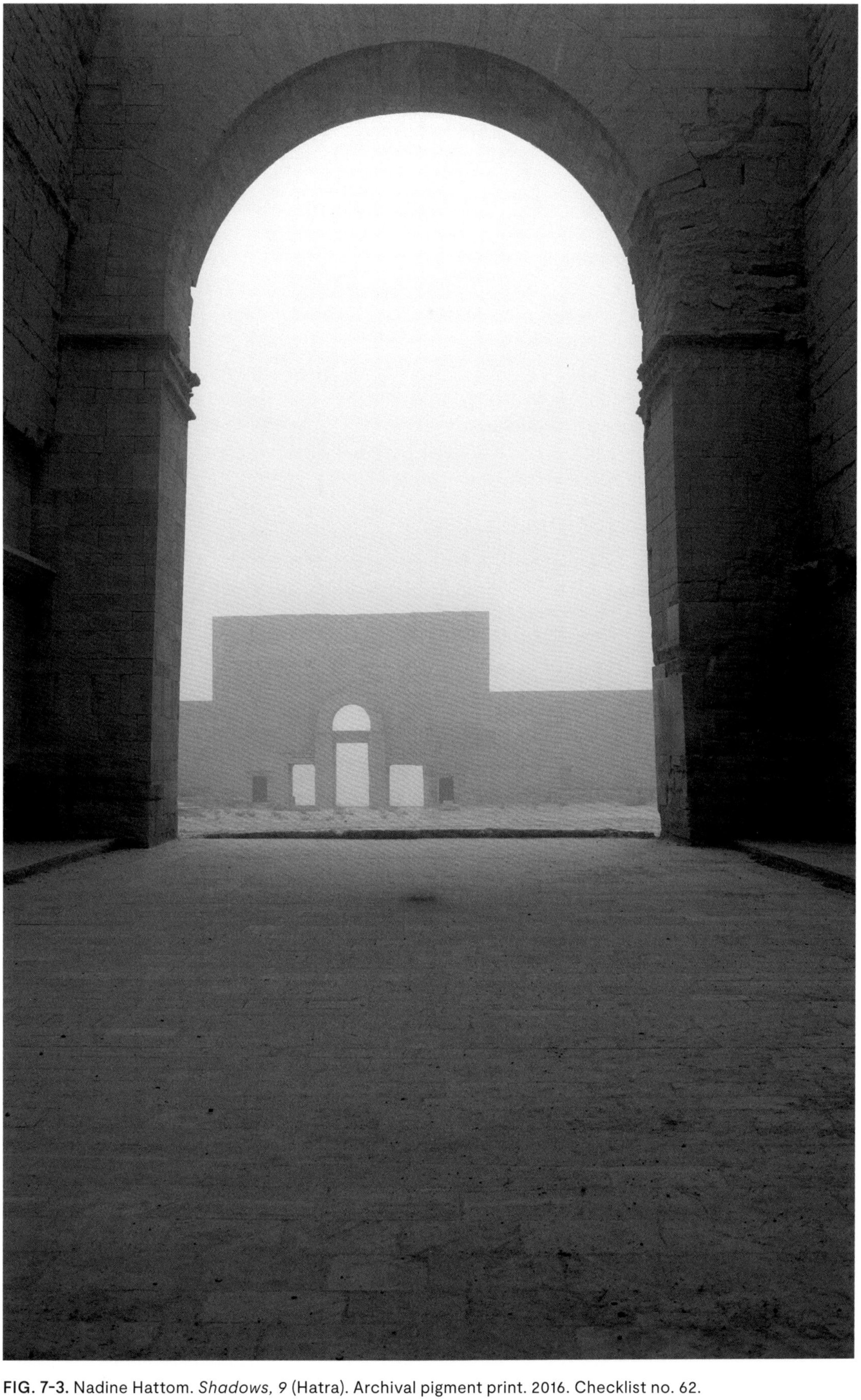

FIG. 7-3. Nadine Hattom. *Shadows, 9* (Hatra). Archival pigment print. 2016. Checklist no. 62.

soil. I'm loath to even call them *ruins* for that suggests something bygone or destroyed, but to me they seemed just as they were supposed to be right now. I wanted nothing more than to stand there among these stones and share the space that my ancestors inhabited. They would be demolished by ISIS some few years later.

—

I hopped out of the taxi to take a photo of the sprawling Syrian desert in Jordan. The taxi driver stood outside the car impatiently. No doubt perplexed at what I was doing with my analog medium-format camera, the Mamiya RB-67, on a tripod pointing into the vast desert. We stopped some sixty kilometers short of the border. The driver was anxious to return to Amman. And so we turned back.

That was the closest I came to Iraq in the twenty-five years since I had last visited with my mother as a young girl. On that visit, we arrived in 1988 on the eve of the end of the Iran-Iraq war. I remember crouching down in the car on the way from the airport as people celebrated in the streets by firing into the air.

My grandmother's place was a haven or perhaps heaven. There, we slept all together on the floor in the living room. Uncles, aunts, and cousins. A sea of mattresses, pillows, and pajamas. My uncles were telling me jokes.

"An elephant goes to the swimming pool. Then an ant arrives. The elephant goes, what's this now? Kindergarten?!" A little is lost in translation.

One of my aunts was upstairs, recovering from giving birth.

We went to eat at an Italian restaurant.

I was wearing a denim dress, with the word *Love*, in English, sprawled in pink across the front.

I don't remember seeing them, but I can still feel the palm trees that were in the garden.

My parents had planned an elaborate escape at the beginning of the Iran-Iraq war. My father left first. He took a colleague's job offer in Abu Dhabi in the United Arab Emirates and gave the colleague our furniture, which had been bought from the UK retailer Habitat, as a thank-you gift.

Next my mother left, taking me, then still a baby, to London to wait for a visa. My brother was in school and the government wouldn't issue him an exit visa until the school year was out, so he stayed behind for a few months with my grandparents before meeting my mother and me in London.

My father, a budding civil engineer with a master's from Scotland and work experience in Libya, had been called on by Saddam Hussein to fix some bunkers. To which he would be transported blindfolded. My mother said that we needed to leave immediately. And she certainly was right.

—

I downloaded the public-domain image of Hatra. A 1.6MB file with 3,328 x 4,992 pixels. I relished the image on my large computer screen. I could touch the dust. But I felt I couldn't see it all. Something stood in the way. It was the soldier. What if I were to remove the soldier? Could I see more of the image? Would it help me reclaim my invaded homeland? I began to painstakingly, pixel by pixel, approximate the image where the soldier stood, building and filling the space that the soldier occupied to reconstruct the image.

The reconstruction, no matter how "real" or seamless it appeared, could never erase or undo what happened there. What was etched into the earth and its

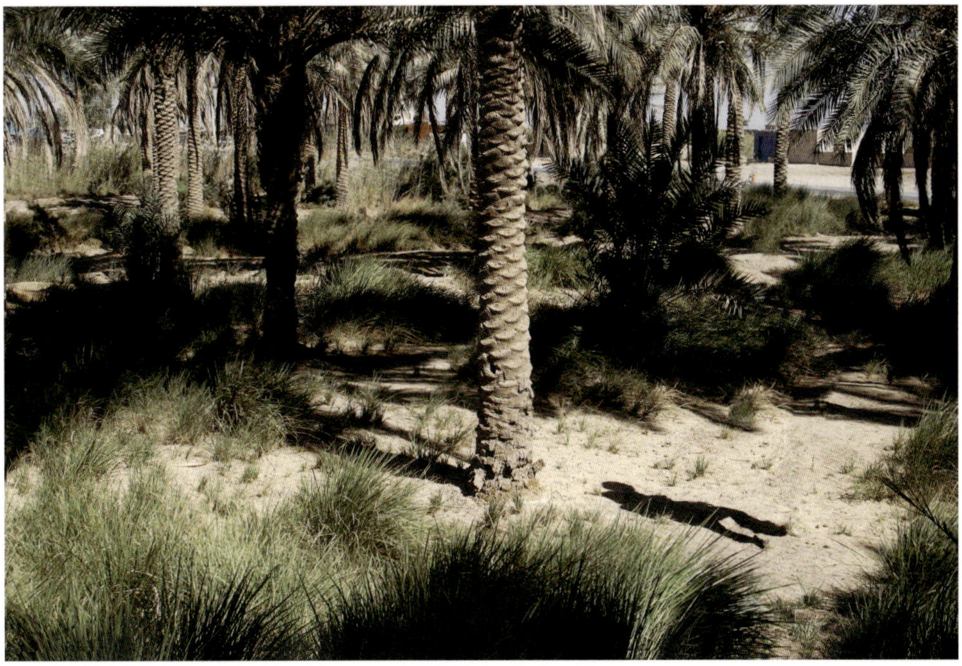

FIG. 7-4. Nadine Hattom. *Shadows, 2* (Fallujah). Archival pigment print. 2016. Checklist no. 55.

history. And the global consequences that followed in the twenty years since. They say that war has a long shadow. So, while I removed the bodies of the soldiers in the images, I left their shadows as a trace of the long shadow that war has left behind.

I then went through the hundreds of US Department of Defense public-domain images documenting Operation Iraqi Freedom. From the entire archive, I chose ten images in total that I modified to reveal the landscape. The photographs taken by combat photographers were beautiful photographs set in the Iraqi landscape. I had never seen such high-resolution images of many of these places before. Fallujah (**FIG. 7-4**), Dulab, Ramadi, Saqlawiyah, Habbaniyah, Hit, Ashur, Diyala, Ziggurat of Ur, and Hatra. They featured sand, palm trees, ancient sites, and structures.

I removed the soldiers from the ten images, some with their shadows so stark and detailed that you can still see the weapons that they bear. Each image carried a caption describing the mission, its purpose, who was involved, when it took place, and of course crediting the photographer.

> *U.S. Marines of Company G, 2nd Battalion, 2nd Marines, fall into a tactical column as they maneuver through a palm grove to conduct a security patrol in Fallujah, Iraq, on Oct. 22, 2005. DoD photo by Sgt. Paul S. Mancuso, U.S. Marine Corps. (Released)*

I realized that the real subject of these images was indeed the landscape itself. In all its beauty. And that when I removed the perceived subject, or the figure, I had created a kind of record of what really happened in each place. Despite the caption's[1] description, or rather together with it, the images told their own story. Their own archive of the events. It isn't an erasure or a lie, but maybe a truth that is carried in the earth itself, on the rays of the sun. And a way to hold both truths—a rich, ancient one, with a dark and devastating one, in one image.

1 Each image from the US Department of Defense public-domain archive is accompanied by a caption that describes the mission documented by the photograph. This caption forms an integral part of the Shadows series, always shown alongside it. The text component of the work is a look at the language of warfare in the public domain and addresses the absence visible in the images.

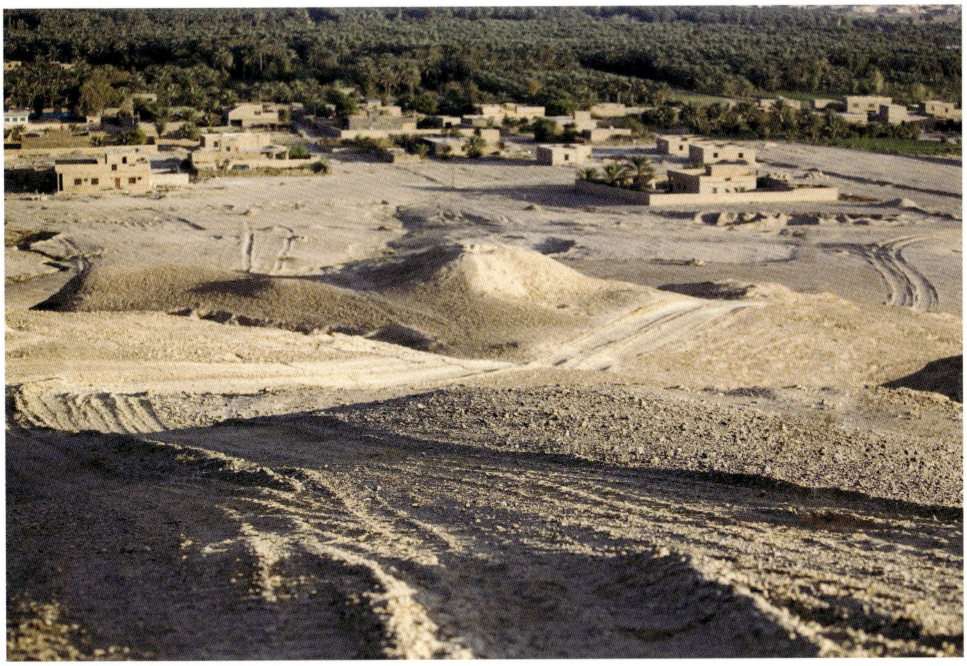

FIG. 7-5. Nadine Hattom. *Shadows, 1* (Dulab). Archival pigment print. 2016. Checklist no. 54. U.S. Marines from 1st Platoon, Alpha Company, 1st Battalion, 7th Marine Regiment patrol from Expeditionary Patrol Base Dulab to a ridge along the outskirts of Dulab, Iraq, Sept. 26, 2007. The Marines are working with Iraqi police in support of Operation Iraqi Freedom in the Al Anbar province of Iraq. (U.S. Marine Corps photo by Cpl. Shane S. Keller).

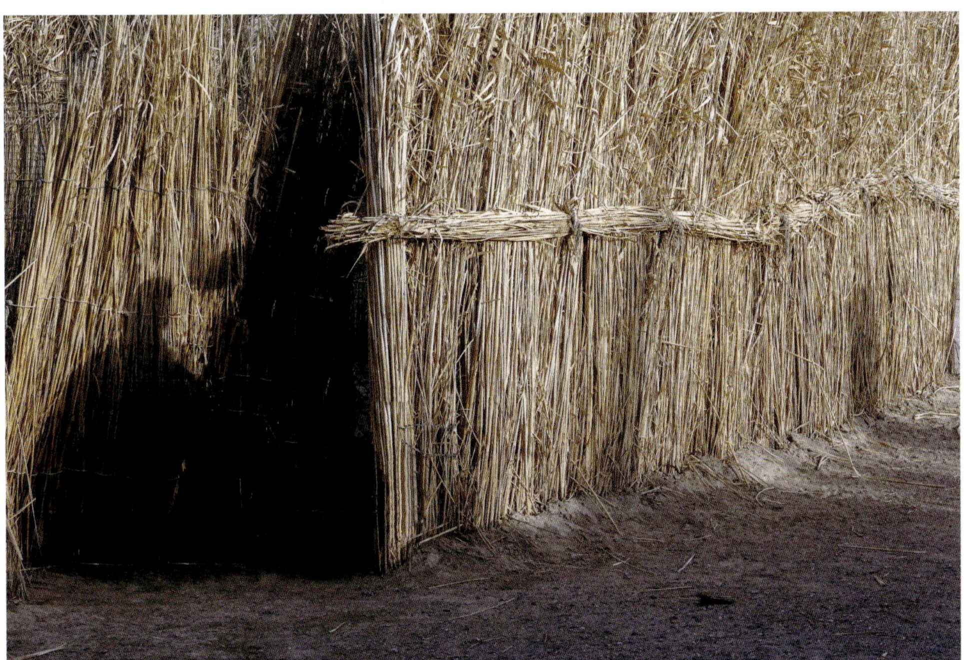

FIG. 7-6. Nadine Hattom. *Shadows, 3* (Ramadi). Archival pigment print. 2016. Checklist no. 56. U.S. Marine Corps Cpl. Julius Mitchell scans the area while on patrol in Ramadi, Iraq, on May 13, 2006. Mitchell is attached to the 2nd Air Naval Gunfire Liaison Company. DoD photo by Petty Officer 2nd Class Samuel C. Peterson, U.S Navy. (Released).

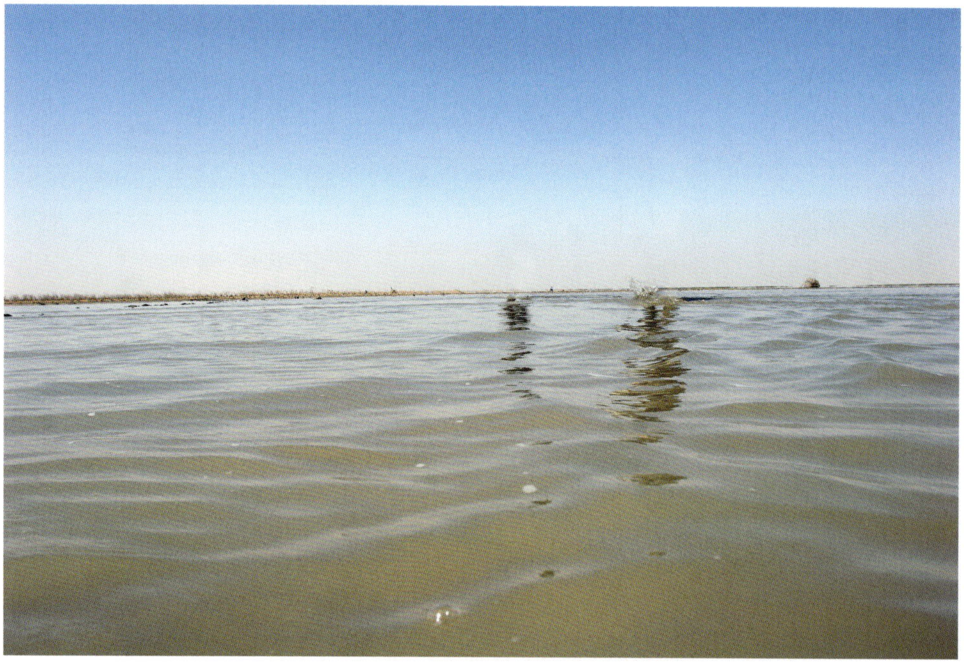

FIG. 7-7. Nadine Hattom. *Shadows, 4* (Habbaniyah). Archival pigment print. 2016. Checklist no. 57. U.S. Sailors with Riverine Squadron 1, Detachment 3, wade to the shore line on Lake Habbaniyah, Iraq, March 19, 2009. U.S. Sailors and Iraqi River Police officers are conducting beach insertions along the lake. (U.S. Marine Corps photo by Sgt. Richard L. McCumber III).

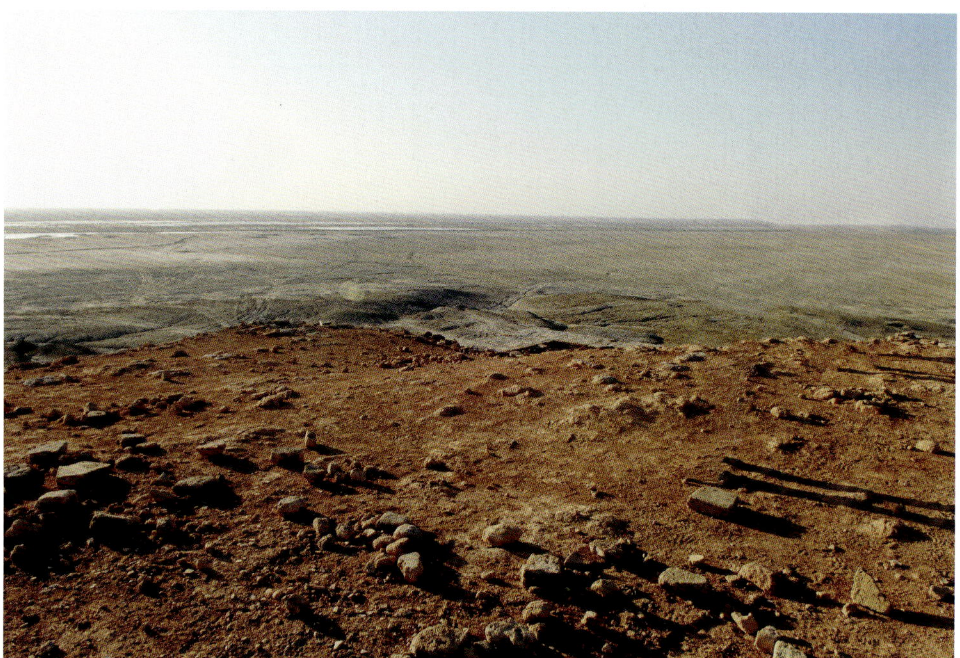

FIG. 7-8. Nadine Hattom. *Shadows, 5* (Ziggurat of Ur). Archival pigment print. 2016. Checklist no. 58. Lt. Gen. Gene Renuart looks out at the landscape from atop the Great Ziggurat of Ur, Iraq, Jan. 19, 2007. The ziggurat was believed to be a place of worship, dedicated to the moon god Nanna in the Sumerian city of Ur in ancient Mesopotamia. Defense Dept. photo by Cherie A. Thurlby.

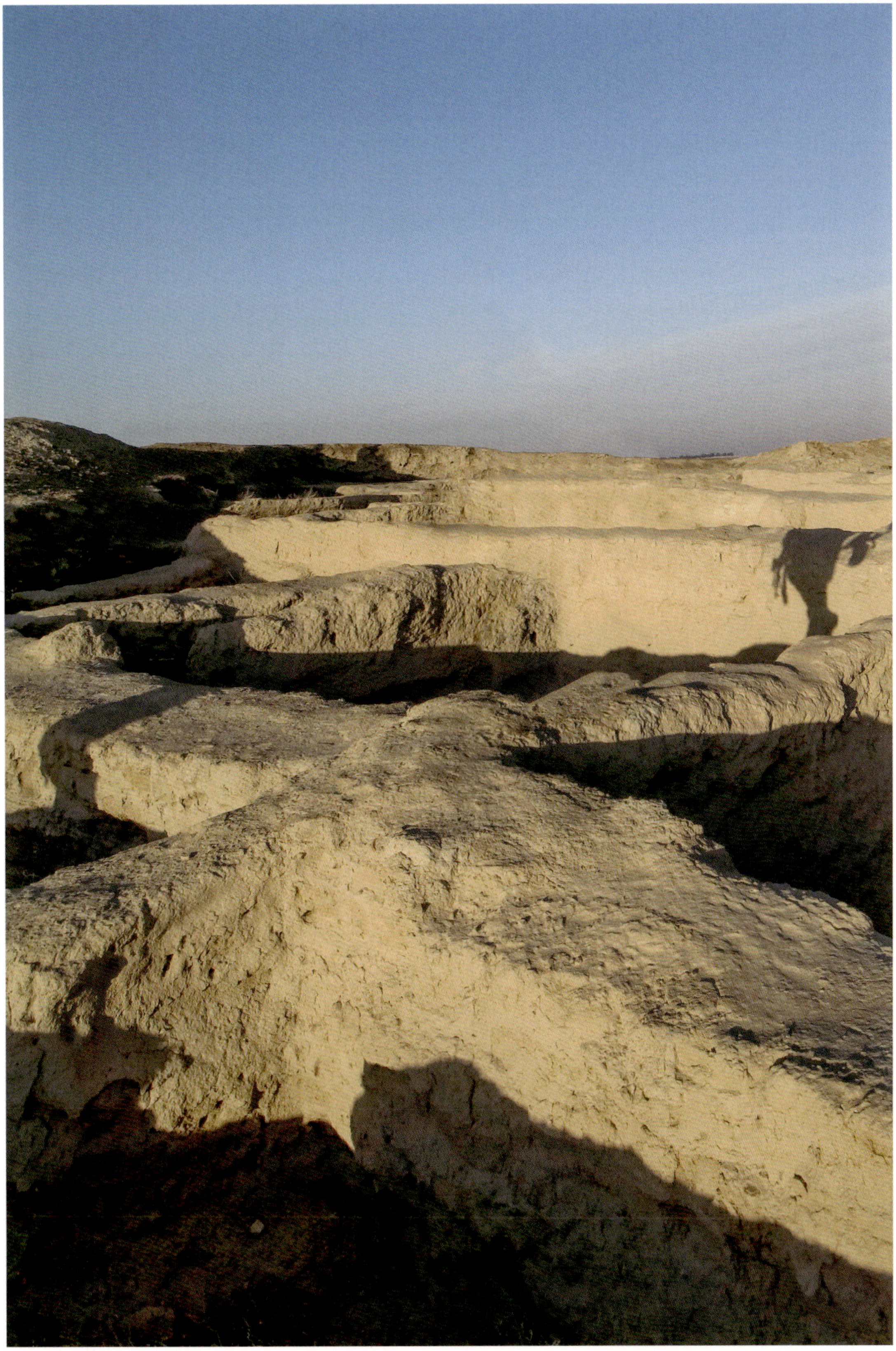

FIG. 7-9. Nadine Hattom. *Shadows, 6* (Diyala). Archival pigment print. 2016. Checklist no. 59. U.S. Army soldiers of 1st Stryker Brigade Combat Team, 25th Infantry Division patrol a section of Iraq's Diyala River Valley on Dec. 27, 2008. DoD photo by Petty Officer Walter J. Pels, U.S. Navy. (Released).

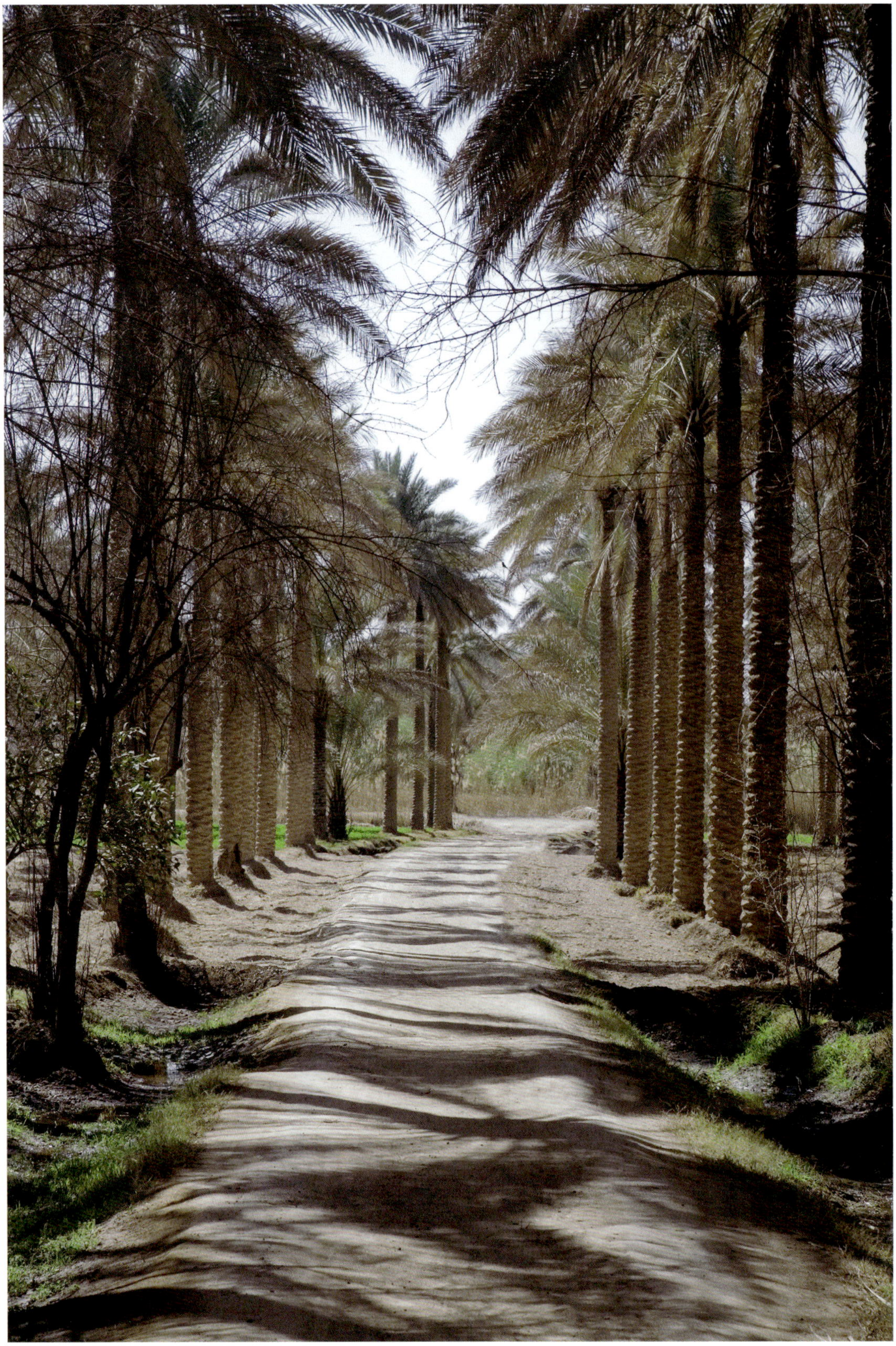

FIG. 7-10. Nadine Hattom. *Shadows, 7* (Hit). Archival pigment print. 2016. Checklist no. 60. A U.S. Marine with 3rd Battalion, 4th Marine Regiment provides security for Marines with 1st Combat Engineers Battalion as they search palm groves for weapon caches outside the city of Hit, Iraq, March 9, 2008. U.S. Marine Corps photo by Cpl. Tyler Hill. (Released).

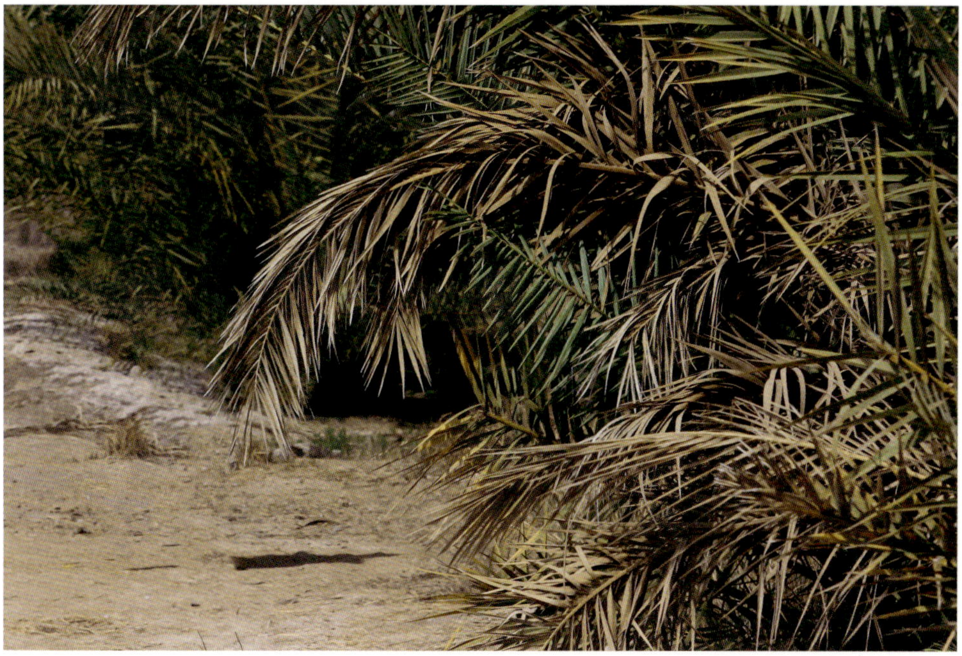

FIG. 7-11. Nadine Hattom. *Shadows, 8* (Saqlawiyah). Archival pigment print. 2016. Checklist no. 61. Marines 2nd Battalion, 6th Marine Regiment, Regimental Combat Team 5, step into a palm grove while they patrol the farmlands of Saqlawiyah, Iraq during Operation Jaws V. Marines pushed out into the rural areas to pursue insurgents placing improvised explosive devices and setting up mortar firing positions. Photo by Cpl. Adaecus Brooks.

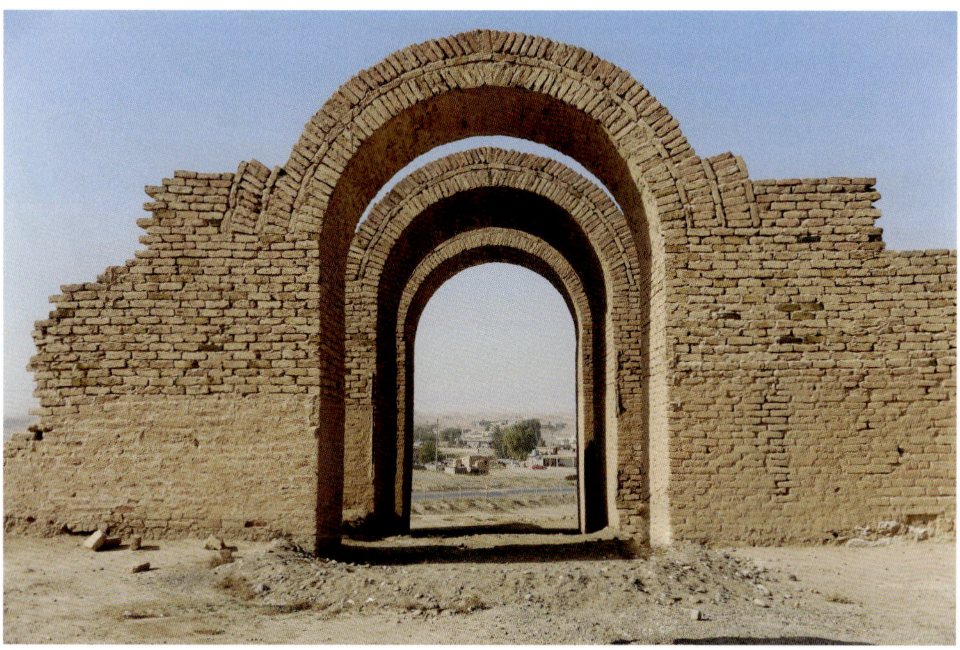

FIG. 7-12. Nadine Hattom. *Shadows, 10* (Ashur). Archival pigment print. 2016. Checklist no. 63. U.S. Army soldiers from 1st Squadron, 3rd Armored Cavalry Regiment provide security for a provincial reconstruction team and representatives of the United Nations Educational Scientific and Cultural Organization as they visit the ancient city of Ashur in Iraq on Nov. 21, 2008. Shura, also known as Qalat Shergat, is one of three areas in Iraq that is a World Heritage site. DoD photo by Staff Sgt. JoAnn S. Makinano, U.S. Air Force. (Released).

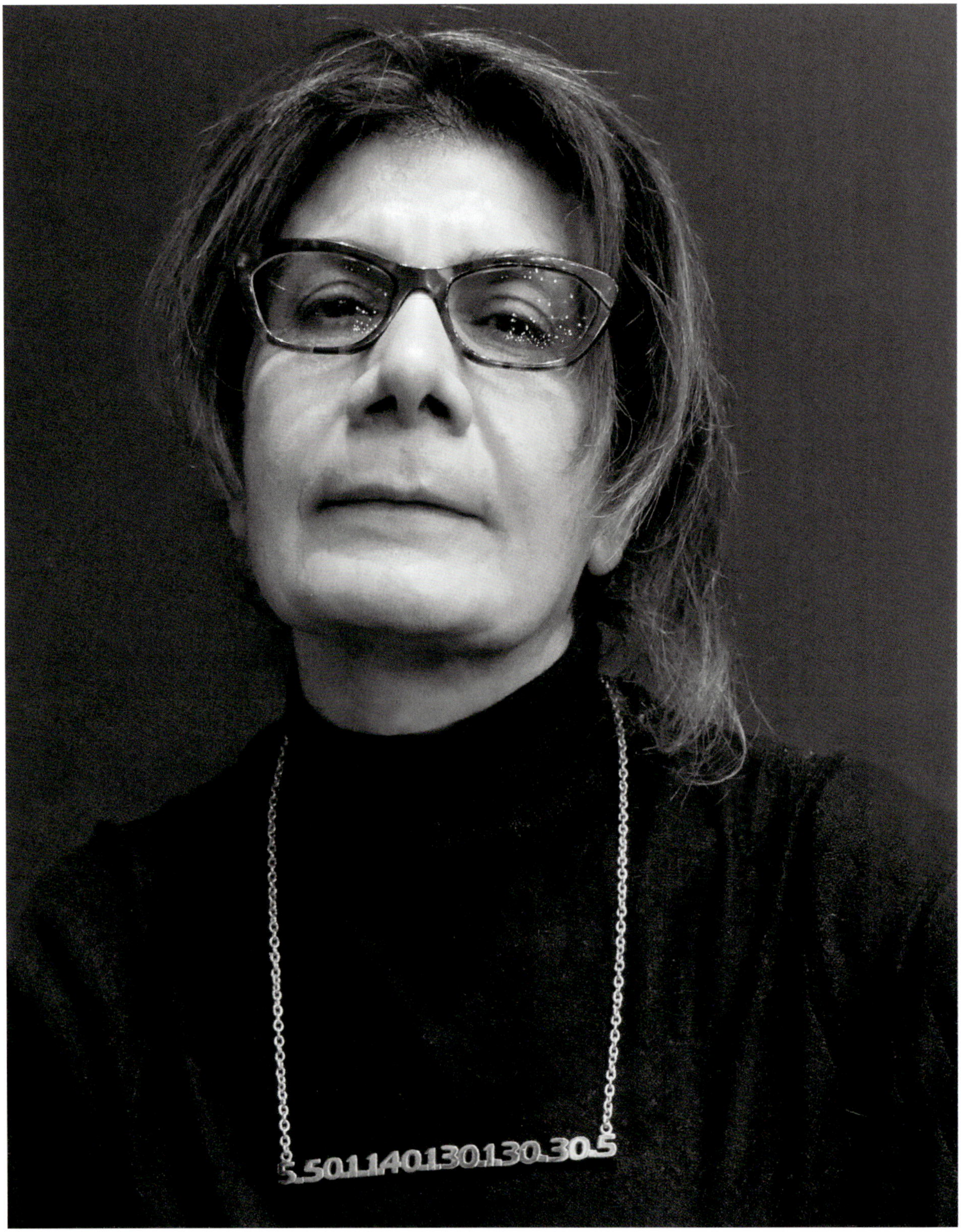

CHAPTER 8

ON RUINS AND RUBBLE:

RUIN AS A TRAJECTORY FOR FUTURES

Hanaa Malallah

My practice addresses one subject in particular—Ruins—but from various aspects: my own physical experience having lived amongst ruins in Iraq for most of my life, both archaeological Mesopotamian ruins (**FIG. 8-2**) and the rubble left by wars. My work reflects both these landscapes—Ruins and Rubble—which make up Iraq. From my experience, Mesopotamia is no longer defined as a land between

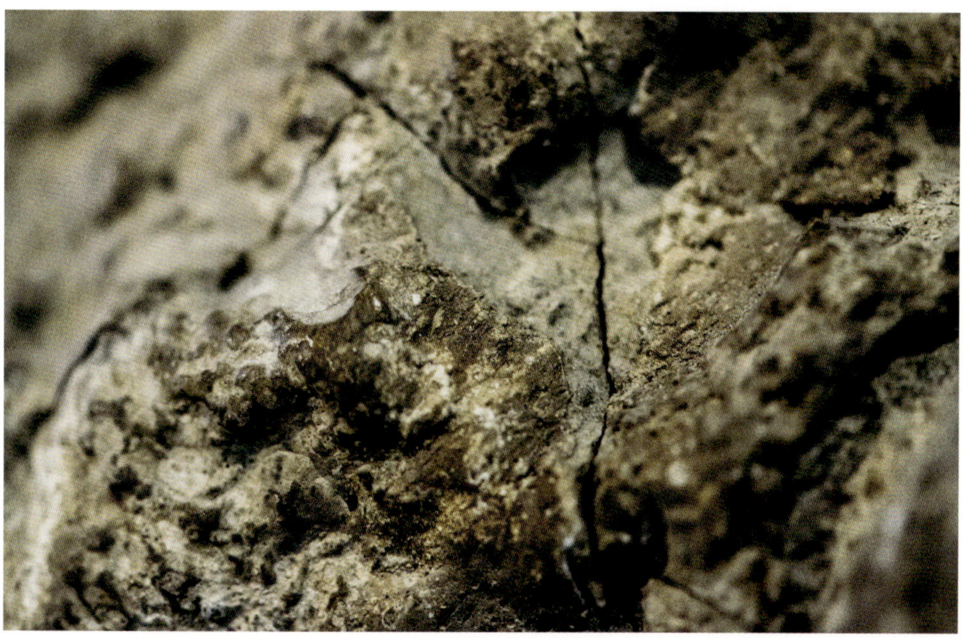

OPPOSITE: FIG. 8-1. Portrait of Hanaa Malallah. Digital image. 2023. **ABOVE: FIG. 8-2**. Betoul Amin. Detail of Al Warka temple wall. Baghdad, The Iraq Museum. Digital image. 2019.

two rivers, but as a landscape reduced, by archaeological pillaging and repeated wars, to ruins and rubble. Now that I live outside Iraq, the distance gives me space to examine this different perspective.

In my practice, the tasks of doing research and producing visual work always proceed in tandem. Using different techniques to conduct it, I work both individually and collaboratively. This approach to practice as research becomes a tool toward understanding, communicating my questions around the subject through my artistic responses.

"In the case of the ruin, the fact that life, with its wealth and its changes once dwelled here constitutes an immediately perceived presence."[1]

I chose Mesopotamia as a site of my research subject to focus on the concept of ruins: Mesopotamia with its extensive time span, and "among the longest continuously inhabited urban settlements in human history,"[2] gives a scope to examine my hypothesis that ruins are not merely the site "of life from which life has departed"[3] but also exist as a kind of development and process, as a function of time. I approach ruination as "Time Travel" and ruins as a physical form of a time machine, often understood as a "portal connecting distant points in time."[4] The question here: Could Mesopotamian Ruins be seen or used as a hypothetical time machine . . . as a Vehicle?[5] I call it fluidity of time on matter. I approach the concept of ruins as a symptom of time and ecology effects, and sequences of currents, which allow me (us) to understand and experience an incessant dialectical process between ruination, rejuvenation, and existence as "a process of life . . . [that] effects transformations within that process."[6]

—

In December 2018, after two rainy days, I went with my research team to visit the ancient archaeological site of Nippur (**FIG. 8-3**). We had been advised not to as the surface of the site after rain becomes very fragile, unstable, and hard to walk on; nevertheless, we went. We immediately were faced with the most

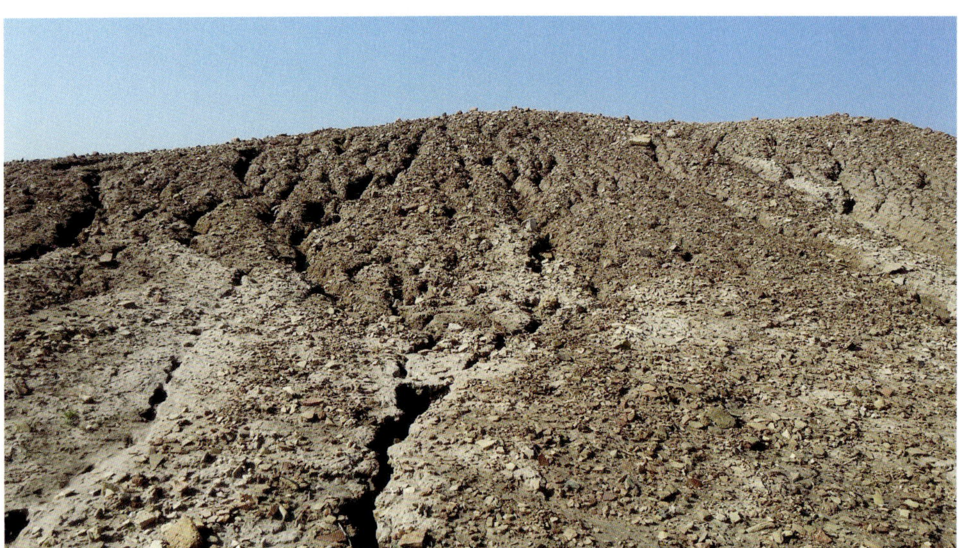

FIG. 8-3. Hanaa Malallah. Nippur/Nuffar/Al-Qadisiyah. Digital image. December 2018.

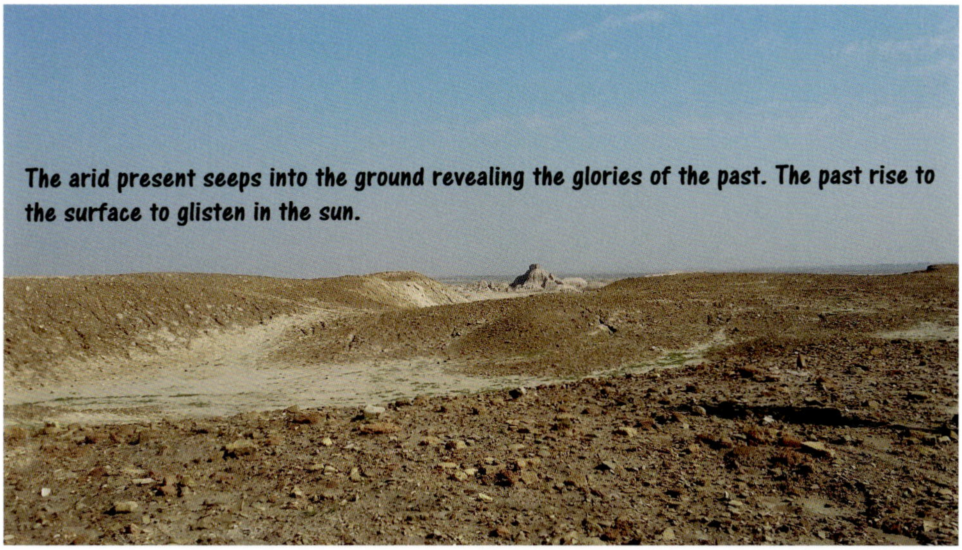

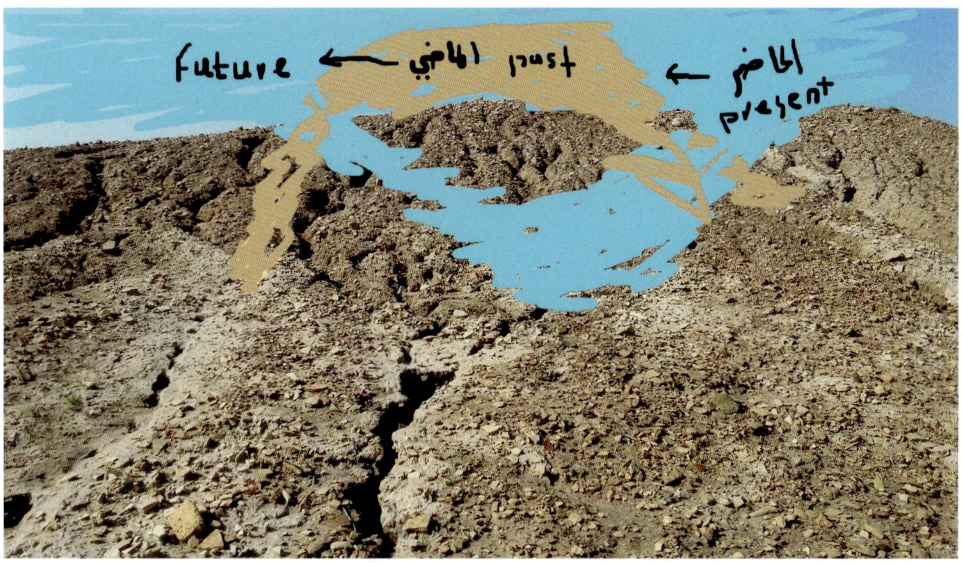

TOP: FIG. 8-4. Hanaa Malallah. "The arid present seeps into the ground revealing the glories of the past. The past rises to the surface to glisten in the sun." Illustrated digital image. 2018. **BOTTOM: FIG. 8-5.** Annotated photo taken with the artist's mobile at Nippur/Nuffar/Al-Qadisiyah showing the suggestive trajectory: Present → Past → Future. Digital image. December 2018.

bewitching, breathtaking, and unforgettable landscape structured into many mounds formed by the rain. The surface was indeed very fragile, exposing many ancient fragments of archaeological significance; all now glistening in the sunrise like plants (**FIG. 8-4**).

The very landscape of Mesopotamia, littered with its ancient ruins, allows me (us) to encounter contradictory forces of past and present as experienced in equilibrium, where "that struggle between above and below comes to a standstill . . . with its incessant moving up and down, its constant shifting of boundaries, and the playing of the inexhaustible forces in it, one against the other"[7] (**FIG. 8-5**). In this way I am able to tap the innermost energy of Mesopotamian ruins and exploit their rejuvenation power rather than approaching them merely as ancient relics. Ruination now is understood as just a change in material state, not as annihilation.[8]

As an artist and researcher, I focus on Mesopotamian ruins as shaking off, avoiding the "reductionist thinking"[9] of most archaeologists, instead of applying the preconceptions (of archaeologists) that might otherwise give premature shape and thereby "convert every certainty into a question."[10] Obviously our technique to approach the ancient ruins is not a technique typically used by archaeologists to collect data of the past, but to learn how to experience the Ruins & Ruination and get (what I call) "practice Knowledge" or to collect knowledge directly from the ruins at the sites. And we shape that as research papers and visual works. In a nutshell, could archaeological ruins be approached to extrapolate the future, not just to collect past data?!

"The trauma is the present, the therapeutic located in the past, in the last vestiges of Mesopotamian archaeological sites."[11]

But modern Iraq is not only a landscape of ancient ruins; it is also littered with the effects of its more recent wars. Here we encounter ruination as forms of rubble—evidenced in its modern cities as destruction and death; here we find a loss of culture and identities, all is chaos and destruction with little hope for any future. Here is where we understand Baudrillard's notion of the lethal energy in ruins,[12] all is laid waste. On the contrary, turning to Iraq's ancient sites, these antiquities are not experienced as debris and destruction but as sites that are alive and full of hope; they are evidence of our past which is active in the present. Here we find hope and life.

Here is a possible dialogue between the status of Mesopotamian ruins and that evidenced as the ruins have been perpetuated by the violence of recent wars in Iraq. My endeavor is to discuss these differences where the archaeological ruins become sites of positivity (forces of existing/life power/transformation), giving hope in the present and shaping more positive futures counteracting the lethal energy of rubble (as disintegration) that is experienced as modern Iraq. Underneath and alongside the debris that is modern Iraq lie the remnants of past powerful and rich cultures which are still vibrating with possibilities for more positive futures. Here I find a "relation of the ruin to a future or futures: its capacity to invent or imagine a time to come, even as it seems to fall back into time past."[13] My project is to attend to this past in order to imagine a future that is yet to come, where "the past is littered with debris of these futures, while our present incorporates the unstable collective memory of hopes that have long since been abandoned."[14]

Now, I consider this ongoing state of ruination in its greater global context, the ruination which we all occupy in a postcolonial context. I am concerned to address the possibilities for addressing ruins as a new aesthetic which attends to this history (the latent power of ruins القوة الكامنة للخرائب) in the present, as that which might provide the foundations for a new relation between past and present, one which dislocates the traditional spatial-temporal continuity—of history—of time—of sequences. We attend to the past-present-future trajectory as a possible dissolve, as now in flux, as open to new becoming (according to Deleuzian theory). This past is not our present but our future; we inhabit this ongoing state of ruination; we explore this state as offering other kinds of futures, other modes of temporality; as artist/researcher, I inhabit an ongoing state of ruination as powerful, as potential for rejuvenation, as enabling dialogue between our experiences of antiquities, colonial occupation, and the ruins of war. I mine the past in our performances of the present, producing artworks which delineate new relations to the past and to possible futures. Could the archaeological ruins give us the opportunity to extrapolate our future?

—

This practice-based research project approaches the ruins and rubble of Babylon as a site which "evokes an image of power, wealth, and splendour—and decadence . . . [a] city whose image of oppression and wantonness persisted and flourished long after the city itself had crumbled into piles of dust."[15] We explore Babylon,

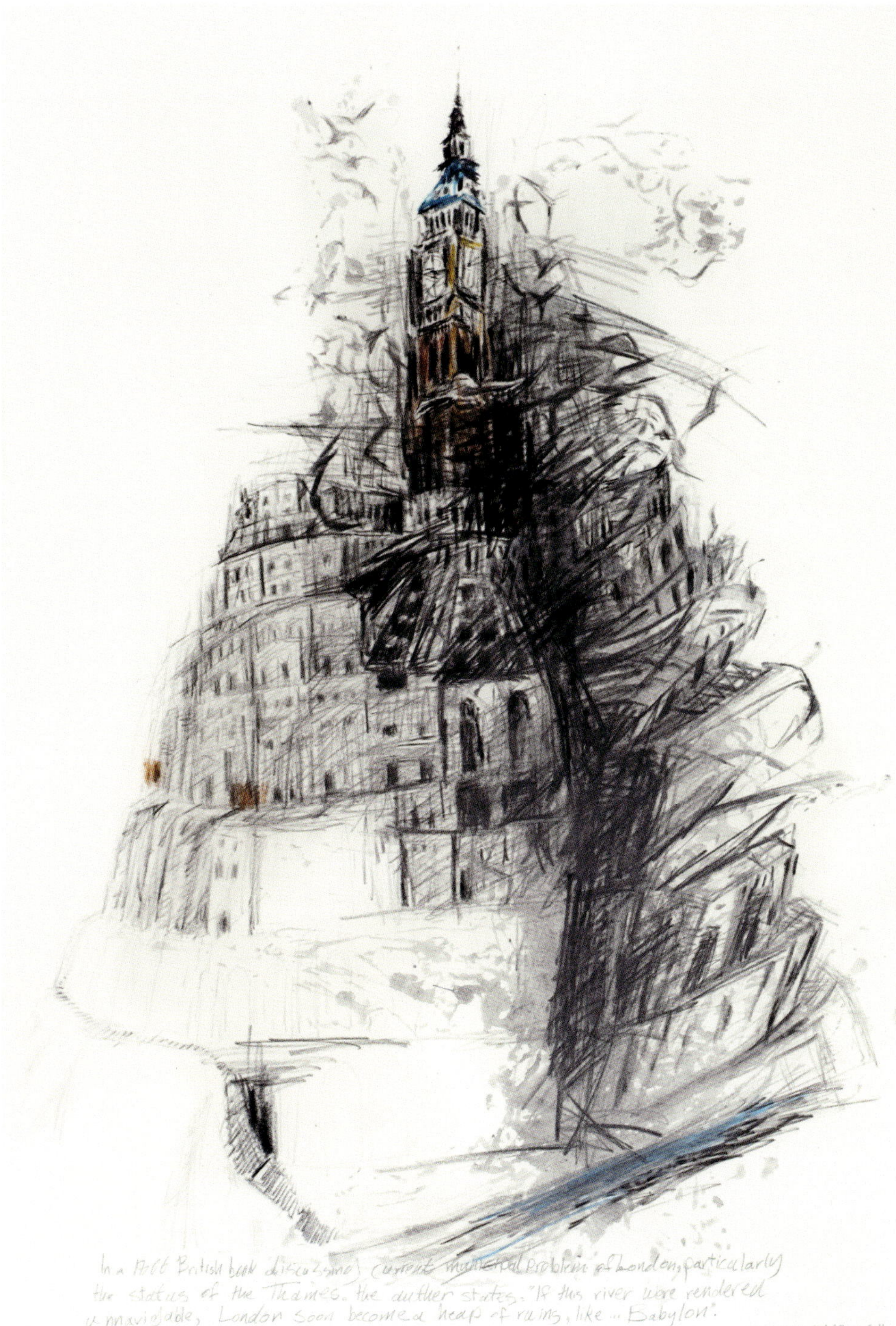

FIG. 8-6. Hanaa Malallah. *Babylon Curse I*. Charcoal, pencil, colored pencil, and acrylic on paper. 2023. Checklist no. 23.

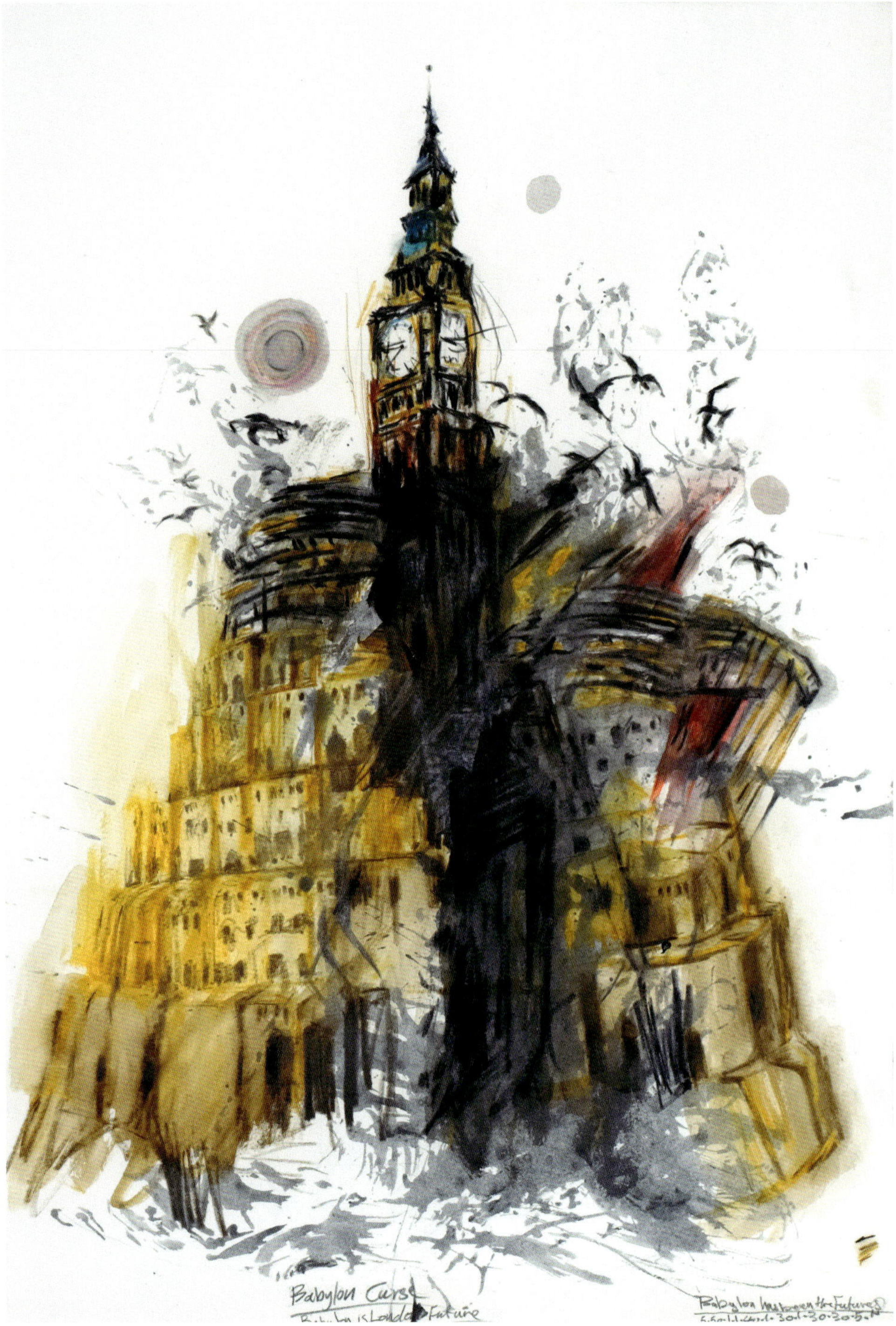

FIG. 8-7. Hanaa Malallah. *Babylon Curse II.* Charcoal, pencil, colored pencil, and acrylic on paper. 2023. Checklist no. 24.

with its magnitude, drama, and complexities, as simultaneously Past, Present, and Future. We work directly from our firsthand experience of this ancient site to produce our artistic responses.

I came across an extract in an 1806 British book discussing current municipal problems of London, particularly the status of the Thames, in which the author states: "If the river were rendered unnavigable, London would be soon become

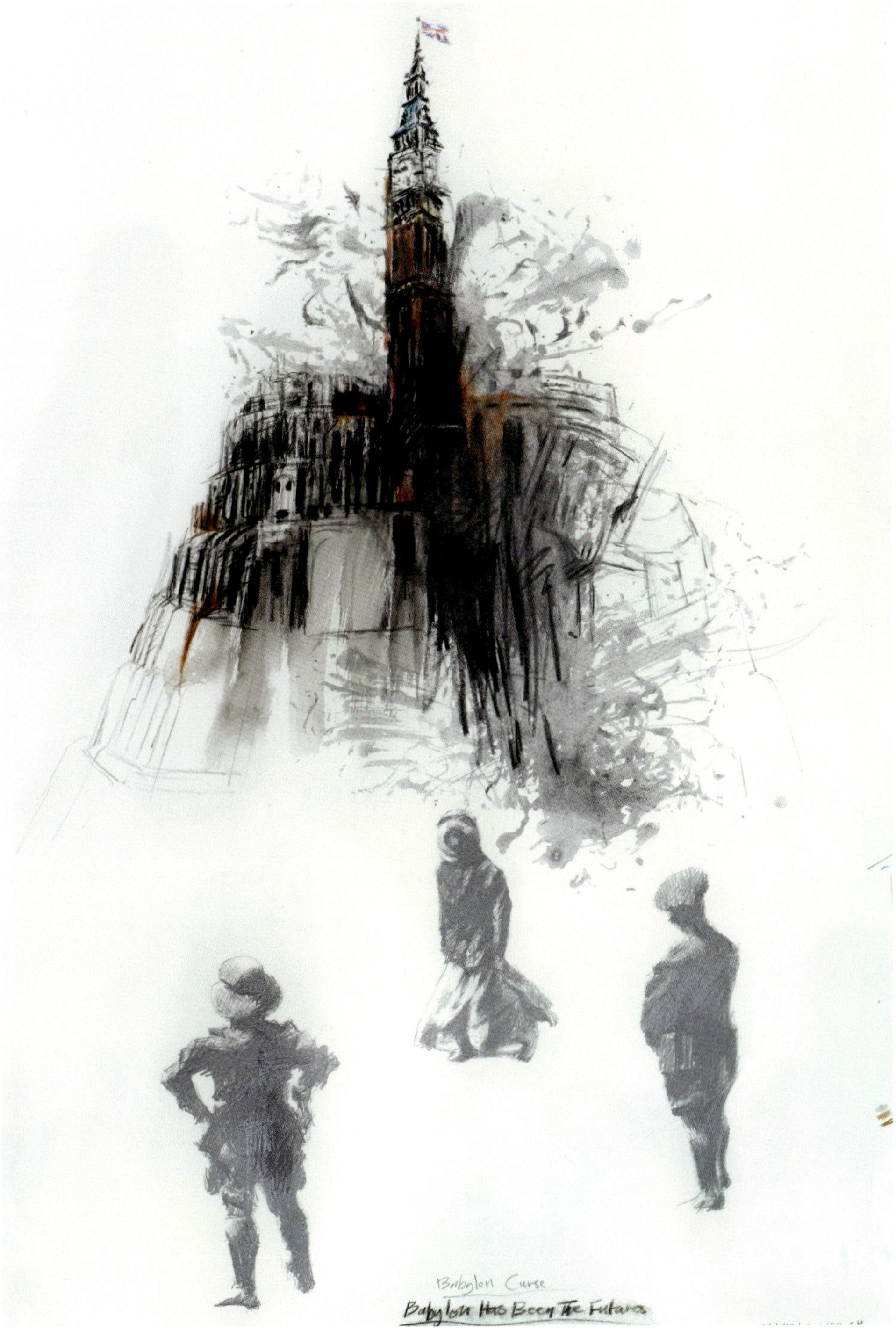

FIG. 8-8. Hanaa Malallah. *Babylon Curse III*. Charcoal, pencil, colored pencil, and acrylic on paper. 2023. Checklist no. 25.

a heap of ruins, like Nineveh or Babylon."[16] In Eugene Roche's poem "London in a Thousand Years" (1830), Revelation's destroying angel brings the end upon London. Somehow the narrator survives, to awaken a thousand years later to find "Babylon" covered in a green mantle, and starts recollecting about the sinful place that was once London. My immediate response to this comparison of London and Babylon was to produce a series of drawings titled *Babylon Curse* and

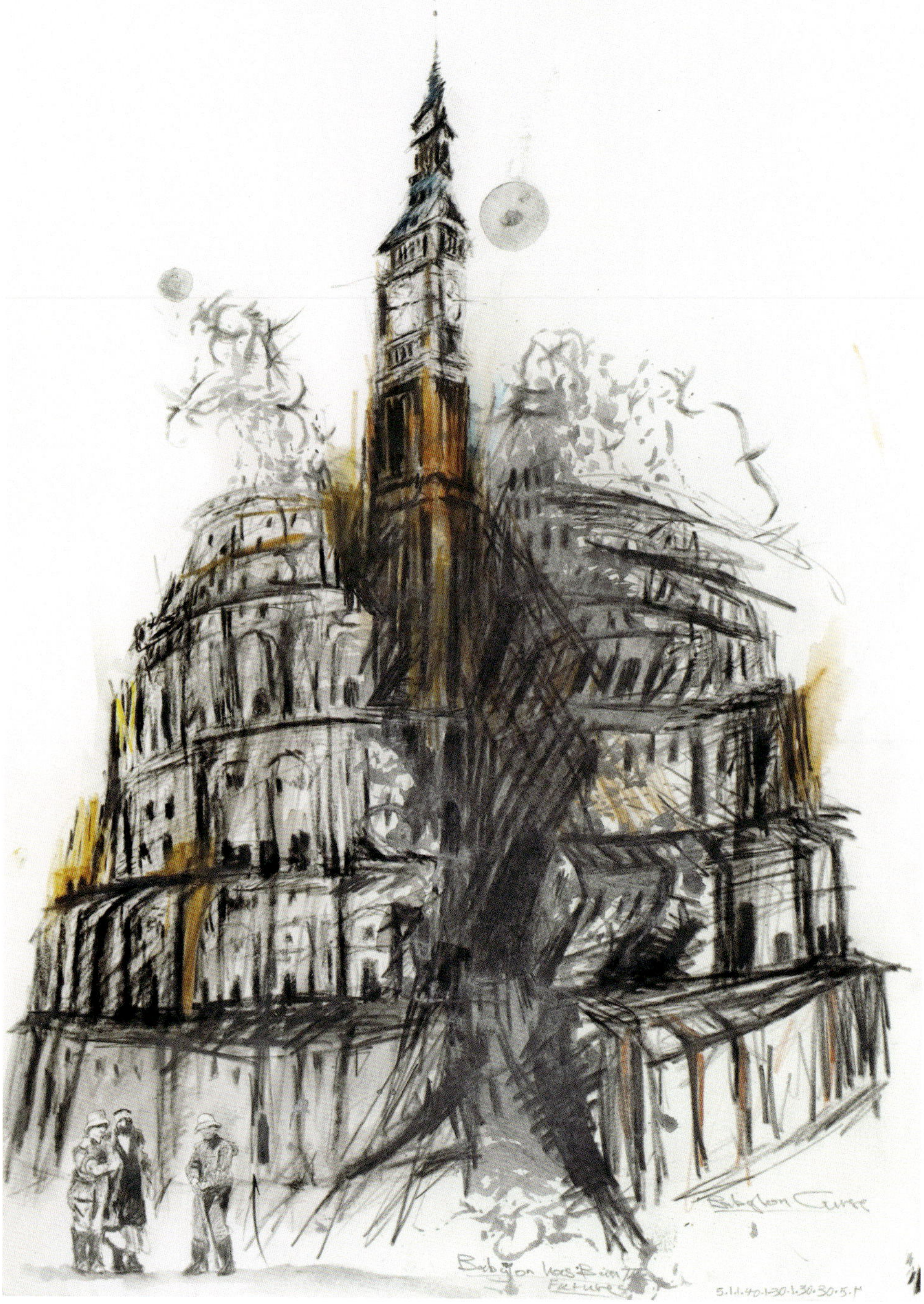

FIG. 8-9. Hanaa Malallah. *Babylon Curse IV.* Charcoal, pencil, colored pencil, and acrylic on paper. 2023. Checklist no. 26.

a homonymous video, trying to illustrate the idea (FIGS. 8-6 through 8-10). While exhibiting some of these drawings in London in April 2022,[17] a strange incident occurred: I had just visited Tate Modern in London with a friend, Walid Siti, when we came upon protestors by the river Thames holding banners that read "When Babylon Falls" (FIG. 8-11).

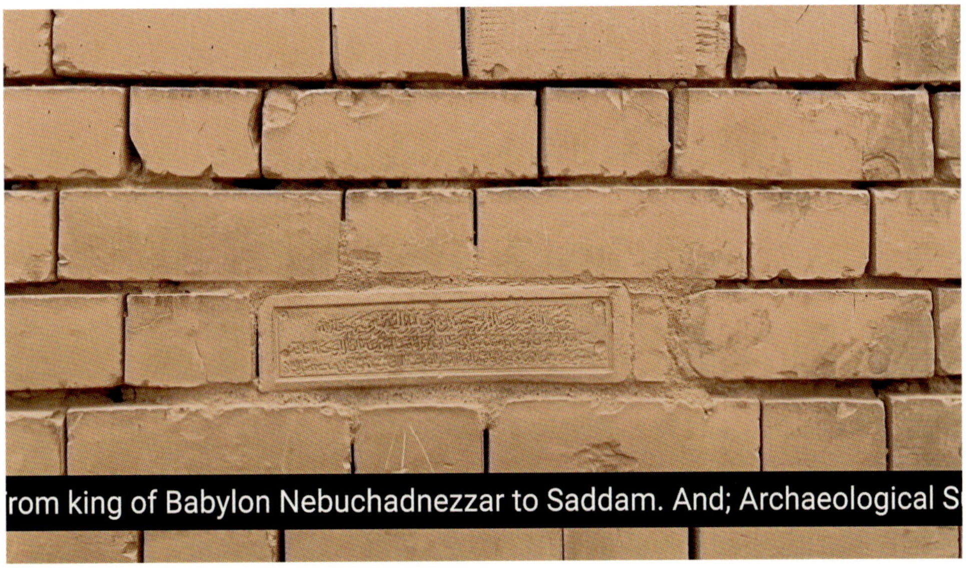

FIG. 8-10. Hanaa Malallah. *Babylon Curse.* Still from video. 2023. Checklist no. 22.

While I was searching social media to find out how Iraqis use images of Mesopotamia in order to protest the misery of their present life, I discovered an archival video showing British troops entering the Babylon site in 1917. I tracked down the original to the video archives of the Imperial War Museum, London.

Then, in May and November 2022, I made two visits to the Babylon archaeological site and experienced it quite differently than on my previous, frequent visits. The research team and I had been shuttling between the ancient Babylon site and the neighboring city of Hillah and felt the power of encountering those

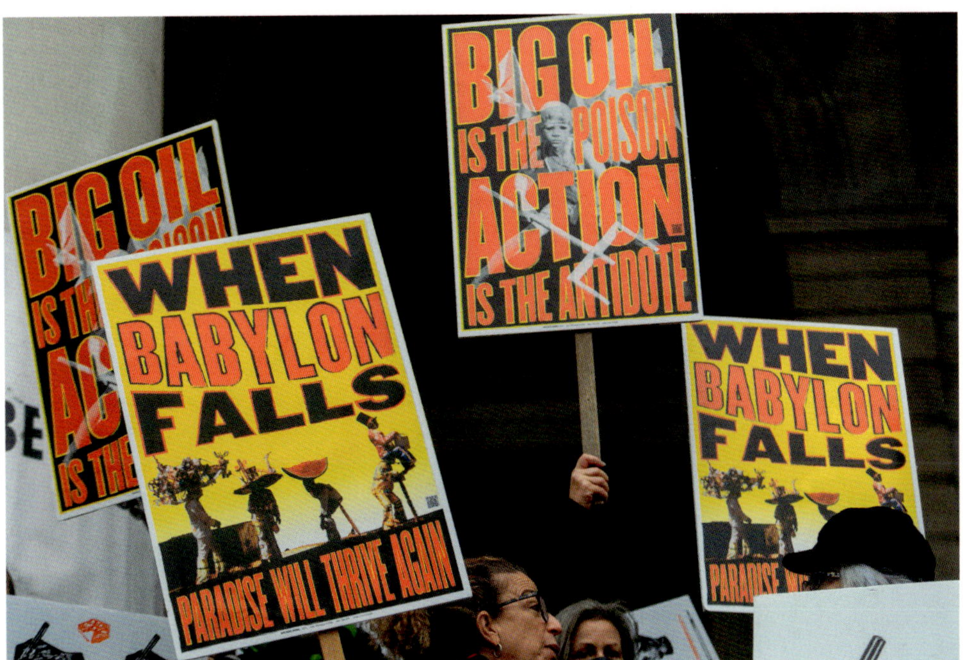

FIG. 8-11. Climate activists outside the Bank of England for a rally on Global Day of Action for Climate Justice, London. November 6, 2021. Credit: Stephen Chung / Alamy Live News.

contradictory forces of past history and present reality: Hillah as evidence of our current impoverished lives situated in close contrast to those antiquities which were once the glorious empire of Babylon. We know that the current archaeological site is but the tip of the iceberg, with much of its treasures still to be unearthed—a site for our hypothetical futures. That feeling could be matched or contradicted by Gertrude Bell's remark that through our experience of the East, "[We] have learnt to reckon with the unbroken continuity of its history. Conqueror follows upon the heels of conqueror, nations are overthrown and cities topple down into the dust, but the conditions of existence are unaltered and irresistibly they fashion the new age in the likeness of the old . . . . Past and present are woven so closely together, the habitual appreciation of the division of time slips insensibly away."[18]

—

We (I) use a drone and other technologies to produce our artworks, and that helps us to extrapolate and then develop a new textual and visual work for the project. For instance, during our visit to the Babylon site, a drone was used to film from above to give us a bird's-eye view of the site. When the drone was circumnavigating over the Babylon Borsippa towers and came closer to them, suddenly tens of doves which dwell inside the towers were disturbed and started to hover under the drone, giving me the title: *Dove – Drone Hovering above Babylon Borsippa Two Towers*. The image of the drone as a signifier of the present digital age with its multitasking use of surveillance, both military and civic, clashes in sharp contrast to that of the dove and its ancient symbol as a token of peace. I later hear of a new device called the Dove Drone, recently used for spying. In a similar way we might now understand the archival video from the Imperial War Museum as the colonialist's tool to claim ownership of ancient sites such as Babylon. For the video *Dove – Drone Hovering above Babylon Borsippa Two Towers*, we used a normal drone to conduct it, but we animated the Dove Drone in the video to deliver the concept of the clash between two symbols: Dove Drone as machinery of intelligence and natural doves seeking peace at the site (**FIGS. 8-12** and **8-13**).

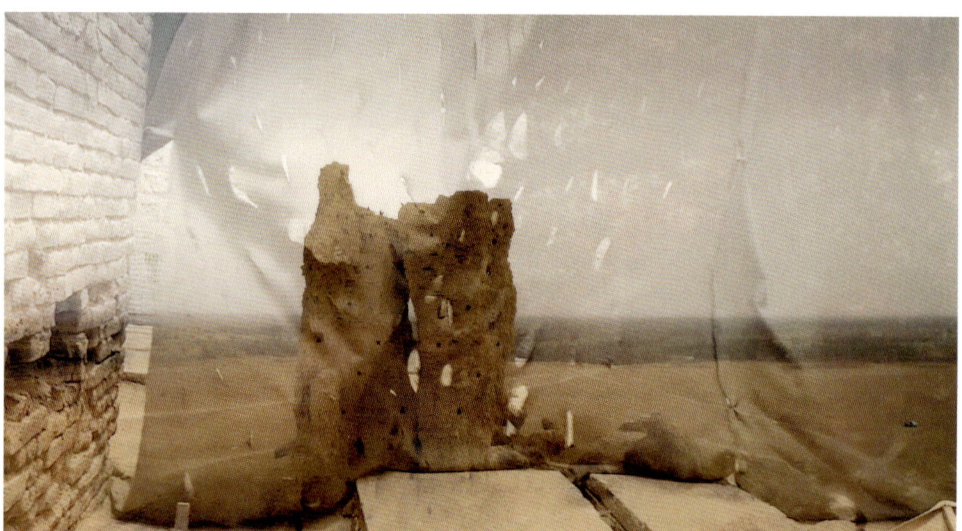

FIG. 8-12. Hanaa Malallah. *Dove – Drone Hovering over Babylon Borsippa Twin Towers*. Still from video. 2023. Checklist no. 19.

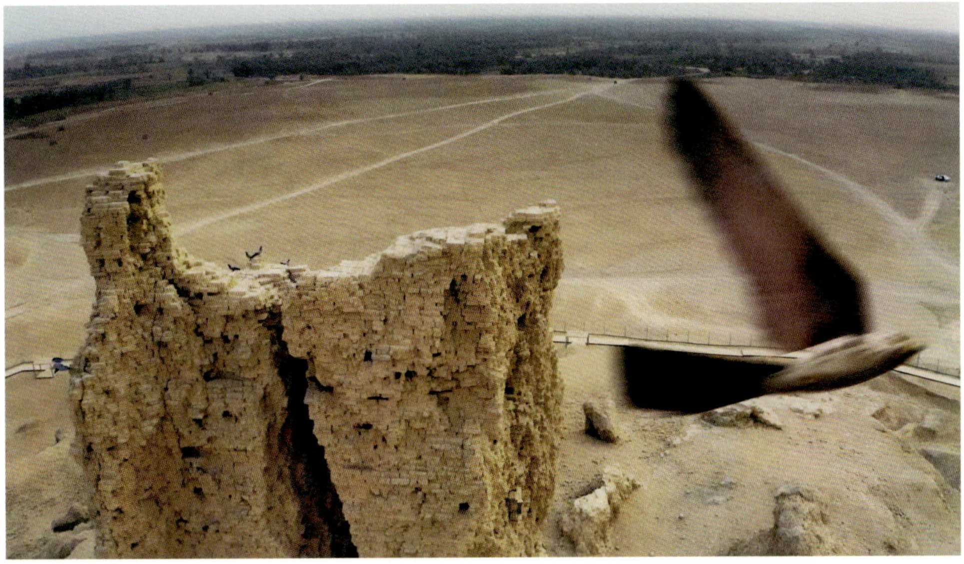

FIG. 8-13. Hanaa Malallah. *Dove – Drone Hovering over Babylon Borsippa Twin Towers.* Still from video. 2023. Checklist no. 19.

1 Simmel 1958.

2 Bryce 1995, 1.

3 George Simmel, The Ruin (1911), quoted in Dillon 2011, 23.

4 For more on space-time theories see Harvey and Tillman 2022.

5 See Wells 1895, 2.

6 Ingold 2013, 3.

7 See note 2.

8 Ingold 2013, 2.

9 See Bridle 2022, 56.

10 Ingold 2013, 2.

11 Hanaa Malallah quoted in Nysten 2020.

12 Jean Baudrillard, *The Anorexic Ruins* (1989), quoted in Dillon 2011, 67.

13 Dillon 2011, 11.

14 Nina Power, "Waiting for the Future," quoted in Dillon 2011, 218.

15 See note 1.

16 Feltham 1806, 301.

17 *Co-existent Ruins: Exploring Iraq's Mesopotamian Past through Contemporary Art*, SOAS, University of London, January 18–March 19, 2022; https://www.soas.ac.uk/about/event/co-existent-ruins-exploring-iraqs-mesopotamian-past-through-contemporary-art

18 Bell's *Amurath to Amurath*, quoted in Bernhardsson 2005, 26.

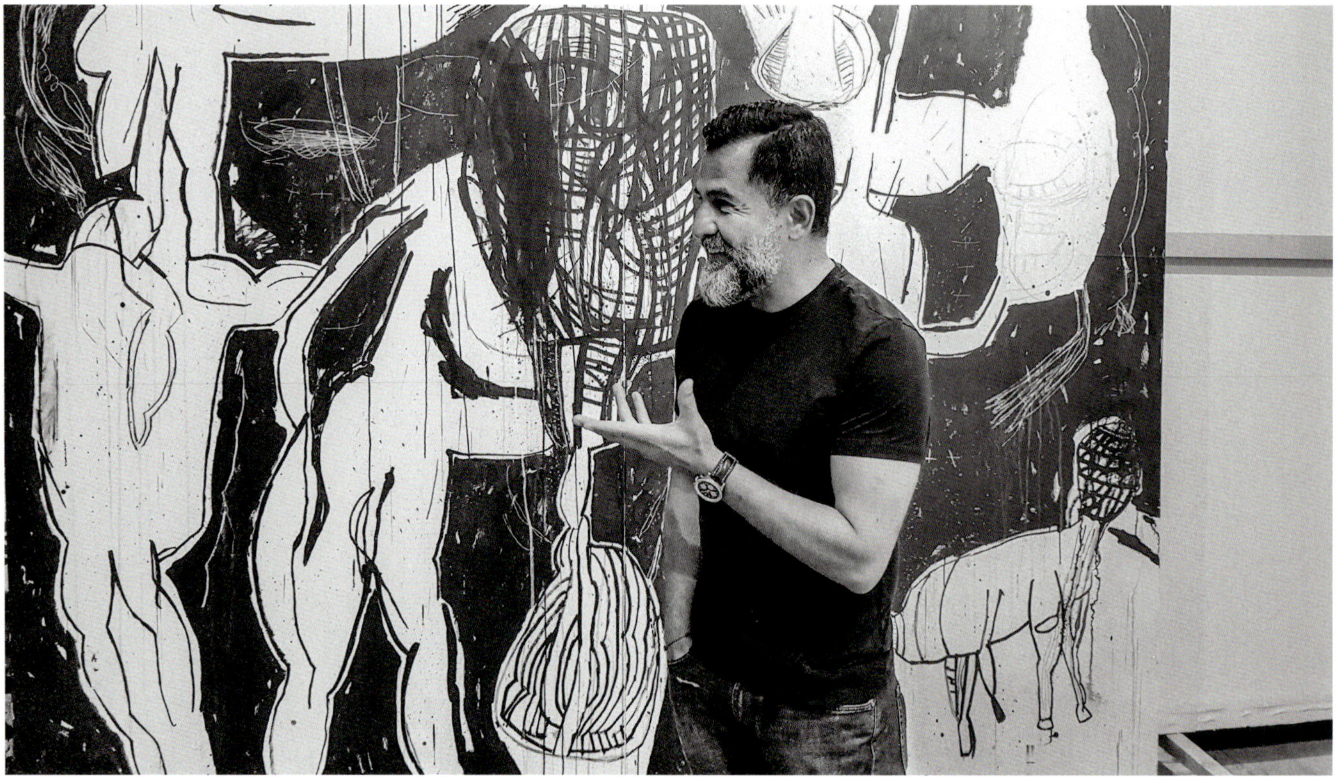

CHAPTER 9

DEFRAGMENT

Mahmoud Obaidi

At times I feel that I was marked for sorrow, for my earliest memories were of war; even now, after the dust has settled and the sky has cleared, it taints me. I cannot abandon the guilt, the fear, or the anger. I cannot abandon my former self so I carry him with me. I re-create the items stolen or destroyed after the invasion, so that he can hold them with both his hands. I cast them in bronze so that they are everlasting—he will not fear losing them. *Fragments* is not a virtue to the art scene, but a devotion to myself—it is a defense mechanism, a promise that not all that I had known has been erased.

The items re-created in *Fragments* range from valuable historical artifacts to mundane, seemingly trivial household items, for everything had been looted or destroyed in the midst of the chaos and war (**FIGS. 9-2** and **9-3**). It almost acts as a record of history, a report that states Iraq was once more than rubble—it is a homage to a six-thousand-year civilization, credited with some of the most important developments in human history. *Fragments* is a declaration of tenderness for both my country and my former self.

An extension of this project is *Compact Home*. During my early childhood, I developed the habit of living out of a suitcase, as my father had to travel regularly due to the nature of his work. Years later, after fleeing from Iraq, I picked up this habit once more, as I had no place to call home. I lived a lifestyle that could only be described as nomadic, as I moved from place to place—I was refused entry from most. The places that I stayed in had strict visa regulations, so I cycled between them (from Thailand to Jordan to Tunisia) as I waited to return to Iraq. During those few years, I lived out of two suitcases, I only kept possessions that were absolutely necessary, significant, or sentimental to me—I stripped my closet down to one shirt, one pair of pants, one pair of shoes, one winter jacket. Even books were not

FIG. 9-1. Mahmoud Obaidi in his studio, 2023.

exempt from this rule; I would rip out the pages and keep only the cover once I was finished reading them. In 2003, I began to buy things again—my possessions were no longer disposable. This was not because I finally thought I could come back to Iraq, but because I finally realized I couldn't. For years, I carried my things around with me, in anticipation of a return that was no longer possible. *Compact Home* is an art installation that recognizes this era of my life—it is a collection and archive of newspaper clippings, sketches, torn fabric, and other futile items I had gathered since leaving Iraq, compressed and portable.

I often find myself referring to an imagined conversation my dear friend Dia al-Azzawi wrote in 2016, inspired by our frequent conversations about returning home:

> He tells me between now and then: I want to go back! Yet, where to?
> To a space called homeland, to morning bread loaves near the Tigris.
> However, I forgot to tell him that closed spaces would never make a homeland.
> After all these years, haven't you been surprised by this fib between now and then?
> He asked me: Listen to the sound of destruction and to what is there in the pants of the thieves. Yet, this time, I'll migrate to a land that guarantees sleep to me, that erases the memories of the siege.
> And for the homeland, I will hold a great funeral.
> I forgot to tell him, however: Why are you in a hurry? Not a single cloud has not been overwhelmed by the blueness of the sky.

Every so often, I catch myself fantasizing about home, plotting a return to the Baghdad I once knew. To my bedroom, where knickknacks gathered dust on the shelves and the window stayed open on cool summer days. The world then was

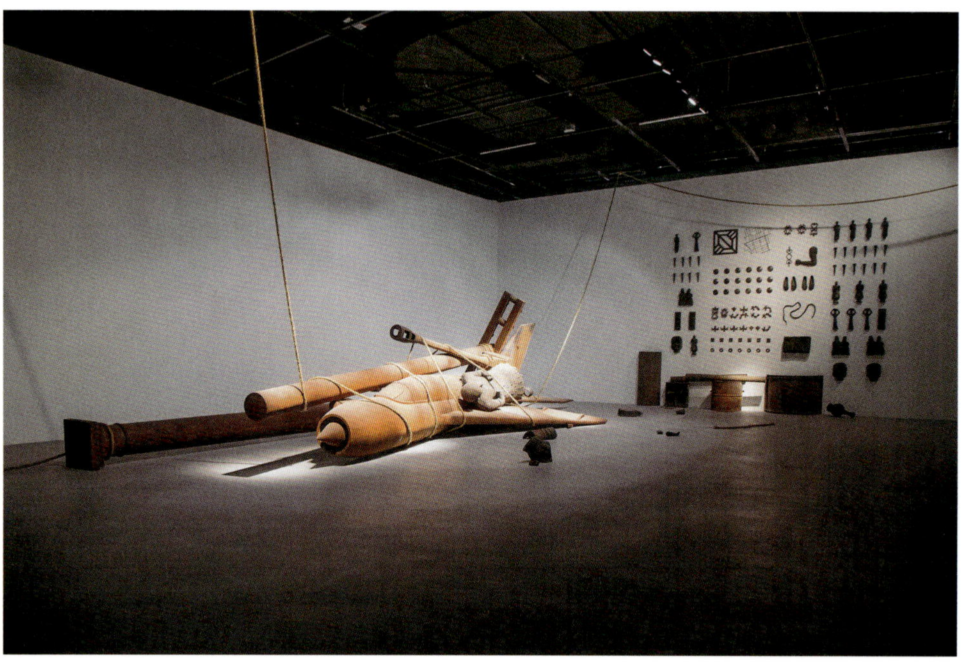

FIG. 9-2. Installation view of Mahmoud Obaidi's *Fragments* at Qatar Museums Gallery – Katara, 2016. Checklist no. 64.

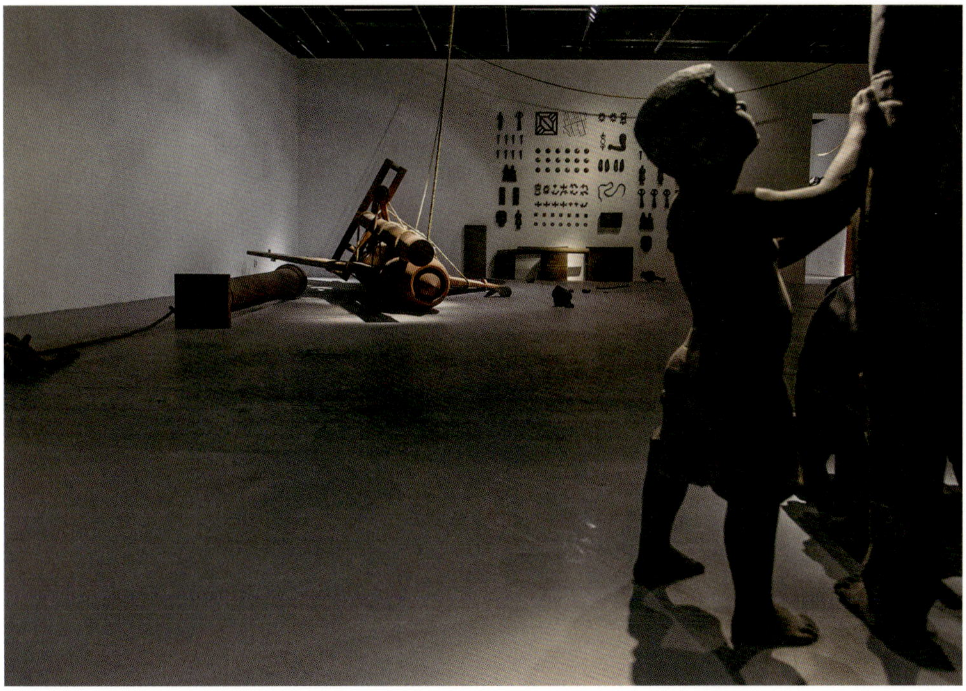

FIG. 9-3. Installation view of Mahmoud Obaidi's *Fragments* at Qatar Museums Gallery – Katara, 2016. Checklist no. 64.

no larger than my books, my tapes, my novelty keychains, the posters on my wall. I play handball on the driveway with my friend Ali until the streetlights come on. I worry about fourth-period algebra class, the local football team, what I was going to have for dinner that night. When I was thirteen, a jet dropped a bomb on Ali's house. Ali always wore the same red flannel shirt, and when I went over to check on him, this shirt was all that was left of him. The world did not seem so small now. That marked the day the Baghdad I had known began to rot, to decay from the inside, until it had become a husk of its previous self—entirely unrecognizable. Still, I would entertain these fantasies of home and allow myself to indulge; perhaps it was for my own sanity.

In 2017, I finally embraced the truth that there is, in reality, no place called home, no place in which I could permanently reside, no place that I could honestly and sincerely call mine. *Compact Home* had, at that point, become more than just a project, but was instead my own personal philosophy. I cannot find home, because home is not a physical space, it is not four walls; home is a familiar song, a candle that smells like your grandmother's perfume, a television that plays your favorite film through a stranger's window. Home can be found within the pages of a book, in the murmurs of a crowd—home is everywhere, if you look for it.

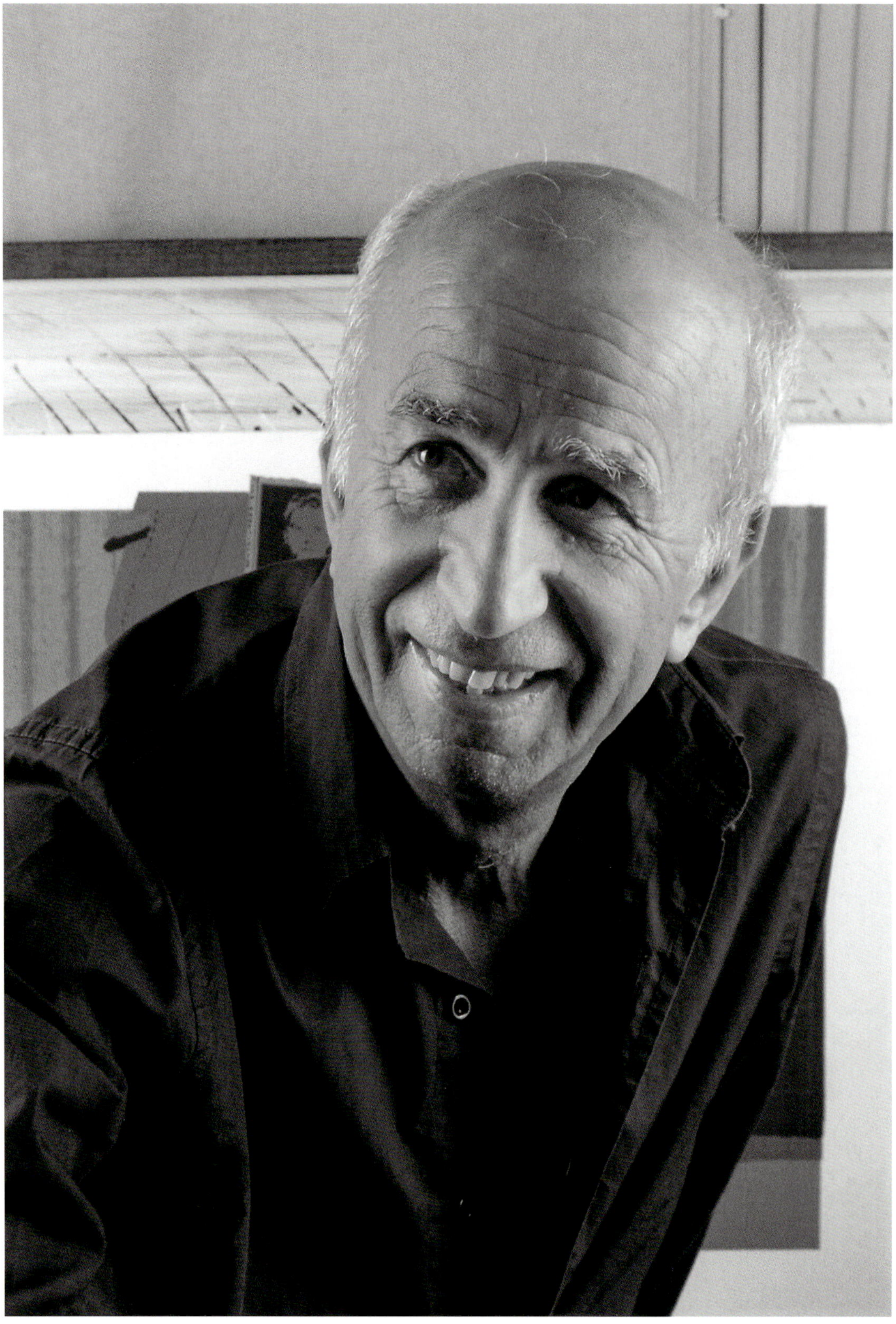

CHAPTER 10

BRITTLE BUILDS: THE HORIZONTALIZING ICONOGRAPHY OF VERTICALITY

Nat Muller

Walid Siti (b. 1954, Duhok, Iraqi Kurdistan) has been fascinated by towers for many years. On bus rides back home to Duhok in the early 1970s, when he was a young student at the Institute of Fine Arts in Baghdad, he would see the majestic spiraling mud-brick minaret, the *malwiya*, of Samarra's Great Mosque (**FRONT COVER, FIG. 10-2**). Built in the ninth century CE during the reign of the Abbasid Caliph Al-Mutawakkil, scholarship suggests the *malwiya*'s unique conic design echoes the ziggurats of Mesopotamia, anchoring its form in a very specific geo-cultural context and infusing it with Babylonian architectural influences.[1] Once the largest mosque of the Islamic world, the Great Mosque marked the move of the Abbasid empire's seat of power from Baghdad to the city of Samarra, a newly created capital designed to enhance the prestige of the Abbasid dynasty by ostentatiously displaying luxurious grandeur, military prowess, and religious authority.[2] Largely destroyed in 1278 CE by invading Mongol forces, little remains of the mosque complex except for the minaret and its boundary walls.[3] Today, its enduring towering presence on the east bank of the Tigris River persists, but stands strangely in a landscape of ever expanding urban sprawl and traffic. Nevertheless, the *malwiya* (**FIG. 10-3**) continues to bear witness to cycles of turbulent history, be they of a long-gone past or more recent upheavals. During the US invasion of Iraq in 2003, the *malwiya* served as an American military base, and in 2005 a terrorist attack destroyed some of the architectural features of its summit.[4] At the center of Walid Siti's varied oeuvre lies a practice of making visible the entrenched entanglements of sovereignty, architectural form, landscape, violence, and historical narration. However, Siti does much more than tell us stories about the machinations of power; he renders power and the soaring architectural structures representing it porous. As such, he performs an egalitarian gesture that flattens the notion of

FIG. 10-1. Portrait of Walid Siti, 2019.

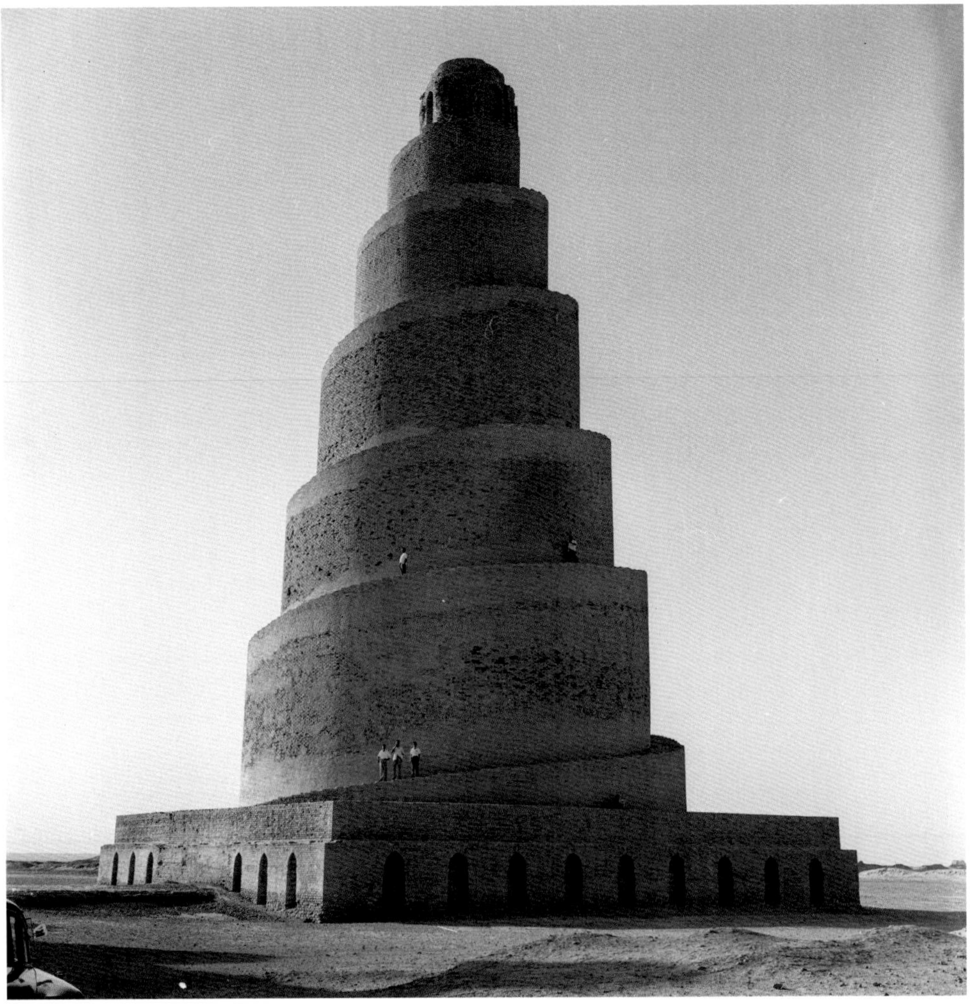

FIG. 10-2. Latif Al Ani. Samarra, the spiral minaret of the Great Mosque. Gelatin silver negative on cellulose acetate film. 1960. AIF: 0190an00115. Checklist no. 79.

hierarchy and exclusion, so often associated with verticality. The verticality that marks Siti's work is humble and inclusive. His builds are made with cheap and throwaway materials such as cardboard, twigs, straw, and plywood. His use of materials reflects the intent to address social and historical inequity and points to the precarity of hard-won freedoms.

Siti knows a thing or two about loss of freedoms. Growing up in a Kurdish and politically active leftist family, he experienced firsthand how the liberties of minorities and those opposing the Ba'ath party were squelched under Saddam Hussein. In the 1970s, when Siti was studying in Baghdad (FIG. 10-4), Iraq turned rapidly more totalitarian and opportunities for those who did not explicitly support the Ba'ath regime were scant. Enrollment in a postgraduate degree program at the prestigious Academy of Fine Arts was an impossibility for those who were not party members.[5] Left with few options other than leaving the country, Siti embarked on undergraduate and postgraduate degrees at Ljubljana's Academy of Fine Arts in the former Yugoslavia. Unfortunately for Siti and his fellow Iraqi students, ties between Yugoslavia and the Ba'ath regime were warm and it was unsafe for him to return back home. In 1984 he received political asylum in London, where he resides to this day.[6] The shape of the *malwiya*, as a signifier of a home

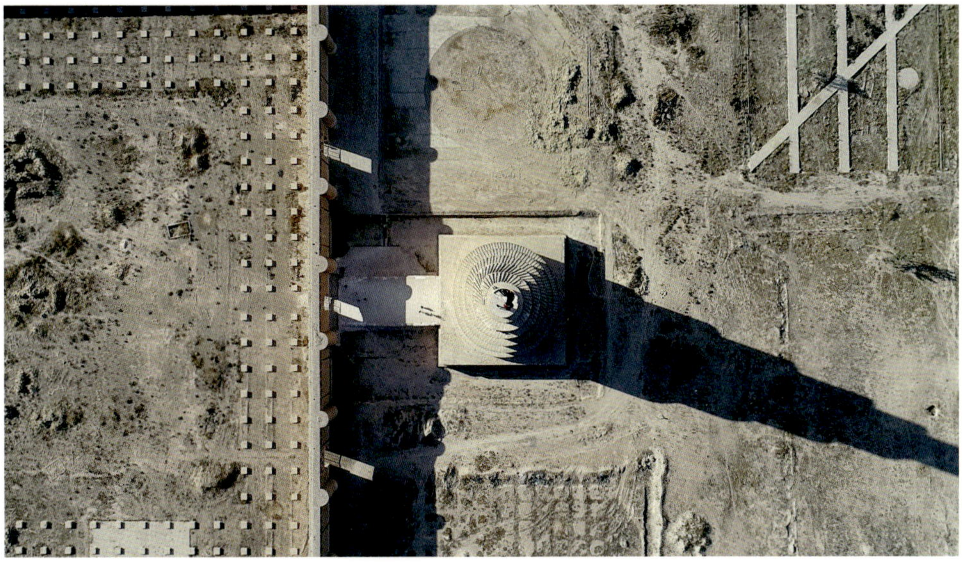

FIG. 10-3. Walid Siti, Still from *To the Unknown Architect*. Video (sound). 2022. Checklist no. 76.

lost, would continue to haunt him and his work. He was only able to climb the stairs of the *malwiya* in Samarra for the first time in 2019 (**FIG. 10-5**); an experience he describes as "overwhelming, mind-blowing and beautiful."[7] The footage he shot during that visit became the backbone of Siti's second video work to date, *To the Unknown Architect* (2022), in which he poignantly underlines the tension between ascending and descending movement. Here, that tension becomes much more than simply climbing up and down the stairs of the *malwiya*. It becomes a comment on social mobility and how very precarious it is for marginalized groups to dream of possibility. The video is framed by an opening sequence that takes us by car from Baghdad to Samarra, akin to the journey the young Siti would have taken returning home during term break. Filmed through the car window with a shaky handheld camera, the video takes us past Jewad Selim's (1919–1961) mural *Freedom Monument (*1961), one of central Baghdad's most iconic monuments and landmarks celebrating the overthrow of the monarchy and the creation of the Iraqi Republic in 1958. Here Siti provides a conscious visual reference to Selim, a prominent modernist artist and founder of the visionary Baghdad Modern Art Group. The latter was pivotal in the 1950s and advocated—in the spirit of a newly minted national consciousness—the concept of *istilham al-turath* (seeking inspiration in tradition), which called for a distinct Arab aesthetic that would honor heritage and tradition but also be modern.[8] While Siti shares with Selim an interest in heritage and ancient historical landscape, his art moves, as scholar Zainab

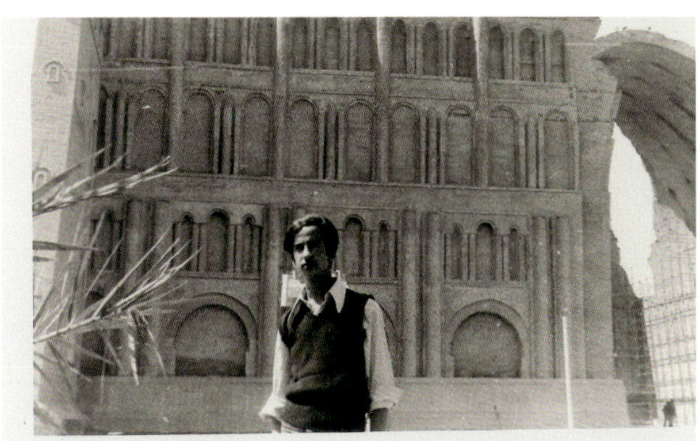

FIG. 10-4. Walid Siti at Ctesiphon, the ruins of the Tāq Kasrā (Arch of Ctesiphon), 1971.

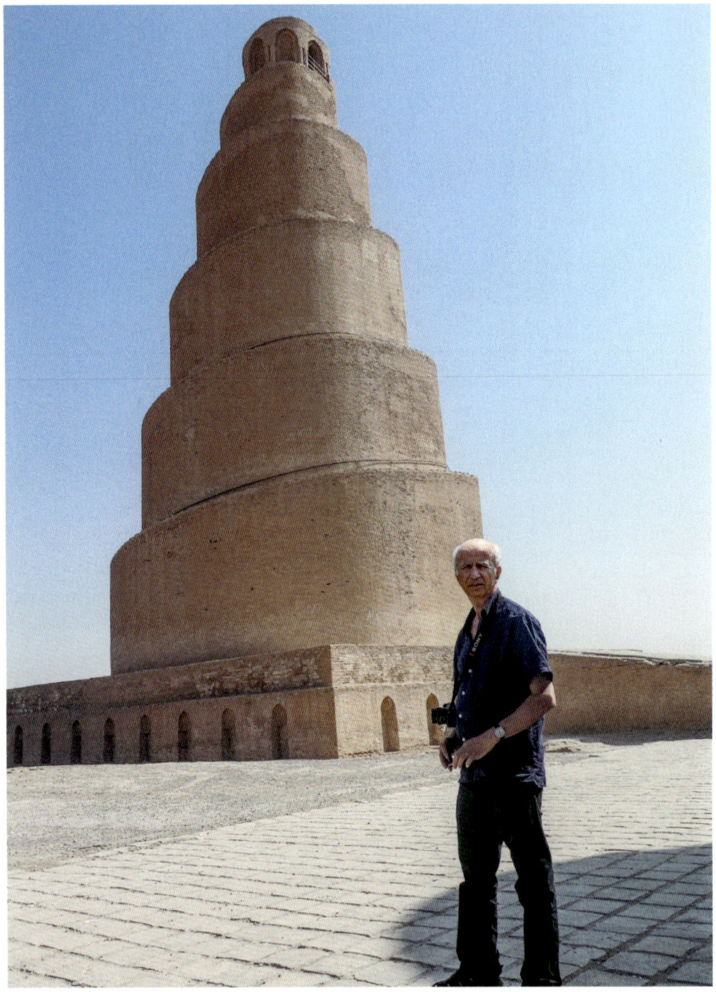

FIG. 10-5. Walid Siti visiting Samarra, October 2019.

Bahrani observes, "into another direction, and reflects another historical experience of place that came afterwards . . . What we see is a complexity of identity in his work, and an art that also often brings to mind the troubled experience of exile and displacement, despite a strong link to the land."[9]

To the Unknown Architect is propelled, as is most of Siti's oeuvre, by a quality of fragility. This is cleverly underlined by the video's voice-over during a trip from Baghdad to Samarra, which recounts an Mesopotamian folk tale that serves as a memento mori (**FIG. 10-6**). In this well-known story, a merchant's servant attempts to trick Death in Baghdad by fleeing to Samarra, but ends up meeting Death in Samarra anyhow, hence not escaping his fate. War, brutality, and conflict have sadly dominated much of Iraq's recent history, in particular since 1968 with the coming to power of the Ba'ath party and the dictatorship of Saddam Hussein, and the political instability following the US invasion in 2003. Siti poetically conceptualizes the notion of demise and extends it to the land and its natural and built environment. Whether we encounter mountains, ziggurats, or towers, Siti renders their soaring monumentality into something brittle but delicately beautiful. A rotating miniature model of the *malwiya*, dexterously fashioned out of twigs, dances across the screen, collapsing in and out of form. In the video, this sense of ephemerality is further enhanced by ever-changing points of view. The camera

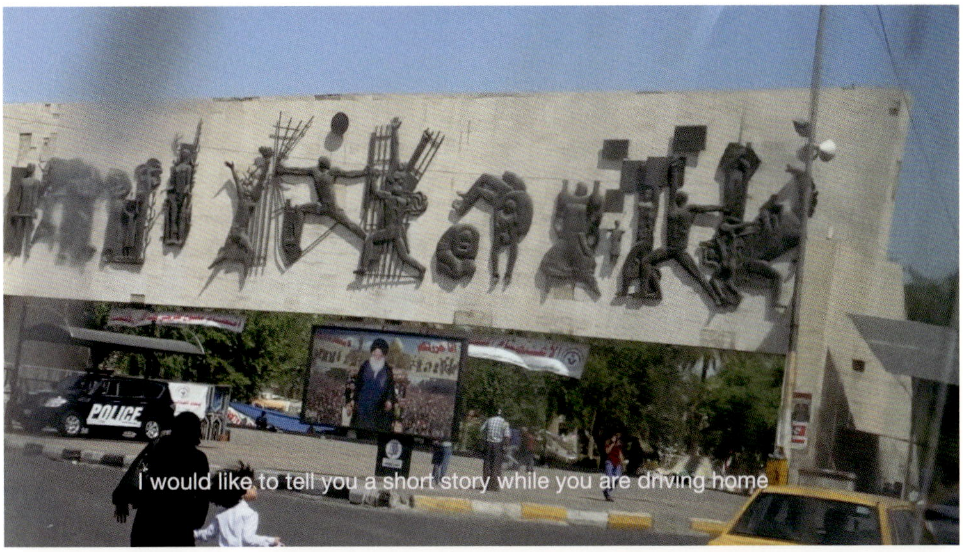

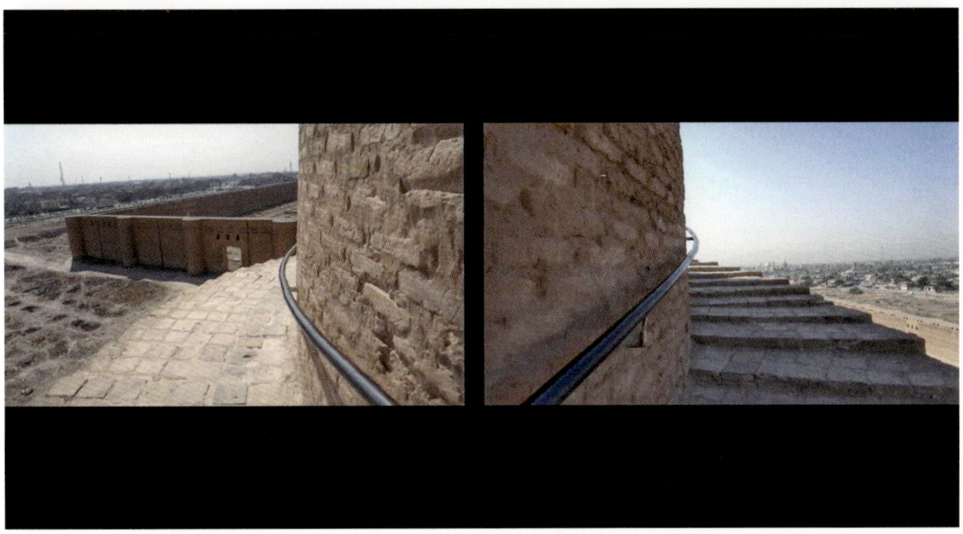

TOP: FIG. 10-6. Walid Siti. Still from *To the Unknown Architect*. Video (sound). 2022. Checklist no. 76. **BOTTOM: FIG. 10-7.** Walid Siti. Still from *To the Unknown Architect*. Video (sound). 2022. Checklist no. 76.

pivots from sweeping aerial perspectives, shrinking the human scale, to shaky handheld camerawork that records the labored breathing of the artist while he climbs up and down the *malwiya*, bringing everything back to human scale. The camerawork replicates the twisting and turning of the building. Nothing in this video is ever static. Siti intersperses the images with intertitles that provide historical context. What follows is a spectral image of the Great Mosque complex, on which his cursor obsessively draws repetitive ziggurat shapes across the screen: ascending and descending staircases that result in a landscape of zigzagging towers that provide a lens on how to read history, landscape, and identity as always jagged and messy (**FIG. 10-7**).

This approach is saliently articulated in Siti's works on paper: distinct sketches on brown packing paper mainly intended as studies for future projects. Jotted down in a frenzy with black marker, quick strokes of dripping acrylic paint, or smudged swipes of crayon, the spiring shapes exude a dynamic energy (**FIG. 10-8**).

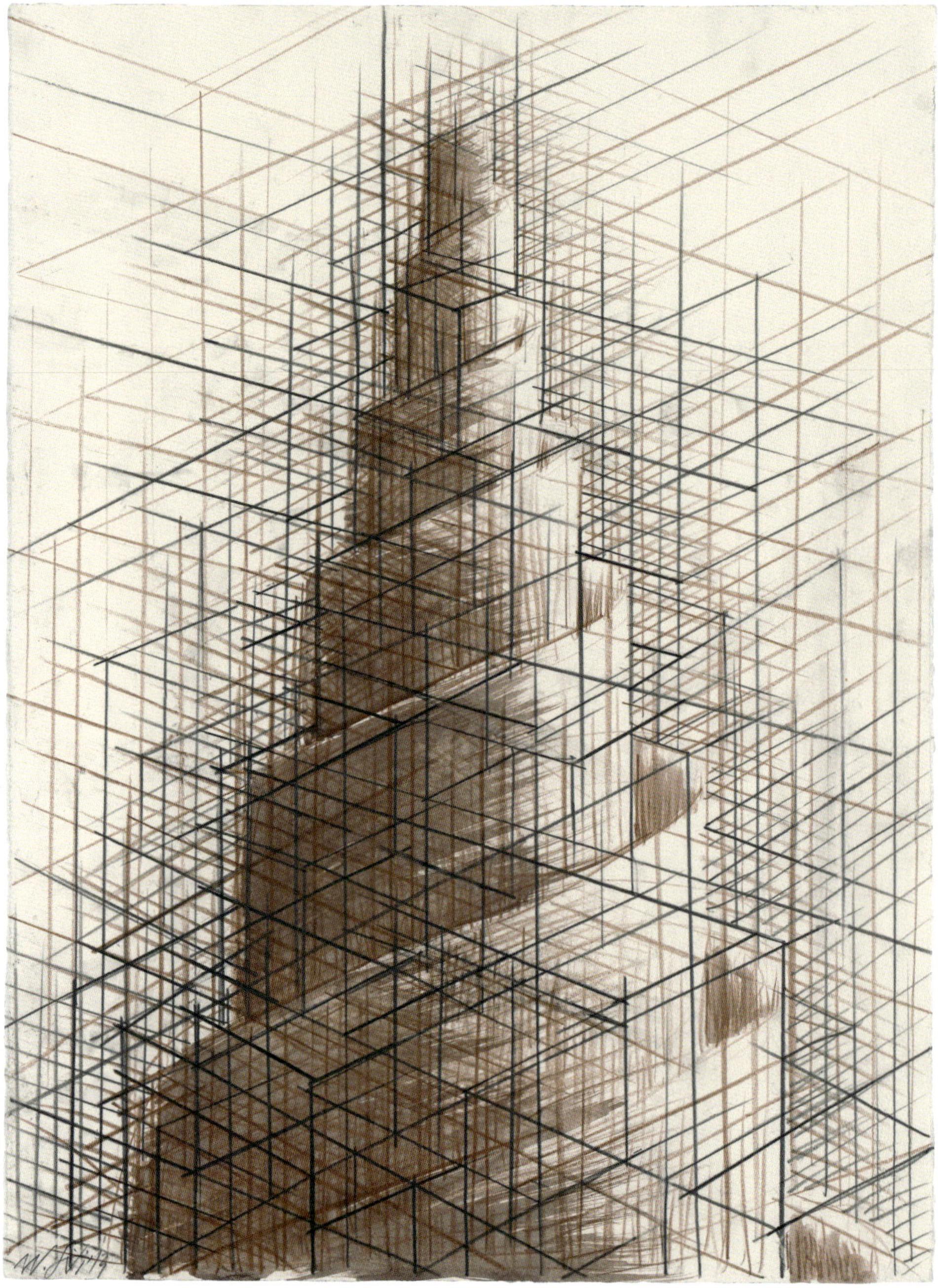

FIG. 10-8. Walid Siti. *The Seven Towers, I Series*. Graphite, colored crayon, and acrylic wash on paper. 2013. MMA: 2014.429. Gift of Ipeknur and Shwan Ibrahim Taha, 2014. Checklist no. 77.

The viewer can actually sense the artist working through a particular idea. I have written elsewhere that these drawings divulge the architectural grammar of Siti's visual language, and in them we can always discern a specific form: a square, a rectangle, an oval, a cone, an arch, or simply a line.[10] Nevertheless, these building blocks remain characteristically fragile. In the work on view in this exhibition, *Tower Series* (2020), the curvature of the winding tower is produced by black vertical lines meeting white horizontal lines (**FIG. 10-9**). The black lines seem sharp as daggers, while the white lines bleed paint across the page. This charged encounter—in this case between two different types of lines and between acrylic and crayon—lies

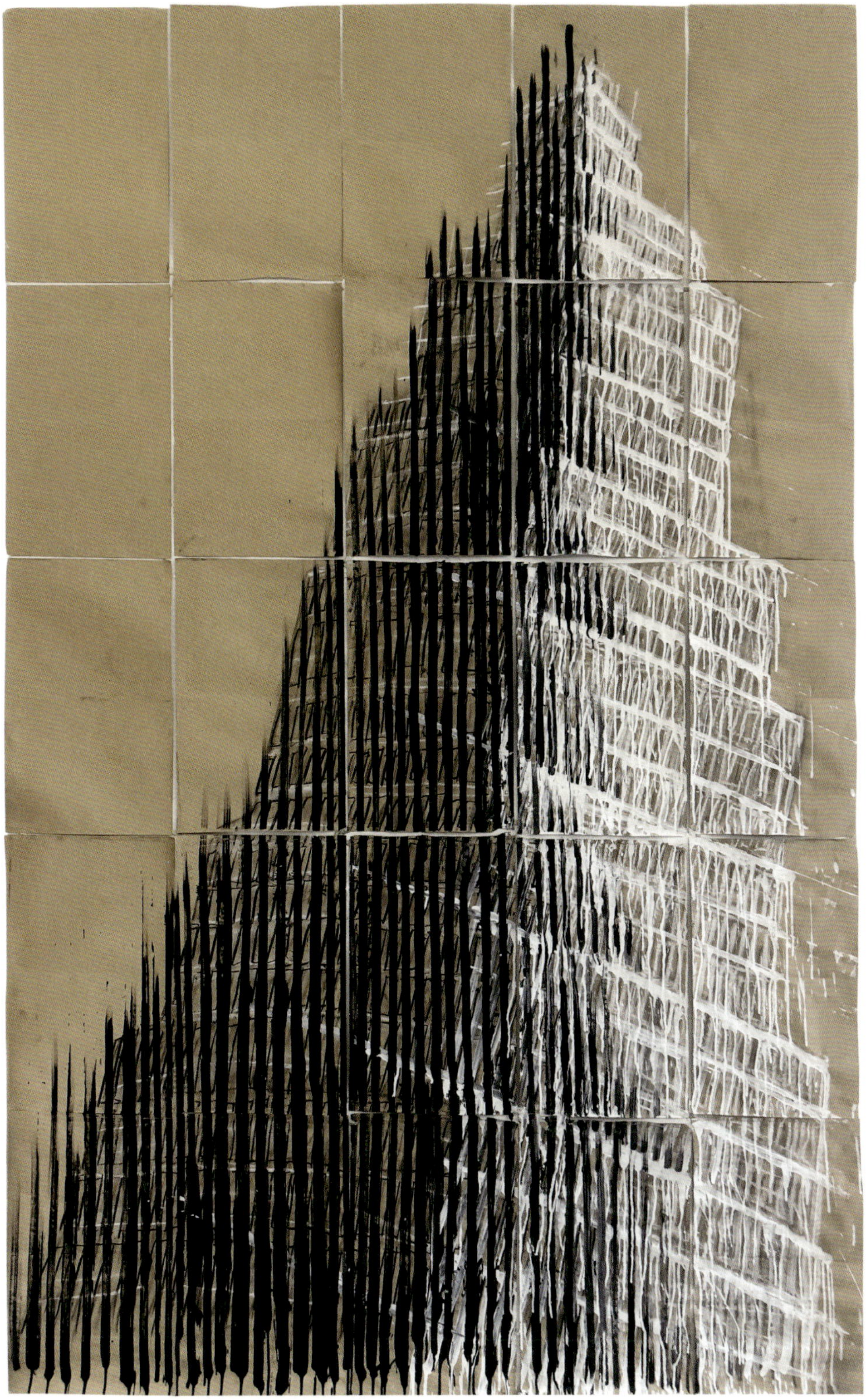

FIG. 10-9. Walid Siti. *Tower Series*. Acrylic and crayon on paper. 2020. Checklist no. 75.

at the base of much of Siti's practice. By complicating ways of seeing, the artist shows how aspirational possibility can turn into violent destruction. The two seem inextricably intertwined throughout his oeuvre, but this is not to say that his works

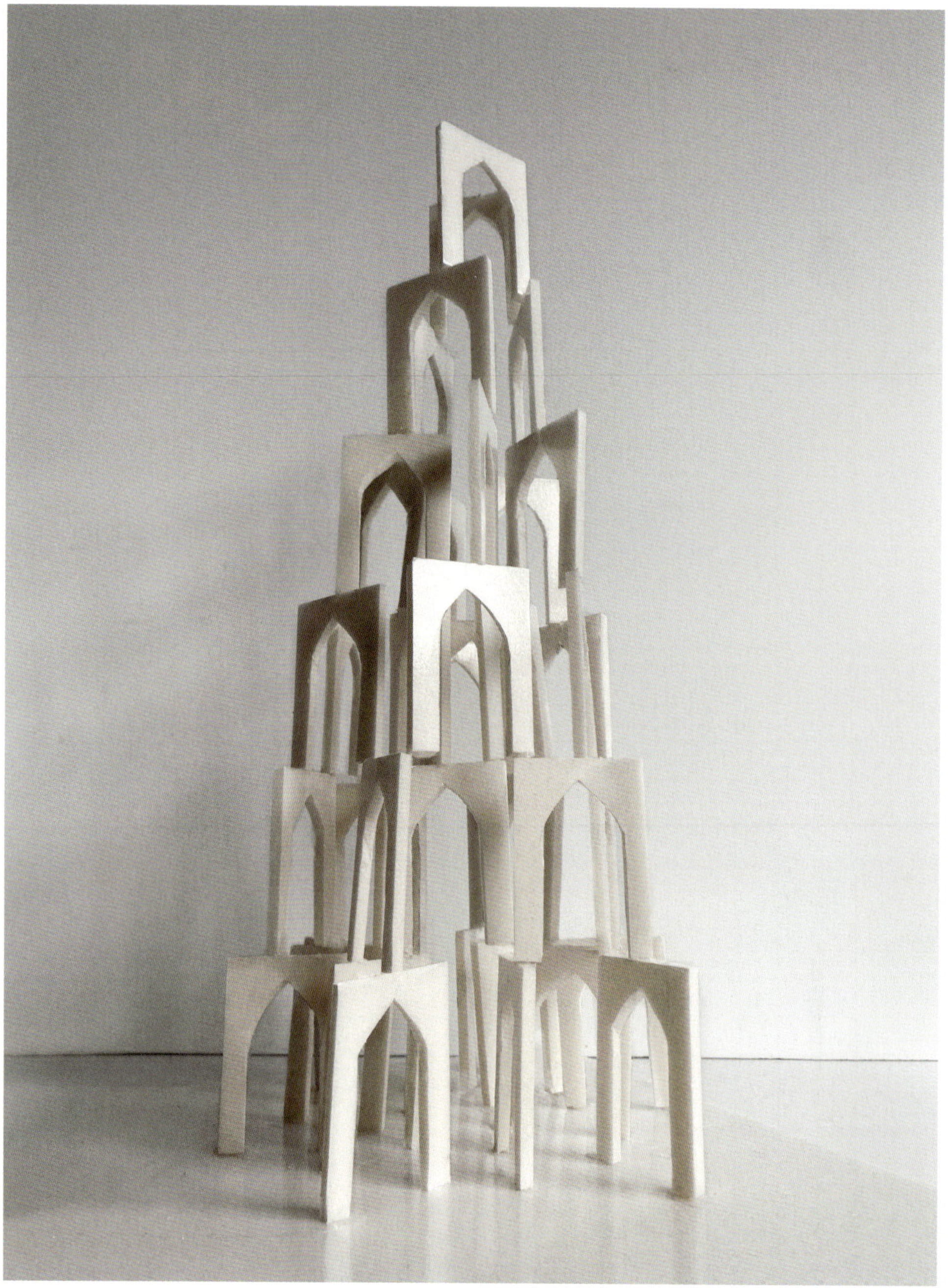

FIG. 10-10. Walid Siti. Maquette of *Arched Tower*. Insulation board and plaster of paris. 2023. Checklist no. 1.

are devoid of hope. On the contrary, his practice is truly an art of scaffolding in which loss—signified by negative space—also becomes a foundational constituent. Siti's voids are therefore always meaningful: they trouble our perception of time and space. A rupture might be looming, but so might potential. This sense of breakability is further enhanced in *Tower Series* by the drawing being cut up into twenty-five rectangles and then reassembled like a frail puzzle. The dividing lines between the fragments stay faintly visible, which suggests the object will never be quite whole again. The towers Siti shows us are still magnificent but perhaps a little less mighty.

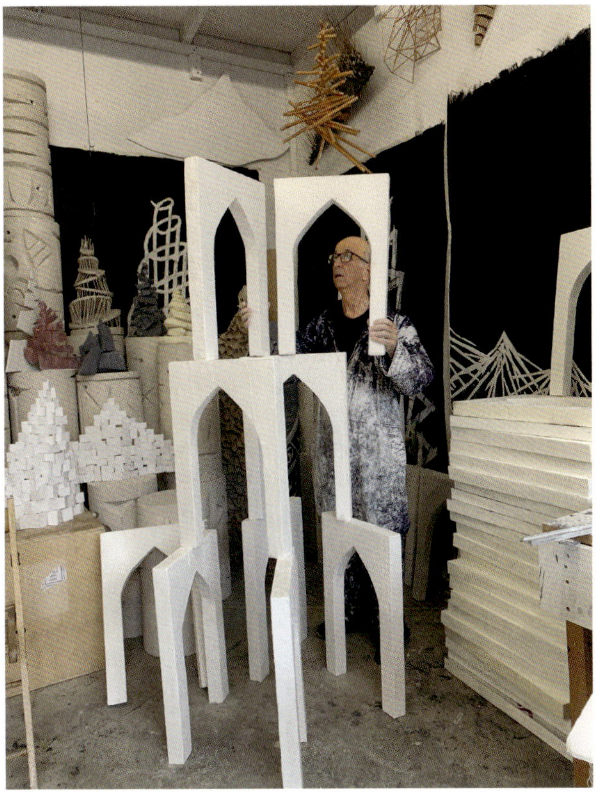

FIG. 10-11. Walid Siti working on the *Arched Tower* in his studio. London, 2023.

This is also true for the newly commissioned large-scale installation *Arched Tower* (2023). Here the *malwiya* is fashioned out of forty-one pointed arches made from insulation board and plaster (**FIGS. 10-10** and **10-11**). Stacked one on top of another, not only are they the building blocks of the towered structure, they also open multiple gateways into it. The viewer can peer through, and engage with, the installation from many different angles. Here, too, the artist's subtle repetition of form proffers an ever-changing perspective. Though large in scale, this particular work—like many of Siti's more site-specific sculptures—meets us at eye level and allows for a horizontal interaction. Our gaze is not only trained upward, but the pervious quality of the work blends with its surroundings and therefore forces us to become more conscious of the latter. Indeed, these towers, so firmly rooted in the landscape of Siti's home country, feel slightly out of place in an exhibition context—as if Siti's own involuntary exile were extended to the objects he crafts and is then shared with the viewer. The tower coils like a slow vortex, gently drawing the viewer in. Ultimately the work demonstrates how the force of verticality comes undone as a hubristic pillar of power and gradually transforms into an exercise in humility, openness, and transience. The absolute verticality of the tower is broken by a horizon of possibility, with the caveat that change often seems to come with costs: disquiet, violence, and defeat. Siti does not shy away from these aspects but poetically instills them in his work.

Many of Siti's projects can be read as an homage to those who are forgotten and written out of history, such as the architects, craftspeople, and laborers who built the marvels of Islamic architecture but are never named, as expressed in the title of his video *To the Unknown Architect*. Across his oeuvre, and originating in his own lived experience, he foregrounds disenfranchised minorities and other groups who have been silenced. Siti's work makes these absences implicitly present by focusing on the interstitial and drawing out what is "there and not there."[11] Here the word *implicitly* is of importance. Siti's work is never didactic. Rather, as in the installation *Arched Tower* and the *Tower Series* drawing, he presents us with a form that is skeletal, stripped to its bare bones. Simultaneously playing with the material and the immaterial, his work places the onus on the viewer to contemplate and commemorate the omissions of the past and those which, undoubtedly, will come in the future.

1 Al-Qahtany 2009, 450–53.

2 El-Hibri 2021, 132–35.

3 Ahmad and Aslam 2020, 296.

4 Alfarra 2020.

5 Tripp 2007, 186–276.

6 For an extensive biographical essay of Siti, see Porter 2020, 20–25.

7 Interview with the artist, June 6, 2023.

8 Shabout 2007, 27–29.

9 Bahrani 2020, 75.

10 Muller 2017, 10.

11 Bahrani 2020, 77.

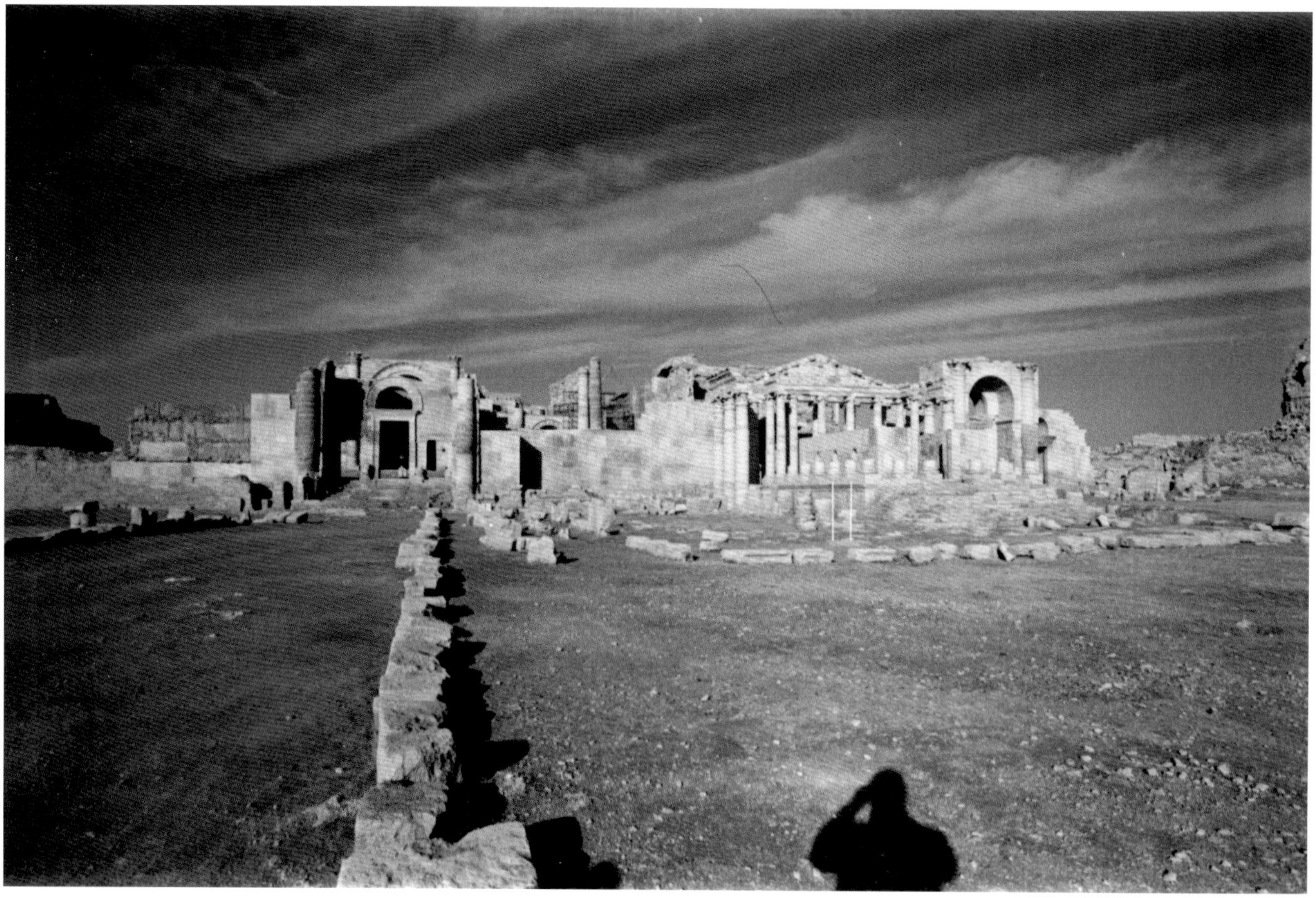

Latif Al Ani. Hatra, the Great Iwans. Gelatin silver negative on cellulose acetate film. Ca. 1960.
AIF: 0190an01786. Checklist no. 68.

BIBLIOGRAPY

Unless otherwise noted, all websites were active at the time of publication.

Abd al-Latif 2012
Abd al-Latif, S. *Limadha tajahal alealami aluathari aleiraqiu alkabir hurmz rasaaman?* لماذا تجاهل العالم.. الآثاري العراقي الكبير هرمز رسام (Why did the World Ignore the Great Iraqi Archaeologist Hormuz Rassam?). December 15, 2012. https://www.ahewar.org/debat/show.art.asp?aid=336707

***Ahl al-Naft* 1951a**
"The Venture/Adventure." *Ahl al-Naft*, no. 1 (August 1951): 3.

***Ahl al-Naft* 1951b**
"Noah's Ark." *Ahl al-Naft*, no. 5 (December 1951): 13–14.

***Ahl al-Naft* 1955**
"Baghdad in 1960." *Ahl al Naft*, no. 50 (September 1955): 12–13.

***Ahl al-Naft* 1956**
"Cement: Iraq's New Builder." *Ahl al-Naft*, no. 59 (June 1956): 42–43.

***Ahl al-Naft* 1957**
"Roads and Bridges." *Ahl al-Naft*, no. 68 (May/June 1957): 16–20.

***Ahl al-Naft* 1959**
"The Science of Archaeology and Irrigation in Iraq."*Ahl al-Naft*, no. 81 (March 1959): 19–21.

Ahmad and Aslam 2002
Ahmad, Zahid Tauqeer, and Seemin Aslam. "Comparative Study of Architecture of the Great Mosque at Samarra, Iraq and Ibn Tulun Mosque at Cairo, Egypt." *Journal of Islamic Thought and Civilization* 10, no. 2 (2020). https://doi.org/10.32350/jitc.102.16.

Al-Quraishi and Al-Ajmi 2021
Al-Quraishi, Youussef Ibrahim, and Khairallah Mohammed Al-Ajmi. *Aihtimam biritania bathar aleiraqiati: Almasi bil ain-mudhaja* اهتمام بريطانيا بآثار العراقية: المس بيل انموذجا;ة:اهتمام بريطانيا بآثار العراقية: المس بيل انموذجا (Britain's interest in Iraqi antiquities: Miss Bell as a model). *Journal of Education College Wasit University*, no. 13 (2021): 62–76.

***Al Amiloon Fil Naft* 1969**
Al Amiloon Fil Naft 9, no. 89 (November 1969): 1.

Alfarra 2020
Alfarra, Jehan. "Discover the Malwiya Minaret of Samarra, Iraq." *Middle East Monitor*, October 3, 2020. MiddleEastMonitor.com.

Al-Humaidhi 2020
Al-Humaidhi, Ghassan Salih. *Tarikh altanqib fi madinat ashur(qaleat alsharqati) wabruz natayijah* تاريخ التنقيب في مدينة اشور(قلعة شرقاط) وابرز نتائجه ، (History of the Excavations in the City of Ashur [Sharqat Citadel] and its Most Prominent Results). *Sirr Man Ra'a Journal* (Samarra University) 16, no. 62 (2020): 783–819.

Al-Majdhub 1951
Al-Majdhub, Ahmad Saadi. "Ibn Battuta . . . Did He Know Oil?" *Ahl al-Naft*, no. 5 (December 1951).

Al-Nakib 2013
Al-Nakib, Farah. "Kuwait's Modern Spectacle: Oil Wealth and the Making of a New Capital City, 1950–90." *Comparative Studies of South Asia, Africa and the Middle East* 33, no. 1 (2013): 1–25.

Al-Nassery 2019
Al-Nassery, S. *Hurmz rssam walttnqybat al'athri* هـرمـز رسّـام والـتّـنـقـيـبـات الأثـريـة (Hormuz Rassam and Archaeological Excavations). October 10 (2019). https://sabahalnassery.wordpress.com/2019/10/.

Al-Qahtany 2009
Al-Qahtany, Hani Mohammed. "Islamic Architecture as a Reflection of Functionalism and Interactionism: Conceptual Origins in Culture and Sociology." *Contemporary Arab Affairs* 2, no. 3 (2009): 450–53.

Al-Sabbagh 2012
Al-Sabbagh, Mahmoud. "Alem al athar aleslami: bedayat u Tabaat" محمود الصباغ، علم الآثار الإسلامي: البدايات والتبعات، الحوار المتمدن-العدد (Islamic Archaeology: Beginnings and Consequences). *Hewar Motamaden*, no. 7353 (Aug 27, 2022). https://www.ahewar.org/debat/show.art.asp?aid=633241.

Al-Saadi n.d.
Al-Saadi, Kathem Nasser. *Al-Mada* (Baghdad), n.d. https://almadapaper.net/sub/06-424/p11.htm.

Al-Shammari 2015
Al-Shammari, Hamid. *Sariqat hadarat altiyn walhajri, kitab ahmir ghayr rasmiin*سرقة حضارة

الطين والحجر، كتاب احمر غير رسمي (Theft of the Civilization of Mud and Stone: An Unofficial Red Book). Baghdad: Dar Adnan, 2015.

Al-Suff 2009
Al-Suff, Behnam Abu. *Altaarikh min batin al'arda, athar wahadarat aiemaal maydania* االتاريخ من باطن الأرض، اثار وحضارات واعمال ميدانية (History from the Ground: Archaeology, Civilization, and Field work). Amman: Al-Adeeb, 2009.

Al-Tameemi 2020
Al-Tameemi, Rasha. "Urban Planning in the Middle East: Analyzing Al-Tahrir Square as a Public-Political Space in Iraq," *Design Discourse on Culture and Society: Re:Research* 5 (2019): 138–70.

Azara 2012
Azara, Pedro. *Antes del diluvio: Mesopotamia, 3500–2100 BC / Before the Flood: Mesopotamia, 3500–2100 BC*. Barcelona: Polígrafa, 2012.

Bahrani 2020
Bahrani, Zainab. "Walid Siti: Landscape, History and War." In Muller 2020, 75–79.

Bahrani, Çelik, and Eldem 2011
Bahrani, Zainab, Zeynep Çelik, and Edhem Eldem: *Scramble for the Past: A Story of Archaeology in the Ottoman Empire, 1753–1914*. Istanbul: Salt/Garanti Kültür A.S., 2011.

Baqer 2012
Baqer, T. *Almoqadam fi tarikh Alhathrat Alqadima*. 2nd ed. Baghdad: Dar Alrwaq, 2012.

Bernhardsson 2005
Bernhardsson, Magnus T. *Reclaiming a Plundered Past: Archaeology and Nation Building in Modern Iraq*. Austin: University of Texas Press, 2005.

Botta 1845
Botta, P.-É. *Lettres de M. Botta sur ses découvertes à Khorsabad près de Nineve, publiés par M. J. Mohl*. Paris: Imprimerie royal, 1845.

Bridle 2022
Bridle, James. *Ways of Being: Animals, Plants, Machines; The Search for a Planetary Intelligence*. [England]: Penguin Random House, 2022.

Bryce 1995
Bryce, Trevor. *Babylonia: A Very Short Introduction*. Oxford: Oxford University Press, 1995.

Chakravarti 1950
Chakravarti, N. P. "The Story of Indian Archaeology." In *Archaeology in India*. Delhi: Bureau of Education, 1950.

Chalabi 2017
Chalabi, Tamara. "Interview with Latif Al Ani." In Tamara Chalabi, Morad Montazami, and Shwan Ibrahim Taha, *Latif Al Ani*. Antwerp: Hannibal, 2017.

Chalabi and Van Cauteren 2015
Chalabi, Tamara, and Philippe Van Cauteren, eds. *Invisible Beauty*. Milan: Mousse, 2015.

Chesney 2002
Chesney, Francis Rawdon. *Report on the Euphrates Valley Railway*. London, 1857.

Chevalier 2002
Chevalier, Nicole. *La recherche archéologique française au moyen-orient, 1842–1947*. Paris: Editions recherche sur les civilisations, 2002.

Chevalier 2008
Chevalier, Nicole. "Les fouiller archéologique françaises au Xixe siècle." In *Catalogue Babylone*, 513–15. Paris: Musée du Louvre, 2008.

Damluji 2022
Damluji, Mona. "Latif al Ani: A Life Behind the Lens." In "Latif al Ani: Baghdad, 'A Modern Place.' Barcelona: La Virreina, Centre de la Imatge, 2022. ajuntament.barcelona.cat/lavirreina/sites/default/files/2022-04/PDM%20ENG.pdf.

Damrosch 2007
Damrosch, David. *The Buried Book: The Loss and Rediscovery of the Great Epic of Gilgamesh*. New York: Henry Holt, 2007.

Dillon 2011
Dillon, Brian, ed. *Ruins*. London: Whitechapel Gallery and MIT Press, 2011.

El-Hibri 2021
El-Hibri, Tayeb. *The Abbasid Caliphate: A History*. Cambridge: Cambridge University Press, 2021.

Fawzi 1951
Fawzi, Abd al-Sattar. "Adam: Because He

Knew Oil." *Ahl al-Naft*, no. 4 (November 1951): 4–5.

Feltham 1806
Feltham, John. *The Picture of London for 1806*. London: Roden and Lewis, 1806.

Forged Components Inc. 2023
"Distillation Columns Used in Crude Oil Refining." Forged Components Inc., 2023. https://forgedcomponents.com/distillation-columns-used-in-crude-oil-refining.

Fuccaro 2013
Fuccaro, Nelida. "Introduction: Histories of Oil and Urban Modernity in the Middle East." *Comparative Studies of South Asia, Africa and the Middle East* 33, no. 1 (2013): 1–6.

Fuccaro 2023
Fuccaro, Nelida. "The Oil Company's Fields of Vision: Public Relations and Labour Images in the Arab World." In *Life Worlds of Middle Eastern Oil: Histories and Ethnographies of Black Gold*, edited by Nelida Fuccaro and Mandana E. Limbert, 87–119. Edinburgh: Edinburgh University Press, 2023.

Fügert and Gries 2019
Fügert, Anja, and Helen Gries. "'The Men Who Wrought the Baked Brick, Those Were Babylonians': A Brief History of Molded and Glazed Bricks," in *A Wonder to Behold: Craftsmanship and the Creation of Babylon's Ishtar Gate*, edited by Anastasia Amrhein, Clare Fitzgerald, and Elizabeth Knott (New York: Institute for Study of the Ancient World, 2020), 41–54.

Kitan 2018
Kitan, Samira Shalaan. "Hakadha bada'at biritania bialbahth ean athar aleiraq mulahiq jaridat almadaa alyawmia" September 16. هكذا بدأت بريطانيا بالبحث عـن آثار العراق (How Britain Began Searching for the Antiquities of Iraq). https://www.almadasupplements.com/view.php?cat=20289.

Habab 2012
Habab, B. S. *Alasir almasihiat fi almawsil* الاسر المسيحية في الموصل (Christian Families in Mosul). Erbil.

Ibrahimi Collection, n.d.
Ibrahimi Collection, Amman. S.v., "Qutaiba al-Sheikh Nouri." http://www.ibrahimicollection.com/node/69.

Harvey and Tillman 2022
Harvey, Alisa, and Nola Taylor Tillman. "What Is Wormhole Theory?" *Space.com*, January 13, 2022. https://www.space.com/20881-wormholes.html.

Ingold 2013
Ingold, Tim. *Making: Anthropology, Archaeology, Art and Architecture*. London: Routledge, 2013.

Khalil 1991
Khalil, E. J. "Al'anshitat al'athariatu: altanqib ean alathar" الأنشطة الاثارية: التنقيب عن الاثار (Archaeological Activities: Excavations for Antiquities). *Mosul Civilization Encyclopedia* 1, (1991): 492–94.

Larsen 1996
Larsen, M. T. *The Conquest of Assyria: Excavations in an Antique Land, 1840–1860*. London: Routledge, 1996.

Layard 1849
Layard, Austen Henry. *Niniveh and Its Remains*. 2 vols. New York, 1849.

Marcus 1975
Marcus, Harold G. *The Life and Times of Menelik II: Ethiopia, 1844–1913*. Lawrenceville, NJ: Red Sea Press, 1975.

Margron 1986
Margron, J. C. *Alathar fi mizubutamya* الاثار في ميزوبوتاميا (Antiquities in Mesopotamia). Translated by Yosif Habi. Baghdad.

Meskell 2002
Meskell, Lynn. "The Intersections of Identity and Politics in Archaeology." *Annual Review of Anthropology* 31 (2002): 279–301.

Montazami, Chalabim, and Taba 2017
Montazami, Morad, Tamara Chalabim, and Shwan Ibrahim Taba. *Latif Al Ani*. Cannibal/Hannibal, 2017.

Muller 2017
Muller, Nat. *The Black Tower*. Berlin: Zilberman Gallery, 2017.

Muller 2020
Muller, Nat, ed. *Walid Siti*. Heidelberg: Kehrer Verlag, 2020.

Nye 1994
Nye, David E. *American Technological Sublime*. Cambridge, MA: MIT Press, 1994.

Nysten 2020
Nysten, Anastasia. “Hanaa Malallah: Treasure in Ruins; Treasure of Ruins; Treasure in&of Ruins.” *Selections Art*, May 1, 2020. https://selectionsarts.com/hanaa-malallah-treasure-in-ruinstreasure-of-ruins-treasure-inof-ruins.

Office of the Special Inspector General for Iraq Reconstruction 2007
“Al Basrah Oil Terminal, Basrah, Iraq.” *Office of the Special Inspector General for Iraq Reconstruction*, April 26, 2007. https://captainslog.gr/wp-content/uploads/2020/12/Basra-Oil-Terminal.pdf.

Parrot 1953
Parrot, André. *Archéologie mesopotamienne*. Vol. 1, *Les étapes*. Paris: Albin Michel, 1953.

Place 1867–70
Place, Victor. *Ninive et l’Assyrie, avec des essaus de restouration*. 3 vols. Paris: Imprimerie national, 1867–70.

Porter 2020
Porter, Venetia. “Dohuk to London: A Tumultuous Journey.” In Muller 2020, 20–25.

Qazanjy 2015
Qazanjy, Y. F. “Hurmz rssam awl athari fi albilad alearabiati: mulahiq jaridat almadaa alyawmia” هرمز رسام اول آثاري في البلاد العربية;ملاحق جريدة المدى اليومية (Horzmud Rassam: The First Archaeologist in the Arab Lands). July 29. https://almadasupplements.com/view.php?cat=13383

Rassam 1897
Rassam, Hormuzd. *Asshur and the Land of Nimrod*. Cincinnati: Curts & Jennings; New York: Eaton & Mains, 1897.

Reade 1994
Reade, Julian E. “Les relations anglo-françaises en Assyrie.” In *De Khorsabad à Paris: La découverte des Assyriens*, edited by Élisabeth Fontan, 116–35. Paris: Réunion des musées nationaux, 1994.

Rigamonti di Cutò 2018
Rigamonti di Cutò, Angeria. “Latif Al Ani: ‘I was documenting for the sake of archiving. I never thought Iraq would arrive at what it has today.’” *Studio International*, March 1, 2018. StudioInternational.com.

Shabout 2007
Shabout, Nada M. *Modern Arab Art: Formation of Arab Aesthetics*. Gainesville: University Press of Florida, 2007.

Shilla Fire Co. 2019
“Shillafire Foam Equipment.” Incheon, South Korea: Shilla Fire Co., 2019. http://en.shillafire.com.

Sikorski 2019
Sikorski, Suzy. “Latif Al Ani: Through the Lens; Father of Iraqi Photography,” *Mid East Art*, July 23, 2019. MidEastArt.com.

Silberman 1990
Silberman, Neil Asher. “Power, Politics, and the Past: The Social Construction of Antiquity in the Holy Land.” In *The Archaeology of Society in the Holy Land*, edited by T. E. Levy, 9–23. London: Leicester University Press, 1990.

Simmel 1958
Simmel, Georg. “Two Essays.” *Hudson Review* 11, no. 3 (1958): 371–85.

Stanley 2003
Stanley, Bruce. “Iraq’s Oil Terminal Ready for Exports.” *Midland (MI) Daily News*, May 24, 2003. https://www.ourmidland.com/news/article/Iraq-s-Oil-Terminal-Ready-for-Exports-7122780.php.

Taha 2016
Taha, Salam. “Hurmozd Al-Rassam” (in Arabic). *Iraq in History*. https://www.iraqinhistory.com/2016-12-04-12-57-28.

Taleb 2015
Taleb, O. “Hormuzd Entwan Rassam (1826–1911)” (in Arabic). June 29, 2015. https://almadasupplements.com/view.php?cat=13381.

Taylor 2008
Taylor, J. “Les explorateur britanniques au XIXe siècle.” In *Catalogue Babylone*, 508–12. Paris: Musée du Louvre, 2008.

Tripp 2007
Tripp, Charles. “The Ba’th and the Rule of Saddam Husain, 1968–2003.” In *A History of Iraq*, 186–276. 3rd ed. Cambridge: Cambridge University Press, 2007.

U.S. Energy Information Administration, 2023
“Oil and Petroleum Products Explained: Refining Crude Oil.” U.S. Energy Information

Administration, updated February 22, 2023, https://www.eia.gov/energyexplained/oil-and-petroleum-products/refining-crude-oil-the-refining-process.php.

Wells 1895
Wells, H. G. *The Time Machine*. https://en.wikisource.org/wiki/The_Time_Machine_(Holt_text)/The_Time_Traveler_Returns.

Wheeler 1964
Wheeler, Mortimer. *Archaeology from the Earth*. Harmondsworth: Penguin, 1964.

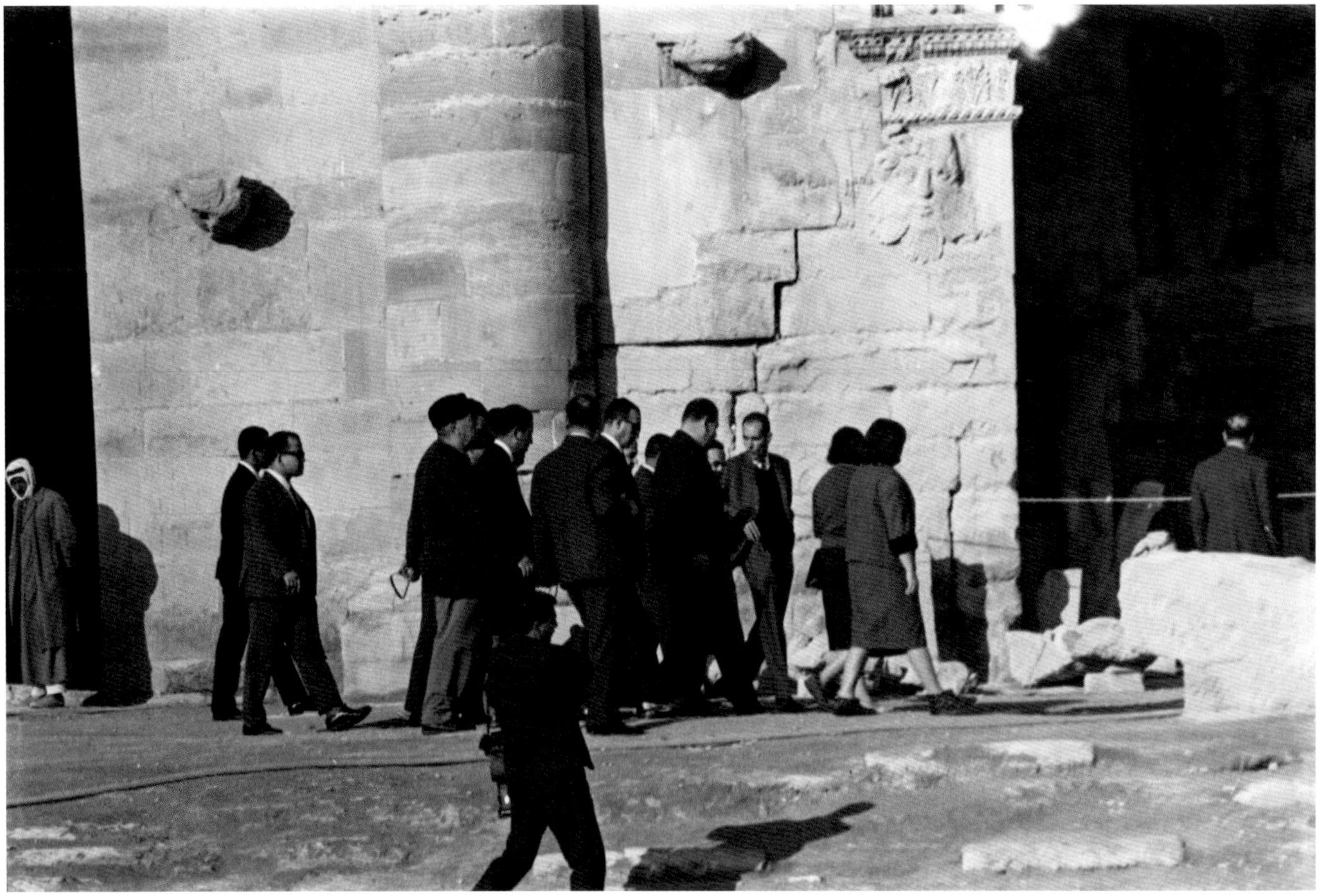

Latif Al Ani. Hatra, a group of visitors at the Great Iwans. Gelatin silver negative on cellulose acetate film. Ca. 1960. AIF: 0190an01789. Checklist no. 70.

EXHIBITION CHECKLIST

1
Walid Siti
Arched Tower
2023
Insulation board, plaster of paris, and acrylic
H. 360 cm; W. 175 cm; D: 175 cm
Courtesy of Walid Siti
(FIG. 10-10)

2
Latif Al Ani
Ziggurat of Dur-Kurigalzu (Agargouf) as seen from a plane
1960
Gelatin silver negative on cellulose acetate film (6 × 6 cm)
Arab Image Foundation
0190an00008b
(FIG. 4-19)

3
Latif Al Ani
Baghdad, Hisham Munir's Endowment Office
1960
Gelatin silver negative on cellulose acetate film (6 × 6 cm)
Arab Image Foundation
0190an00145
(FIG. 4-4)

4
Latif Al Ani
Baghdad, Hisham Munir's El Rawaf Building
1960
Gelatin silver negative on cellulose acetate film (6 × 6 cm)
Arab Image Foundation
0190an01216
(FIG. 4-5)

5
Frederick Charles Cooper
Austen Henry Layard. *A Second Series of the Monuments of Nineveh*. Plate 53: "Painted Bricks" (Nimroud)
1853
Lithograph
H. 38 cm; W. 57 cm
ISAW
N5380 .L3 1853 Folio
(FIG. 1-11)

6
Frederick Charles Cooper
Austen Henry Layard. *A Second Series of the Monuments of Nineveh*. Plate 54: "Painted Bricks" (Nimroud)
1853
Lithograph
H. 38 cm; W. 57 cm
ISAW
N5380 .L3 1853 Folio
(FIG. 1-12)

7
Frederick Charles Cooper
Austen Henry Layard. *The Monuments of Nineveh: From Drawings Made on the Spot*. Plate 84: "Painted bricks from the N. W. Palace – Nimroud"
1849
Lithograph
H. 38 cm; W. 57 cm
ISAW
N5380 .L3 1849 Folio
(FIG. 1-13)

8
8A. Adel Abidin
Debris. IMAM - I 1996
2019
Mixed media on fragments of building blocks
H. 17 cm; W. 16 cm; D. 21 cm
Courtesy of Galerie Tanit
(FIG. 6-4)

8B. Adel Abidin
Debris. IMAM - II 2004
2019
Mixed media on fragments of building blocks
H. 23 cm; W. 17 cm; D. 23 cm
Courtesy of Galerie Tanit
(FIG. 6-4)

8C. Adel Abidin
Debris. IMAM - III 1999
2019
Mixed media on fragments of building blocks
H. 33 cm; W. 17 cm; D. 20 cm
Courtesy of Galerie Tanit
(FIG. 6-4)

8D. Adel Abidin
Debris. IMAM - IV 2005
2019
Mixed media on fragments of building blocks
H. 28 cm; W. 16 cm; D. 24 cm
Courtesy of Galerie Tanit
(FIG. 6-4)

8E. Adel Abidin
Debris. IMAM - V 2008
2019
Mixed media on fragments of building blocks
H. 27 cm; W. 15 cm; D. 23 cm
Courtesy of Galerie Tanit
(FIG. 6-4)

8F. Adel Abidin
Debris. IMAM - VI 2010

2019
Mixed media on fragments of building blocks
H. 26 cm; W. 16 cm; D. 22 cm
Courtesy of Galerie Tanit
(FIG. 6-4)

8G. Adel Abidin
Debris. IMAM - VII 2006
2019
Mixed media on fragments of building blocks
H. 21 cm; W. 17 cm; D. 19 cm
Courtesy of Galerie Tanit
(FIG. 6-4)

8H. Adel Abidin
Debris. IMAM - VIII 2013
2019
Mixed media on fragments of building blocks
H. 22 cm; W. 15 cm; D. 21 cm
Courtesy of Galerie Tanit
(FIG. 6-4)

8I. Adel Abidin
Debris. IMAM - IX 2011
2019
Mixed media on fragments of building blocks
H. 21 cm; W. 17 cm; D. 19 cm
Courtesy of Galerie Tanit
(FIG. 6-4)

8J. Adel Abidin
Debris. IMAM - X 2016
2019
Mixed media on fragments of building blocks
H. 23 cm; W. 17 cm; D. 23 cm
Courtesy of Galerie Tanit
(FIG. 6-4)

8K. Adel Abidin
Debris. IMAM - XI 2009
2019
Mixed media on fragments of building blocks
H. 41 cm; W. 16 cm; D. 22 cm
Courtesy of Galerie Tanit
(FIG. 6-4)

9
Latif Al Ani
Baghdad, Hisham Munir's Villa
1960
Gelatin silver negative on cellulose acetate film (5.7 × 5.7 cm)
Arab Image Foundation
0190an00253
(FIG. 4-6)

10
Latif Al Ani
Baghdad, Hisham Munir's Villa
1960
Gelatin silver negative on cellulose acetate film (5.7 × 5.7 cm)
Arab Image Foundation
0190an00269
(FIG. 4-7)

11
Latif Al Ani
Baghdad, Hisham Munir's Villa
1960
Gelatin silver negative on cellulose acetate film (5.7 × 5.7 cm)
Arab Image Foundation
0190an00268
(FIG. 4-8)

12
Latif Al Ani
Babylon, detail of a mušḫuššu dragon from the Ishtar Gate
ca. 1961
Gelatin silver negative on cellulose acetate film (6 × 6 cm)
Arab Image Foundation
0190an00630
(FIG. 1-14)

13
Frederick Charles Cooper
Austen Henry Layard. *A Second Series of the Monuments of Nineveh*. Plate 3: "Human headed Bull & winged figure from a gateway in the wall surrounding Kouyunjik"
1853
Lithograph
H. 38 cm; W. 57 cm
ISAW
N5380 .L3 1853 Folio
(FIG. 2-11)

14
Frederick Charles Cooper
Austen Henry Layard. *The Monuments of Nineveh: From Drawings Made on the Spot*. Plate 3: "A Winged human headed Lion (Nimroud)"
1849
Lithograph
H. 38 cm; W. 57 cm
ISAW
N5380 .L3 1849 Folio
(FIG. 1-10)

15
Latif Al Ani
Berlin, Vorderasiatisches Museum. Lamassu reliefs from the palace of Tukulti-Ninurta I
1960
Gelatin silver negative on cellulose acetate film (6 × 6 cm)

Arab Image Foundation
0190an01133
(FIG. 2-12)

16
Latif Al Ani
Berlin, Vorderasiatisches Museum. Lamassu relief from the palace of Tukulti-Ninurta I
1960
Gelatin silver negative on cellulose acetate film (6 × 6 cm)
Arab Image Foundation
0190an01132
(FIG. 2-13)

17
Latif Al Ani
Berlin, Vorderasiatisches Museum. Ishtar Gate
1965
Gelatin silver negative on cellulose acetate film (6 × 6 cm)
Arab Image Foundation
0190an01345
(FIG. 2-8)

18
Latif Al Ani
Berlin, Vorderasiatisches Museum. Walking lions from the Procession Street of Nebuchadnezzar II
1965
Gelatin silver negative on cellulose acetate film (6 × 6 cm)
Arab Image Foundation
0190an01348
(FIG. 2-9)

19
Hanaa Malallah
Dove – Drone Hovering over Babylon Borsippa Twin Towers
2023
Video (sound)
Courtesy of Hanaa Malallah
(FIG. 8-13)

20
Latif Al Ani
Babylon, Babel Films shooting an ad for Arab tourism in front of the wall of sacred bulls and mušḫuššu dragons at the Ishtar Gate
1961
Gelatin silver negative on cellulose acetate film (6 × 6 cm)
Arab Image Foundation
0190an00067
(FIG. 4-21)

21
Latif Al Ani
Babylon, musician playing the rebab in front of the city wall
ca. 1961
Gelatin silver negative on cellulose acetate film (6 × 6 cm)
Arab Image Foundation
0190an00763
(FIG. 3-5)

22
Hanaa Malallah
Babylon Curse
2023
Video (without sound)
Courtesy of Hanaa Malallah
(FIG. 8-10)

23
Hanaa Malallah
Babylon Curse I
2023
Charcoal, pencil, colored pencil, and acrylic on paper
H. 60 cm; W. 42 cm
Courtesy of Hanaa Malallah
(FIG. 8-6)

24
Hanaa Malallah
Babylon Curse II
2023
Charcoal, pencil, colored pencil, and acrylic on paper
H. 60 cm; W. 42 cm
Courtesy of Hanaa Malallah
(FIG. 8-7)

25
Hanaa Malallah
Babylon Curse III
2023
Charcoal, pencil, colored pencil, and acrylic on paper
H. 60 cm; W. 42 cm
Courtesy of Hanaa Malallah
(FIG. 8-8)

26
Hanaa Malallah
Babylon Curse IV
2023
Charcoal, pencil, colored pencil, and acrylic on paper
H. 60 cm; W. 42 cm
Hanaa Malallah
(FIG. 8-9)

27
James Felix Jones
Memoirs of Baghdad, Kurdistan and Turkish Arabia: Selections from the Records of the Bombay Government, n.s., no. 63. Map of Nineveh
1857
Hand-colored engraving
H. 127 cm; W. 76.2 cm
Private collection
(FIG. 1-7)

28
James Felix Jones
Memoirs of Baghdad, Kurdistan and Turkish Arabia. Selections from the Records of the Bombay Government, n.s., no. 63. Map of Nimrud and Selamiyah
1857
Hand-colored engraving
H. 127 cm; W. 76.2 cm
Private collection
(FIG. 1-8)

29
James Felix Jones
Memoirs of Baghdad, Kurdistan and Turkish Arabia. Selections from the Records of the Bombay Government, n.s., no. 63. Map of Nineveh, the River Tigris, and the Upper Zab
1857
Hand-colored engraving
H. 127 cm; W. 76.2 cm
Private collection
(FIG. 1-9)

30
Frederick Charles Cooper
Austen Henry Layard. *A Second Series of the Monuments of Nineveh*. Plate 1: "The Palaces of Nimrod Restored: From a Sketch by James Ferguson Esq."
1853
Lithograph
H. 39 cm; W. 60 cm
ISAW
N5380 .L3 1853 Folio
(FIG. 2-10)

31
Philip Henry Delamotte
Mr. Hormuzd Rassam vide Layard's Nineveah
ca. 1854
Reprinted from digital file
Swansea Museum Library, Wales
SWASM:SM1987.845.79
(FIG. 2-1)

32
Frederick Charles Cooper
Austen Henry Layard. *The Monuments of Nineveh: From Drawings Made on the Spot*. Plate 2: "Hall in Assyrian Palace restored"
1849
Lithograph
H. 38 cm; W. 57 cm
ISAW
N5380 .L3 1849 Folio
(FIG. 2-5)

33
Frederick Charles Cooper
Austen Henry Layard. *A Second Series of the Monuments of Nineveh*. Plate 2: "Colossal Lion, Great Entrance (Nimroud)"
1853
Lithograph
H. 38 cm; W. 57 cm
ISAW
N5380 .L3 1853 Folio
(FIG. 2-7)

34
Frederick Charles Cooper
Austen Henry Layard. *A Second Series of the Monuments of Nineveh*. Plate 5: "Basreliefs at an entrance to a small temple (Nimroud)"
1853
Lithograph
H. 38 cm; W. 57 cm
ISAW
N5380 .L3 1853 Folio
(FIG. 2-4)

35
Frederick Charles Cooper
Austen Henry Layard. *A Second Series of the Monuments of Nineveh*. Plate 70: "View of the Mounds of Kouyunjik and Nebbi Yunus and of the Remains of the exterior Walls from the North"; "View of the Mounds of Kouyunjik and Nebbi Yunus and of the Remains of the exterior Walls from Mosul"
1853
Lithograph
H. 38 cm; W. 57 cm
ISAW
N5380 .L3 1853 Folio
(FIG. 2-3)

36
Frederick Charles Cooper
Austen Henry Layard. *The Monuments of Nineveh: From Drawings Made on the Spot*. Plate 98: "Outline of the Mound at Nimroud"
1849
Lithograph
H. 38 cm; W. 57 cm

ISAW
N5380 .L3 1849 Folio
(FIG. 2-6)

37
Latif Al Ani
Ctesiphon, tourists in front of the ruins of the Tāq Kasrā (Arch of Ctesiphon)
1964
Gelatin silver negative on cellulose acetate film (6 × 6 cm)
Arab Image Foundation
0190an00919
(FIG. 1-2)

38
Latif Al Ani
Ctesiphon, tourists in front of the ruins of the Tāq Kasrā (Arch of Ctesiphon) with musician playing the rebab
1964
Gelatin silver negative on cellulose acetate film (6 × 6 cm)
Arab Image Foundation
0190an01178
(FIG. 4-23)

39
Latif Al Ani
Ctesiphon, tourists in front of the ruins of the Tāq Kasrā (Arch of Ctesiphon) with musician playing the rebab
1964
Gelatin silver negative on cellulose acetate film (6 × 6 cm)
Arab Image Foundation
0190an01179
(FIG. 1-3)

40
Latif Al Ani
Ctesiphon, tourists in front of the ruins of the Tāq Kasrā (Arch of Ctesiphon)
1964
Gelatin silver negative on cellulose acetate film (6 × 6 cm)
Arab Image Foundation
0190an00918
(FIG. 1-4)

41
Latif Al Ani
Ctesiphon, tourists in front of the ruins of the Tāq Kasrā (Arch of Ctesiphon)
1964
Gelatin silver negative on cellulose acetate film (6 × 6 cm)
Arab Image Foundation
0190an01181
(FIG. 1-5)

42
Latif Al Ani
Ctesiphon, tourists in front of the ruins of the Tāq Kasrā (Arch of Ctesiphon)
1964
Gelatin silver negative on cellulose acetate film (6 × 6 cm)
Arab Image Foundation
0190an00917
(FIG. 1-6)

43
Latif Al Ani
Ctesiphon, tourists in front of the ruins of the Tāq Kasrā (Arch of Ctesiphon)
1964
Gelatin silver negative on cellulose acetate film (6 × 6 cm)
Arab Image Foundation
0190an01266
(FIG. 4-22)

44
Latif Al Ani
Ctesiphon, tourist in front of the ruins of the Tāq Kasrā (Arch of Ctesiphon) with musician playing the rebab
1964
Gelatin silver negative on cellulose acetate film (6 × 6 cm)
Arab Image Foundation
0190an01177
(FIG. 1-1)

45
Latif Al Ani
Ctesiphon, ruins of the Tāq Kasrā (Arch of Ctesiphon)
ca. 1964
Gelatin silver negative on cellulose acetate film (6 × 6 cm)
Arab Image Foundation
0190an00655
(P. 1)

46
Latif Al Ani
Ctesiphon, ruins of the Tāq Kasrā (Arch of Ctesiphon) with musician playing the rebab
ca. 1964
Gelatin silver negative on cellulose acetate film (6 × 6 cm)
Arab Image Foundation
0190an00560
(FIG. 4-20)

47
Latif Al Ani
Ctesiphon, aerial view of the ruins of the Tāq Kasrā (Arch of Ctesiphon)
1960
Gelatin silver negative on cellulose acetate film (6 × 6 cm)
Arab Image Foundation
0190an00032
(FIG. 3-8)

48
Latif Al Ani
Ctesiphon, view of the site
ca. 1964
Gelatin silver negative on cellulose acetate film (6 × 6 cm)
Arab Image Foundation
0190an01595
(FIG. 4-16)

49
Latif Al Ani
Ctesiphon, ruins of the Tāq Kasrā (Arch of Ctesiphon)
1965
Gelatin silver negative on cellulose acetate film (6 × 6 cm)
Arab Image Foundation
0190an00975
(P. 158)

50
Latif Al Ani
Ctesiphon, the ruins of the Tāq Kasrā (Arch of Ctesiphon) from a Bedouin tent; a *dallah* in the foreground
1965
Chromogenic process film negative on cellulose acetate film (6 × 6 cm)
Arab Image Foundation
0190an00980
(FIG. 4-17)

51
Latif Al Ani
Ctesiphon, tourist in front of the ruins of the Tāq Kasrā (Arch of Ctesiphon)
1964
Gelatin silver negative on cellulose acetate film (6 × 6 cm)
Arab Image Foundation
0190an00977
(FIG. 4-11)

52
Latif Al Ani
Ctesiphon, tourist in a Bedouin tent in front of the ruins of the Tāq Kasrā (Arch of Ctesiphon)
ca. 1964
Gelatin silver negative on cellulose acetate film (6 × 6 cm)
Arab Image Foundation
0190an01593
(FIG. 4-24)

53
Latif Al Ani
Ctesiphon, tourist in front of the ruins of the Tāq Kasrā (Arch of Ctesiphon)
1964
Gelatin silver negative on cellulose acetate film (6 × 6 cm)
Arab Image Foundation
0190an00978
(FIG. 4-12)

54
Nadine Hattom
Shadows. 1. Dulab
2016
Archival pigment print
H. 46 cm; W. 66 cm
Courtesy of Nadine Hattom
(FIG. 7-5)

55
Nadine Hattom
Shadows. 2. Fallujah
2016
Archival pigment print
H. 46 cm; W. 66 cm
Courtesy of Nadine Hattom
(FIG. 7-4)

56
Nadine Hattom
Shadows. 3. Ramadi
2016
Archival pigment print
H. 46 cm; W. 66 cm
Courtesy of Nadine Hattom
(FIG. 7-6)

57
Nadine Hattom
Shadows. 4. Habbaniyah
2016
Archival pigment print
H. 46 cm; 66 cm
Courtesy of Nadine Hattom
(FIG. 7-7)

58
Nadine Hattom
Shadows. 5. Ziggurat
2016
Archival pigment print
H. 46 cm; W. 66 cm
Courtesy of Nadine Hattom
(FIG. 7-8)

59
Nadine Hattom
Shadows. 6. Diyala
2016
Archival pigment print
H. 46 cm; W. 66 cm
Courtesy of Nadine Hattom
(FIG. 7-9)

60
Nadine Hattom
Shadows. 7. Hit
2016
Archival pigment print
H. 46 cm; W. 66 cm
Courtesy of Nadine Hattom
(FIG. 7-10)

61
Nadine Hattom
Shadows. 8. Saqlawiyah
2016
Archival pigment print
H. 46 cm; W. 66 cm
Courtesy of Nadine Hattom
(FIG. 7-11)

62
Nadine Hattom
Shadows. 9. Hatra
2016
Archival pigment print
H. 46 cm; W. 66 cm
Courtesy of Nadine Hattom
(FIG. 7-3)

63
Nadine Hattom
Shadows. 10. Ashur
2016
Archival pigment print
H. 46 cm; W. 66 cm
Courtesy of Nadine Hattom
(FIG. 7-12)

64
Mahmoud Obaidi
Fragments
2015
Weathering steel
Dimensions vary
Courtesy of Mahmoud Obaidi
Obaidi 2015 1/3 + AP
(FIGS. 9-2 and 9-3)

65
Latif Al Ani
Hatra, The Great Iwans
ca. 1960
Gelatin silver negative on cellulose acetate film (3.5 × 2.5 cm)
Arab Image Foundation
0190an01784
(FIG. 4-14)

66
Latif Al Ani
Hatra, The Great Iwans
ca. 1960
Gelatin silver negative on cellulose acetate film (3.5 × 2.5 cm)
Arab Image Foundation
0190an01788
(FIG. 4-15)

67
Latif Al Ani
Hatra, Temple (Iwan) of the sun god Shamash
ca. 1960
Gelatin silver negative on cellulose acetate film (3.5 × 2.5 cm)
Arab Image Foundation
0190an01781
(P. 8)

68
Latif Al Ani
Hatra, The Great Iwans
ca. 1960
Gelatin silver negative on cellulose acetate film (3.5 × 2.5 cm)
Arab Image Foundation
0190an01786
(P. 142)

69
Latif Al Ani
Hatra, tourist in front of the statue of Abu Bint Deimun, Wife of Santruq I
ca. 1960
Gelatin silver negative on cellulose acetate film (6 × 6 cm)
Arab Image Foundation
0190an00648
(FIG. 4-13)

70
Latif Al Ani
Hatra, a group of visitors at the Great Iwans
ca. 1960
Gelatin silver negative on cellulose acetate

film (3.5 × 2.5 cm)
Arab Image Foundation
0190an01789
(P. 148)

71
Latif Al Ani
Hatra, head of statue
1960
Gelatin silver negative on cellulose acetate film (6 × 6 cm)
Arab Image Foundation
0190an00707
(FIG. 3-6)

72
Latif Al Ani
Hatra, The Temple (Iwan) of Shamash, mask (architectural decoration)
ca. 1960
Gelatin silver negative on cellulose acetate film (3.5 × 2.5 cm)
Arab Image Foundation
0190an01779
(FIG. 3-11)

73
Latif Al Ani
Hatra, South Iwan (Hall, No. 12), eagle (architectural relief)
ca. 1960
Gelatin silver negative on cellulose acetate film (3.5 × 2.5 cm)
Arab Image Foundation
0190an01776
(FIG. 3-10)

74
Latif Al Ani
Hatra, Statue of Abu Bint Deimun, Wife of Santruq I
ca. 1960
Gelatin silver negative on cellulose acetate film (8 × 6 cm)
Arab Image Foundation
0190an00818
(FIG. 3-9)

75
Walid Siti
Tower Series
2020
Crayon and acrylic on paper
H. 210 cm; W. 142 cm
Walid Siti
(FIG. 10-9)

76
Walid Siti
To the Unknown Architect
2022
Video (sound)
Courtesy of Walid Siti
(FIGS. 10-2, 10-6, and 10-7)

77
Walid Siti
"The Seven Towers" I Series
2013
Graphite, colored crayon, and acrylic wash on paper
H. 76.2 cm; W. 55.9 cm
Metropolitan Museum of Art. Gift of Ipeknur and Shwan Ibrahim Taha, 2014
2014.429
(FIG. 10-8)

78
Latif Al Ani
Samarra, the spiral minaret of the Great Mosque
1959
Gelatin silver negative on cellulose acetate film (6 × 6 cm)
Arab Image Foundation
0190an00048
(FRONT COVER)

79
Latif Al Ani
Samarra, the spiral minaret of the Great Mosque
1960
Gelatin silver negative on cellulose acetate film (6 × 6 cm)
Arab Image Foundation
0190an00115
(FIG. 10-2)

80
Latif Al Ani
Baghdad, Umma Park. Khaled al-Rahal's Motherhood Monument
ca. 1960
Gelatin silver negative on cellulose acetate film (6 × 6 cm)
Arab Image Foundation
0190an00612
(FIG. 1-15)

81
Latif Al Ani
Baghdad, Jewad Selim's Freedom Monument at Tahrir Square.
1961
Gelatin silver negative on cellulose acetate

film (6 × 6 cm)
Arab Image Foundation
0190an00047
(FIG. 3-7)

82
Latif Al Ani
Baghdad, Jewad Selim's Freedom Monument at Tahrir Square
1961
Gelatin silver negative on cellulose acetate film (6 × 6 cm)
Arab Image Foundation
0190an00070
(FIG. 4-18)

83
Latif Al Ani
Baghdad, Arab Biennal. Khaled al-Rahal, Maquette
ca. 1971
Gelatin silver negative on cellulose acetate film (6 × 6 cm)
Arab Image Foundation
0190an00558
(FIG. 4-10)

84
Latif Al Ani
Baghdad, Jewad Selim's Freedom Monument at Tahrir Square
1961
Gelatin silver negative on cellulose acetate film (6 × 6 cm)
Arab Image Foundation
0190an00044
(FIG. 4-9)

85
Photographer unknown
Portrait of Latif Al Ani
1956
Print (12.5 × 10.3 cm)
H. 30 cm; W. 11.81 cm
Arab Image Foundation
0190an00536
(BACK COVER)

86
Sahim Omar Kalifa and Jurgen Buedts
Latif Al Ani
2010–14
Digital still from *Iraq's Invisible Beauty*
Jurgen Buedts
(FIG. 4-1)

87
Sahim Omar Kalifa and Jurgen Buedts
Latif Al Ani
2010–14
Digital still from *Iraq's Invisible Beauty*
Jurgen Buedts
(FIG. 4-2)

88
Sahim Omar Kalifa and Jurgen Buedts
Latif Al Ani
2010–14
Digital still from *Iraq's Invisible Beauty*
Jurgen Buedts
(FIG. 4-3)

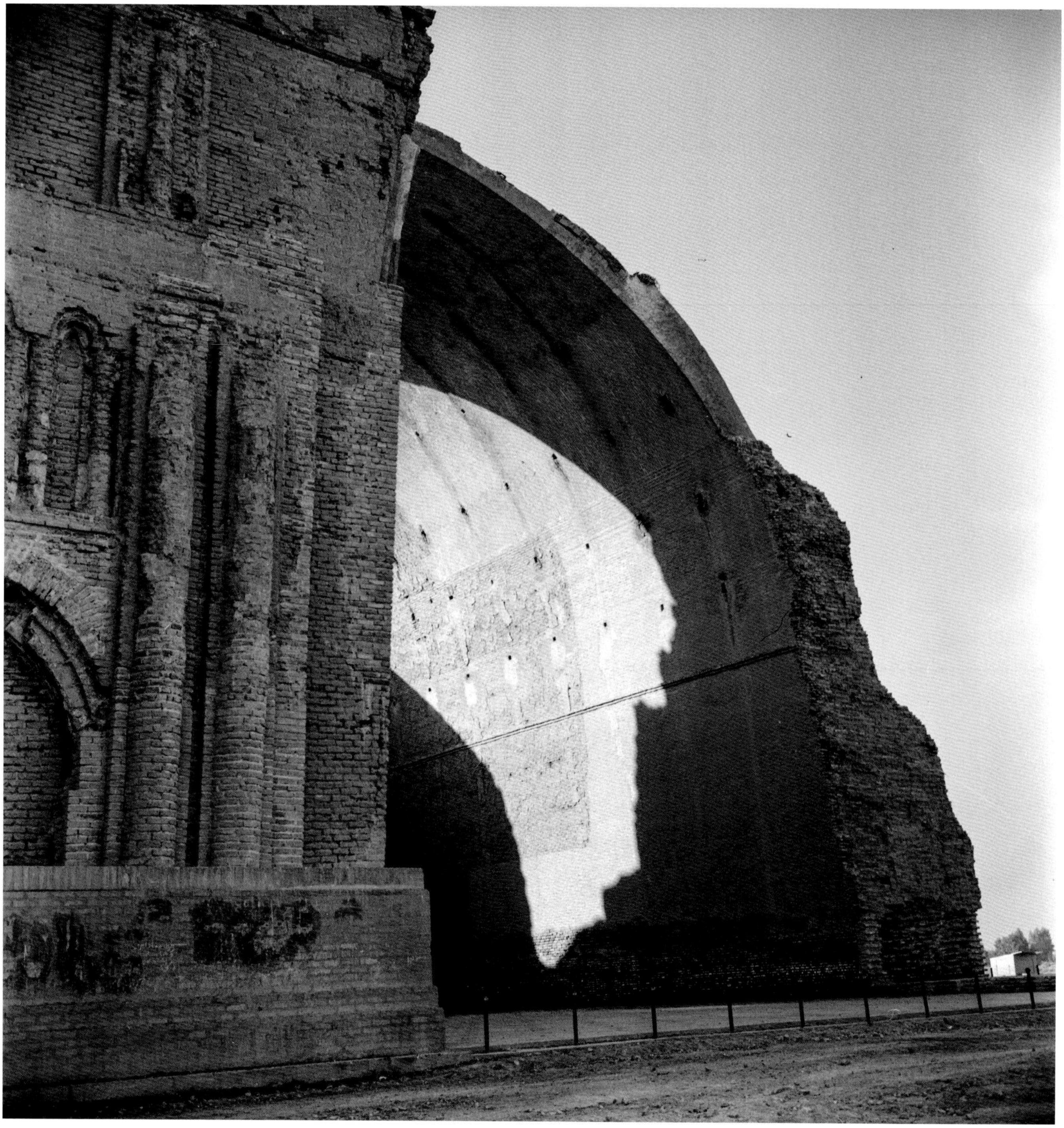

Latif Al Ani. Ctesiphon, ruins of the Tāq Kasrā (Arch of Ctesiphon). Gelatin silver negative on cellulose acetate film. 1965. AIF: 0190an00975. Checklist no. 49.

PHOTOGRAPY CREDITS

Abidin and Galerie Tanit
Image courtesy of Adel Abidin and Galerie Tanit Beirut/Munich: figs. 6-1, 6-2, 6-4, 6-5, 6-6, 6-7, 6-8, 6-9, 6-10, 6-11, 6-12.

Alamy
© Stephen Chung / Alamy Live News: fig. 8-11.

Amin and Darwesh
Image courtesy of Narmin Amin and Abdulrahman K. Darwesh: figs. 2-2, 2-14.

Arab Image Foundation
0190an - Latif el Ani Collection. Courtesy of the Arab Image Foundation, Beirut ©: figs. 1-1, 1-2, 1-3, 1-4, 1-5, 1-6, 1-14, 1-15, 2-8, 2-9, 2-12, 2-13, 3-1, 3-5, 3-6, 3-7, 3-8, 3-9, 3-10, 3-11, 4-4, 4-5, 4-6, 4-7, 4-8, 4-9, 4-10, 4-11, 4-12, 4-13, 4-14, 4-15, 4-16, 4-17, 4-18, 4-19, 4-20, 4-21, 4-22, 4-23, 4-24, 5-1, 10-2, p. 1, p. 8, p. 142, p. 148, p. 158.

Azzawi Archive
Image courtesy of Azzawi Archive, London: figs. 5-2, 5-3, 5-4, 5-5, 5-6, 5-7.

Brooklyn Museum
© Brooklyn Museum, Gift of K. Thomas Elghanayan in honor of Nourollah Elghanayan, 2002.6: fig. 6-3.

Fuccaro
Image courtesy of Nelida Fuccaro and NYU Abu Dhabi: figs. 3-2, 3-3, 3-4, 3-12, 3-13, 3-14, 3-15, 3-16, 3-17, 3-18, 3-19, 3-20.

Getty Images
Ali Al-Saadi / AFP via Getty Images: fig. 6-17.

Hattom
Image courtesy of Nadine Hattom: figs. 7-1, 7-2, 7-3, 7-4, 7-5, 7-6, 7-7, 7-8, 7-9, 7-10, 7-11, 7-12.

Institute for the Study of the Ancient World
Courtesy of the Library of the Institute for the Study of the Ancient World: figs. 1-10, 1-11, 1-12, 1-13, 2-3, 2-4, 2-5, 2-6, 2-7, 2-10, 2-11.

Kalifa and Buedts
Image courtesy of Sahim Omar Kalifa and Jurgen Buedts © 2022 LAS BELGAS: figs. 4-1, 4-2, 4-3.

Malallah
Image courtesy of Hanaa Malallah: figs. 8-1, 8-2, 8-3, 8-4, 8-5, 8-6, 8-7, 8-8, 8-9, 8-10, 8-12, 8-13.

The Metropolitan Museum of Art
Image copyright © The Metropolitan Museum of Art. Image source: Art Resource, NY: fig. 10-8.

Obaidi
Courtesy of Mahmoud Obaidi: figs. 9-1, 9-2, 9-3.

Private collection
Courtesy of a private collection: figs: 1-7, 1-8, 1-9.

Siti
Image courtesy of Walid Siti: figs. 10-1, 10-3, 10-4, 10-5, 10-6, 10-7, 10-8, 10-9, 10-10, 10-11.

Swansea Museum
Courtesy of Cyngor Abertawe: Casgliad Amgueddfa Abertawe. Swansea Council: Swansea Museum Collection: fig. 2-1.

Published by the Institute for the Study of the Ancient World at New York University and distributed by Princeton University Press on the occasion of the exhibition *Through the Lens: Latif Al Ani's Visions of Ancient Iraq*, November 8, 2023 – February 25, 2024.

Institute for the Study of the Ancient World
New York University
15 E. 84th Street, New York, NY 10028
isaw.nyu.edu

Princeton University Press
41 William Street, Princeton, NJ 08540
99 Banbury Road, Oxford OX2 6JX
press.princeton.edu

This exhibition has been organized by the Institute for the Study of the Ancient World at New York University.

The exhibition and its accompanying catalogue were made possible by generous support from the Violet Jabara Charitable Trust and the Leon Levy Foundation. Additional funding provided by Joyce F. Menschel and Mr. and Mrs. Lawrence Tucker.

Managing Editor: Taylor McBride

Copy Editor: Mary Cason

Designer: Laura Grey

Color separations, printing, and binding: Graphius NV, Ghent, Belgium

The book was set in Moderat and printed on Magno volume, 150gsm.

Library of Congress Control Number: 2023945632

ISBN: 978-0-691-97392-0

British Library Cataloguing-in-Publication Data is available.

Printed and bound in Belgium.

10 9 8 7 6 5 4 3 2 1